History of the Grand Orient of Italy

HISTORY

of the

GRAND ORIENT

of

ITALY

---

edited by

EMANUELA LOCCI

Westphalia Press
An Imprint of the Policy Studies Organization
Washington, DC
2019

Westphalia Press
An imprint of Policy Studies Organization
1527 New Hampshire Ave., NW
Washington, D.C. 20036
info@ipsonet.org

ISBN-10: 1-63391-825-4
ISBN-13: 978-1-63391-825-2

Cover and interior design by Jeffrey Barnes
jbarnesbook.design

Daniel Gutierrez-Sandoval, Executive Director
PSO and Westphalia Press

Updated material and comments on this edition
can be found at the Westphalia Press website:
www.westphaliapress.org

A special thanks to the Hur society of Cagliari (1988–2018) for its will to encourage the issue of this valuable volume.

Freemasonry is a school of liberty,
of atonement and brotherhood.

Ettore Ferrari
1912

There is a human feeling called gratitude.

Mine is to Marco Novarino.

A master. My mentor.

CONTENTS

FOREWORD

The initiative to write this volume is derived from the intention to fill a bibliographic gap: a publication in English that fully depicts the history of Italian masonry. To this end, it offers to bridge this gap, and contribute to expanding the Anglo-Saxon audience on the history of a major Obedience in Italy: the Grand Orient of Italy.

This opera combines the knowledge of young Italian scholars that attended the first workshop organised by the Historical Research Centre on Freemasonry in Turin in 2017, who were willing to share their ideas and proficiency on masonic issues. The volume consists of eight chapters, starting with an introduction on the eighteenth century Italy, and the penetration of Freemasonry in the peninsula.

The paper by Giulia Delogu offers a comprehensive review on masonry since '700 to Napoleonic times, and reveals broadly the challenges faced by Freemasonry in its introduction in the early modern Italian domains. Although lodges were established in Rome, Florence, Naples and Milan by the first half of the eighteenth century, almost all of these encountered struggles and even persecutions. The most notable "incident" happened in Florence, where the poet and Freemason Tommaso Crudeli was imprisoned by the Florentine Inquisition. Although subsequently released, he never recovered from the ordeal and died shortly afterwards; thus being the very first martyr of Italian Freemasonry.

Nevertheless, Freemasonry endured and in the '70's gained prominence again, mainly in the Kingdom of Naples, favoured by Queen Maria Carolina, the Grand Duchy of Tuscany under Pietro Leopoldo, and in the Austrian Lombardy. Freemasonry nurtured the birth of cultural networks and contributed to the dissemination of philosophies. A noteworthy example of the intertwinement of cultural, political, and masonic attributes observed in Italy, during the period of enlightenment, is the Neapolitan reformism of Gaetano Filangieri and Francesco Mario Pagano. The revolutionary outbursts gave rise to a period of oppression; masonry, for instance, was banned from all the Austrian territories. Conversely, the advent of Napoleon in 1796 produced a unique dissemination of masonic lodges culminating in the creation of the Grand Orient of Italy in 1805.

Giuseppe Luca Manenti describes in detail the Napoleonic age and Risorgimento, and traces the events of Italian Freemasonry from the period of enlightened despotism to the unification of the peninsula. In addition to providing useful insight on the inner social shift in the lodges, the endorsing or adversary roles the Brethen played from time to time towards the establishment, and the extent of rites and intellectual influences the lodges experienced or acted on, Manenti reports a framework of the historiographical debates on the success in politics and culture of the affiliates in the span under his review. The research critiques a wide and updated compilation of secondary literature—period publishing, trade magazines, pro- and anti-Masonic issues—with the aim of providing a more exhaustive insight on the role Freemasonry played both on the stage of the history and in capturing the fascination of Italians.

The third and fourth chapters by Demetrio Xoccato and Emanuela Locci, respectively, focuses on the history of Italian Freemasonry in the liberal period, from the unification of Italy up to the first decade of the twentieth century. This section is pivotal in the scheme, as it depicts the birth of the first strictly Italian Obedience: the Grand Orient of Italy. The transformation of the Italian Grand Orient as the Grand Orient of Italy facilitated the executive and basic affirmation of the newborn National Obedience. The authors pay particular attention to the merger of Italian Freemasonry under the Grand Orient of Italy. The chapters encapsulate the efforts of three successive Grand Masters who served as the Head of Obedience: Adriano Lemmi, Ernesto Nathan, and Ettore Ferrari. Given their impressive accomplishments, these three leaders have left an indelible mark on the coeval masonry. The Grand Orient of Italy faced many trials, both domestic and in fronting the "profane" world of politics and parties. The split that gave rise to the Great Lodge of Italy 1908, and the resolution of the Socialist Party to expel those belonging to Freemasonry in 1914, represent two such incidences of significance. In conclusion, the fourth chapter will describe the assets of the Obedience in relation to Italy's involvement in the First World War (WWI).

The next chapter, by Nicoletta Casano, offers a comprehensive review of the Grand Orient of Italy during the WWI and outlines one of the gloomiest eras in its history, faced with fascism. The Masonry of Palazzo Giustiniani played a key role in the Italian involvement in the WWI as a part of the Entente. Due to the influential in-house and foreign socio-political role of

Italian Freemasonry in the early twentieth century, this Obedience acted on the public opinion in a more subtle manner than the interventionist political parties. The country actually emerged with a 'mutilated' victory and a deep crisis that profoundly changed the scenario nationwide, leading to Freemasonry to withdraw in light of the emergent fascist dictatorship.

The sixth chapter written by Emanuela Locci, briefly addresses the exile of Italian Freemasonry, and highlights the struggle of the Grand Orient of Italy in managing not to suffer oblivion, which was largely accomplished by some representatives of the Italian masonry fleeing abroad. Particular emphasis is given to the figure of Augusto Albarin, the first Grand Master of exiled masonry.

The seventh chapter anew by Emanuela Locci, centres on foreign lodges of the Grand Orient of Italy, by operating within the frame of Italian communities. He refers to, as case studies, the Italian lodges in Turkey (former Ottoman Empire), Egypt, Tunisia, Libya, and Eritrea. While this section provides a fairly comprehensive description of the history of Italian lodges in Turkey and North Africa, the proposed depiction about Eritrea comes bare, as the research carried out by Locci is currently *in itinere*.

The last chapter is dedicated to the alliance between Freemasonry and secular solidarity. Written by Demetrio Xoccato, the chapter entitled 'Masonic solidarity in the liberal age: education and philanthropy' highlights one of the inherent sides of masonry: the apparatus of worldly charity. The essay offers an overview of the Masonic commitment to social life in the liberal age. Subsequent to the first few years of post-unification and the pursuant attempts to merge the entire Masonic force into one, Freemasonry could finally incorporate its actions within the civil society. To this end, since the late 60s of the nineteenth century, there were several efforts to fund educational and welfare institutions in Italian cities. The issues of schooling, concurrent to occupation and poverty had emerged and prevalent expansively; after several attempts, and some encouragement, the lodges responded mainly in two ways: by following foreign models of intervention (such as Economic Kitchen Houses and Night Shelters); or through specific initiatives, that would lead to different fortunes.

The volume concludes its chronic–historical framing with the banishment of the Grand Orient of Italy during fascism. Subsequent to WWII—and the associated fascism—the Grand Orient of Italy resumed its affairs on

10th June, immediately after the liberation of Rome, where the Obedience regained its name, and disseminated a manifesto stating the rebirth of the masonic communion. Over the decades that ensued, the Grand Orient of Italy has strengthened to reclaim its position as the pivotal Obedience in Italy as demonstrated by its numbers in membership, affiliates, and activities. However, several subsequent issues of bearing, in particular the widely relevant issue concerning Propaganda 2 lodge in '80, has resulted in the negative reputation Freemasonry has in Italy. An additional factor was the split that gave rise to the Grand Regular Lodge of Italy, founded in Rome on April 17, 1993, by some lodges supporting Giuliano Di Bernardo, the Grand Master of the GOI at the time. The chronicles of the Grand Orient of Italy, even the recent volumes, are extensive, the narration of which we hope will be accomplished in future publications.

1. MASONIC NETWORKS IN EARLY MODERN ITALY

Giulia Delogu

1.1 Intro

In the eighteenth century, the Italian masonic history, as well as geopolitics, is divided into many streams.

The absence of a unitary nation did not permit, up to 1805 at least, the building of a masonic group able to overcome the diverse boundaries of local lodges, which remain subdued to the huge European Obedience (English, French, Austrian). Thus, added to the common trials due to changeable nature of masonry itself and its rituals, there is an additional difficulty caused by the fragmentary Italian geography.[1]

In Italy, Masonic ideas, hampered by governments and the papacy, struggle to assert themselves: they are like inner flows carried by European travelers to the most visited cities. It's therefore impossible to depict a unitary draft: here we will sketch out the Masonic presence in the major centers of the Peninsula, from the first lodges' birth, through persecutions, to the establishment, only in 1805 with the foundation of the Grand Orient of Italy by the will of the Napoleonic administration. Hence, we will not dwell on the complexity of rites, Obediences, degrees, but we will try to outline a picture of the Ancient Italian States, which will show the masonic diffusion and the networks stemmed by the lodges.

The networks of the Italian lodges—and some prominent figures of freemasonic environment—allow us to look in the Masonic phenomenon not

---

1   The still definitive reference for the history of Italian Freemasonry since the beginning to the Revolution is Carlo Francovich, *Storia della Massoneria in Italia. Dalle origini alla rivoluzione francese*, La Nuova Italia, Firenze, 1974; a volume assessing the masonry situation from diverse perspective is Gian Mario Cazzaniga (edited), *La Massoneria. Storia d'Italia*, Annali, XXI, Einaudi, Torino, 2006; for a European scenario, see Giuseppe Giarrizzo, *Massoneria e Illuminismo nell'Europa del Settecento*, Marsilio, Venezia, 1994; Antonio Trampus, *La massoneria nell'età moderna*, Laterza, Roma, 2001.

according to a limited and sectorial perspective but within the wider framework of the history of ideas. The masonic networks easily intersects with other multiple webs: cultural, political, and commercial ones. It is in the clash between powers that the first Florentine Masonic persecution broke out. In Naples, it is by linking suggestions from the European Enlightenment that the Masonic intellectuals reflect on what executive reforms can create a more just and equitable society. Again in Naples, it is in the dispute between the pro-Spanish and pro-Austrian supporters that the anti-masonic processes of the '70s are set. It is from the urging to create a new poetry that Tommaso Crudeli, Giuseppe Cerretesi and Antonio Jerocades adapted the universe of Masonic values in lyric. It is by keeping an eye on the development of commerce and of the freeport that the emerging middle-class of Trieste starts a dialogue with the aristocracy and imperial officials in the Masonic lodges. Briefly, the history of Italian Freemasonry in the early modern age, as above mentioned, is indeed the story of the birth and development of lodges and Obediences in major city centers, but it is also and above all a journey made of relationships and networks.

1.2 Rome and Florence

One of the very first centers of Masonic penetration was Rome, then capital of the Papal States, where Freemasonry seems to have already landed in the '30': in the city emblem of Catholicism one of the first Italian lodges arose. It was the meeting point for exiles and British cast out, advocates of the Stuart cause. Deeper evidence was left by the Loge Amis à l'Epreuve, founded in 1776 under the auspices of the *Grande Mère Loge Écossaise*. In 1787, again appointed by the Grande Mère, a singular lodge of artists was raised, La *Réunion des Amis Sincères*, which a few years later, in 1789, went under the rule of Grand Orient. *La Réunion*, which counted only one Italian member, the Marquis Armentiere Vivaldi, was animated by a group of French artists, who in the years of the Revolution became ardent Jacobin.[2]

The papacy in the meantime looked with raising concern to the Masonic activity in Europe and on April 28, 1738, Clemente XII proclaimed the bull *In eminenti Apostulatus specula*, with which "societas, cœtus, coventus, conven-

---

2   On Masonry in Rome, see Anna Maria Isastia, *Massoneria e Logge segrete nello Stato Pontificio*, in Gian Mario Cazzaniga (edited), *La Massoneria. Storia d'Italia*, op. cit., pp. 484–512.

ticola, vulgo de 'freemason, seu Francs Massons" were banned. The imputed guilt was religious tolerance and secrecy. The document, however, remained unheeded, since the Italian and European states refused to enroll it.[3]

The second stage of this brief Italian masonic path is Florence,[4] pounding heart of the primal Freemasonry. In the grand-ducal capital, in 1731-1732 a lodge aroused and, although it had been formed within the English community, soon numbered many Florentine notables and intellectuals, including the poets Tommaso Crudeli and Giuseppe Cerretesi, who can be considered the first two Italian Masonic writers. Exactly in Florence, following a growing inner conflict between free thinkers and Jesuits, the first Italian anti-masonic campaign was carried out, ending up with the poet Tommaso Crudeli detained—as a perfect scapegoat not being an aristocrat and being without any protection—by the Inquisition. After the trial, the Florentine Masonic activity suffered a sharp backlash and the masonic center of Tuscany became first Livorno and then Portoferraio.

1.3 Masonic, Cultural, and Poetic Networks: The Case of Tommaso Crudeli

The case of Crudeli shows how—from the very beginning—the development of Italian Masonic networks was intertwined with that of cultural networks and how masonic lodges were also a laboratory for the development of literature and arts.[5]

The biography of Tommaso Crudeli, the oppression by the Tuscan Inquisition, the imprisonment and premature death which made him the Italian masonic "proto-martyr" are widely known and itemized facts.[6] Crudeli

---

3   On the Catholic Church and Freemasonry, see José Antonio Ferrera Benimeli, *Origini, motivazioni, ed effetti della condanna vaticana*, in Gian Mario Cazzaniga (edited), *La Massoneria. Storia d'Italia*, op. cit., pp. 143–165; Daniele Menozzi, *Cattolicesimo e Massoneria nell'età della Rivoluzione francese*, in Gian Mario Cazzaniga (edited), *La Massoneria. History of Italy*, op. cit., pp. 166–192.

4   On Freemasonry in Tuscany, see Renato Pasta, *Fermenti culturali e circoli massonici nella Toscana del Settecento*, in Gian Mario Cazzaniga (edited), *La Massoneria. Storia d'Italia*, op. cit., pp. 447–483; Fulvio Conti, *La massoneria a Firenze: dall'età dei lumi al secondo Novecento*, Bologna, Il Mulino, 2007.

5   A picture of the interweaving of Freemasonry and literature is found in Francesca Fedi, *Comunicazione letteraria e "generi massonici" nel Settecento italiano*, in Gian Mario Cazzaniga (edited), *La Massoneria. Storia d'Italia*, op. cit., pp. 50–89.

6   Carlo Francovich, *Storia della massoneria in* Italia, op. cit., pp. 31–46; Renato Pasta,

had been a law student of Bernardo Tanucci at the University of Pisa, in the same years during which the Tuscan city had become the center for the spreading of materialistic thought disapproved by the ecclesiastical hierarchy. After a short stay in Venice, he settled in Florence and soon approached masonic circles and, in 1735, he was affiliated to the local lodge. Rather shy, he published very little in life. Confidential and not ambitious, Crudeli even came to refuse the office of Caesarean poet at the court of Naples offered him by Tanucci in 1738.[7] Crudeli claimed the prominence of the bond amid poetry and moral education and the centrality of virtue. His idea of poetry as an agent of education assumed the original traits of a true pathway of civilization toward virtue and reason. Crudeli found himself, unwitting, in the very clash between the new grand-ducal power of Francesco Stefano and the papacy. The affair of the Florentine Masonic lodge actually broke out while the shift between the ancient Medici dynasty—ended in 1737 with Gian Gastone—and the new dynasty of Lorraine was still ongoing, and the enmity amid the two parties sides was high. Strictly considering the bull *In eminenti Apostulatus specula* of 1738, the Tuscan Inquisition began an inquiry on the phenomenon and instructed a trial that, in the first intentions, should have not affected only Crudeli, already unwelcome person since when, in 1735, had declaimed the ode for Buonarroti.

L'Ode Pindarica in morte del Senator Filippo Buonarroti[8] was recited in the *dell'Accademia Funerale per le Lodi del Senatore Filippo Buonarroti fatta dagli Accademici fiorentini il dì 20 Luglio 1735 nel Consolato di Bindo Simone Peruzzi*[9] and then diffused handwritten. There the author outlined two models of virtuous action: Cosimo III, sovereign of peace, who had been able to stem "il furore / del procelloso tempestar del clero"[10]—verses, these, strongly combative against the churchly power the penultimate Grand

---

Fermenti culturali e circoli Massonici nella Toscana del Settecento, in Gian Mario Cazzaniga (edited), *La Massoneria. Storia d'Italia*, op. cit., pp. 447–483.

7   Bernardo Tanucci, *Lettera a Tommaso Crudeli, 21 gennaio 1738*, in Romano Paolo Coppini, Lamberto Del Bianco, Rolando Nieri, (edited), *Epistolario I (1723–1746)*, Edizioni di storia e letteratura, Roma, 1980, pp. 229–230.

8   *The Pindaric Ode in the death of Senator Filippo Buonarroti* [translator's note].

9   Funeral Academy to the Hymn of Senator Filippo Buonarroti made by the Florentine Academicians on July 20, 1735, in the Consulate of Bindo Simone Peruzzi [translator's note].

10   "the fury/of the stormy tempest of the clergy" [translator's note].

Duke Medici had the merit of scaling down and which were censored in the three editions in the eighteenth and nineteenth century—and Filippo Buonarroti, "eroe"[11] who knew how to "rompere le nubi oscure, ove nascosa / e fanatici e Goti / tenner la greca e la romana istoria, / e l'illustre memoria / di quei popoli invitti erger gloriosa / la fronte luminosa".[12] The celebration of Buonarroti, played on the language of glory and honor, was set in a classical frame and in a secular materialistic milieu, where immortality was due to the memory of the "grandi azioni"[13] and "eccelse prove"[14] handed down, also and above all, by the "immortal verso"[15] of the poet.

The arrests had to be three but, due to the turmoil, that of Abbot Bonaccorsi was postponed for infirmity and that of Cerretesi rejected by the Council of Regence. Crudeli, though afflicted with tuberculosis and a severe form of asthma, was detained for three months under inhumane conditions. During inquisitions, weakened physically but not in mind, he rejected the infamous accusations of impiety and sodomy and refused to reveal the Secrets of Freemasonry. In 1740, since he could not be tried for Masonic activity—the papal bull had not been registered yet—he was convicted on charges today may sound minor matters—as having read Lucretius, the life of Sisto V and that of Paolo Sarpi, as well as for having mocked the Sacred Heart of Jesus and Our Lady of Impruneta and eventually for "aver frequentato un'adunanza dove si parlava di Filosofia e Teologia e dove si osservavano vari empi riti e s'insegnano molte eresie"[16]—but in those times they brought him to the confinement. The poet, in very serious health conditions, was interned at Poppi and then at Pontedera; he was allowed to return to Florence only in 1745 and there he died assisted by the Brethen

---

11 "hero" [translator's note].

12 "break the dark clouds, where hid / fanatics and Goths / kept the Greek and the Roman history, / and the illustrious memory / of those folks unbeaten raised glorious / the luminous forehead" [translator's note]. Tommaso Crudeli, Ode Pindarica in morte del Senator Filippo Buonarroti (1735), in Renzo Rabboni, Monsignor/il dottor mordi graffiante, pp. 106–113.

13 "great deeds" [translator's note].

14 "sublime trials" [translator's note].

15 "immortal verse" [translator's note].

16 "having attended a meeting on Philosophy and Theology and where various impious rites were observed and many heresies were taught" [translator's note]. From a report by Giulio Rucellai, Registrar of the Royal Right, in defense of Crudeli and sent to Count Richecourt, Head of the Council of Finance (ASF, Reggenza, filza 339), cit. in Carlo Francovich, Storia della Massoneria in Italia, op. cit., p. 83.

Antonio Cocchi, Luca Corsi, Horace Mann, and Giuseppe Maria Buondel-monti, becoming the first Italian martyr of the masonic cause.

In life, therefore, Crudeli had made public very little that could contribute to outline a personal poetics and an original conception of virtue.. The most interesting result of Crudeli's issues appeared only after his death in the Florentine editions (with Naples as a fake place of printing) of 1746 and 1767. The *editio princeps* was promoted by that "gathering of friends"[17] whom the poet ideally addressed his verses to: Luca Corsi, Pompeo Neri, Giulio Rucellai, Emmanuel de Nay de Richecourt, Antonio Cocchi, Horace Mann, Andrea Bonducci, and Antonio Niccolini, the same group he partook of the Masonic affiliation and lavished in the writing of the dell'*Istoria della carcerazione*[18] (a memory drafted in the 40s to restore the name of Tommaso, and published only in 1782).[19] The poetic collection of 1746, released shortly after poet's death, despite a high editorial front, was actually scarce on the content: a mere "scheletro"[20] of Crudeli's poetic genius, as Bernardo Tanucci told: "a chi sa quanto compose l'infelice amico e quanti capitoli ei fece che erano il più vivace della di lui poesia, comparisce questa edizione solamente uno scheletro che può servire per eccitare il desiderio".[21] Few texts—and heavily censored, not to incur the ire of the Inquisition and to hand down an "orthodox" image of the lost friend: de facto unnecessary precautions since the Rhymes were immediately blacklisted by a decree dated October 7, 1746. The next printing of 1767, although in small format and economic paper, was, as we will see, much yielding, while maintaining the *princeps* censorship.

The real manifesto of Crudeli's thought, the ode *Il Trionfo della ragione*, was printed for the first time in 1767. The poem had been composed in 1740

---

17 "gathering of friends" [translator's note].

18 "History of the arrest" [translator's note].

19 Renzo Rabboni (edited), Il calamaio del padre inquisitore: istoria della carcerazione del dottor Tommaso Crudeli di Poppi e della processura formata contro di lui nel tribunale del S. Offizio di Firenze, Istituto di studi storici Tommaso Crudeli, Udine, 2003, p. 9.

20 "skeleton" [translator's note].

21 "who knows how much [my] unhappy friend composed and how many chapters he made and were the most lively of his poetry, this edition only appears a skeleton to excite desire" [translator's note]. Bernardo Tanucci, *Lettera al Signor Martinelli, 3 giugno 1746*, in Epistolario II (1746–1752), Romano Paolo Coppini, Rolando Nieri (edited), Roma, Edizioni di storia e letteratura, Roma 1980, p. 49.

and though known to Corsi and Neri, however not included it in the first edition. The ode, dedicated to Lady Walpole, probably to thank her for having mediated for a less harsh prison regime, overcame the circumstance to reflect on the meaning of poetry and the role of the artist. Pivotal was the theme of virtue as the main object of artistic creation, bond with reason. As stated in the opening, poetry was called to become "sonante di virtù"[22] and to educate "alme atroci, e spirti inculti"[23] to the laws of "ragion".[24] Crudeli looked at the model of the poet-civilizer per excellence: Orpheus, who taught to a "popol fiero, e sanguinoso"[25] le "leggi d'Amore / leggi eterne di sapienza / di concordia, e di mercé".[26] Virtue was not just the object of poetry, but the aim: the poet, thus, moved, with his verses, to "accende[re] l'alme a virtù".[27]

Virtue and wisdom were, to Crudeli, mutually beneficial: guided by reason "quel che è mal risorge in bene, / quel che è vizio esce in virtù"[28] and by the poetry of virtue, the laws of reason were taught. The virtue of the Tuscan poet, thus, was the skill to dominate "i torbidi tumulti"[29] of the heart, not meant as Christian penance, but as rational response and as the Epicurean "prudenza"[30] of the forementioned madrigal.

In *Il Trionfo della ragione*, Epicurean positions of moral philosophy were expressed - ideas well known to Crudeli since the Pisan studies - but it was also a text rich in more contingent references to the historical and personal reality of the author. The education to virtue—and the subsequent triumph of reason titling the ode— was not in fact a simple path of personal improvement, but (at least ideally) the civilization of the whole society. Reason and virtue were the cure so that clergy abuses—foreshadowed

---

22 "resonant of virtue" [translator's note].

23 "atrocious souls, and uncultivated spirits" [translator's note].

24 "reason" [translator's note]. This quote and the following, till a new reference, are taken from Tommaso Crudeli, *Il trionfo della ragione* (1767), in Renzo Rabboni, *Monsignor/il dottor mordi graffiante*, pp. 147–154.

25 "proud people, and bloody" [translator's note].

26 "the proud and bloody laws of Love / eternal laws of wisdom / concord, and mercy" [translator's note].

27 "[re]ignite the spirit to virtue" [translator's note].

28 "what is bad rises in good, / that which is vice goes out in virtue" [translator's note].

29 "turbulent tumults" [translator's note].

30 "concern" [translator's note].

by the "furia anguicrinita"[31]—which the poet had suffered and continued to, did not repeat themselves. The end of the "oppression livida e nera"[32] should have been working to "altrui felicità",[33] through the use of the "social provvido affetto".[34] That "social provvido affetto"[35] also referred to the reach of brotherly love and care Freemasonry tie was based on: a social and behavioral model that was intended to be extended to the whole of society.

1.4 Venice, Genoa, and the Kingdom of Sardinia

In Venice, in the early '50s, there seems to have been a lively masonic environment.[36] Although there was not a proper masonic lodge, the lagoon city was, in 1730s–1750s, a cluster for outstanding Freemasons, such as Giacomo Casanova, Scipione Maffei, Antonio Conti, and Francesco Algarotti, who all had joined to lodges during European journeys and then had brought Masonic knowledge home. To his, a precocious literary attention to the masonic phenomenon must be added: first, the insertion of term "Free Masons" in the *Nuovo dizionario scientifico e curioso sacro-profano*[37] by Gianfrancesco Pivati in 1747 and then the openly filo-masonic comedies of Carlo Goldoni and Francesco Griselini, *Le donne curiose e I liberi muratori*,[38] respectively, of 1753 and 1754.

Goldoni's comedy plot develops around the prying of some women toward a sect they are kept out. Significant, in the Goldoni's piece, is scene IV from act III,[39] and above all the dialogue where Pantalone, Ottavio, Lelio, Florindo, and Leandro explain to Flaminio the essence of Freemasonry, whose main value are friendship and mutual help amid Brethen. The text of Griselini, instead, is a rooting description of freemasons as philanthro-

---

31 "reptilian fury" [translator's note].

32 "livid and black oppression" [translator's note].

33 "others' happiness" [translator's note].

34 "social provident care" [translator's note].

35 *Ibidem.*

36 On Freemasonry in the Republic of Venice, see Piero Del Negro, *La Massoneria nella Repubblica di Venezia*, in Gian Mario Cazzaniga (edited), *La Massoneria. Storia d'Italia*, op. cit., pp. 399–417.

37 New scientific and rare sacred and profane dictionary [translator's note].

38 A curious mishap: a comedy in three acts.

39 Alessandra Di Ricco (edited), *Carlo Goldoni, Le donne curiose*, Marsilio, Venezia, 1995, pp. 160–162.

pists, moved to the needy and willing to recreate the "golden age." Even in the Republic of Venice, however, Freemasonry did not have an easy start and in 1755, the Inquisition sentenced Giacomo Casanova—as impious, libertine, and freemason—to five years imprisonment in Piombi, a prison the adventurer managed to escape from 15 months later.

In 1772, the birth of "L'Unione" [*The Union*], the very first Venetian lodge was followed by others in Verona, Vicenza, Brescia, and Padua. As stated by a 1774 report of the Inquisition, The Union had a markedly cosmopolitan and transversal profile and gathered "ebrei, tedeschi, inglesi e anche gentiluomini veneziani",[40] hence it was a room for dialogue amid different nationalities as well as different classes in town, welcoming aristocrats, officials of the Republic, professionals, and traders. In May 1785, however, the State Inquisition declared all the "conventicole"[41] banned, commanding to dissolve the existing lodges. These measures did not imply singular trials and persecutions: lodges were suspended till the Republican Triennium, even though Freemasonry kept favors in the flourishing Venetian publishing industry.[42]

In the independent Republic of Genoa, since 1747, two lodges seem to have existed, probably by the initiative of French troop officers.[43] Already in 1751, effective the papal bull, investigations took place; however, the masonic works deepened until 1762, when a new lodge founded by doctor Andrea Repetto is appraised, counting alongside foreigners, many Genoese. The first facts on this lodge derive, once again, from trial records relating to the proceeding—and imprisonment—against some free masons, including the founder. As already in Florence, the detained subdued to a long judicial quarrel opposing the State to the Inquisition—defeated at the very end since the charge for heresy was denied. The events of 1762 did not prevent the ongoing Masonic activity and, in August 1781, in Genoa emerged another lodge linked to the Torinese and Lyonsian lodges. Repetto, still involved and recidivist, was again imprisoned. In 1787, however, another lodge was already active, promoted in the traders' class by a French

---

40 "Jews, Germans, Englishmen and even Venetian gentlemen" [translator's note].

41 "cabal" [translator's note].

42 Piero Del Negro, *La massoneria nella Repubblica di Venezia*, op. cit., pp. 414–416.

43 On Freemasonry in the Republic of Genoa, see Calogero Farinella, *Per una storia della Massoneria nella Repubblica di Genova*, in Gian Mario Cazzaniga (edited), *La Massoneria. Storia d'Italia*, op. cit., pp. 418–446.

merchant, Alexis Bouillod who moved among Livorno, Corsica, and Genoa and, between 1792 and 1793, would have been jailed as accused of Masonic and revolutionary activity. The case of Bouillod shows, on one hand, the common transition more markedly political functions in the post-1789 scenario, on the other the fears of the governments that fully embraced the conspiracy theories according to which the revolutionary excesses that resulted in the regime of the Terror and in the beheading of the king and queen of France had been caused by a diabolical plan promoted by the philosophes and the Masons.[44]

The Kingdom of Sardinia was, at the dawn of Italian Freemasonry, a place of intense activity thanks to the contiguity with France, of which it was influenced. The first lodge we are acknowledged is the *Saint Jean des trois Mortiers of Chambery*, created by the will of Count François Noyel de Bellegarde, Marquis des Marches, in 1749. Bellegarde had been initiated as early as 1739 and was patented a Grand Master for Savoy and Piedmont from England. Only in 1765, however, the Mother Lodge of Chambery profited of its powers and began to establish others: the lodge of the Savoy regiment, *La Vraie Amitié* of Rumilly and *La Mystérieuse* of Turin. Since 1771, the Turin lodge, under the authority of physician Sebastiano Giraud, assumed a more markedly occultist and alchemical temper, becoming the Italian beacon of Martinez de Pasqually thought.[45]

1.5 The Triumph of Freemasonry in Eighteenth-Century Naples

N aples was the most relevant masonic center of the Italian Peninsula in the eighteenth century.[46] In 1749–1751, the Parthenopean capital saw the development of a vast net of masonic lodges where eminent

---

44 Charles Porset, *Franc-maçonnerie, Lumières et Révolution*, Edimaf, Paris, 2001, p. 17.

45 On the peculiar figure of Giraud, a native of Pinerolo—doctor, academic, mason, and alchemist—a friend of Martinez de Pasqually, Willermoz, and Mesmer, see Pierre-Yves Beaurepaire, *L'Europe des francmaçons, XVIIIe–XXIe siècles*, Belin, Paris, 2002 , pp. 85–90; Giuseppe Giarrizzo, *La massoneria lombarda*, op. cit., pp. 364–365. About Mesmer, in particular, see Robert Darnton, *Mesmerism and the End of the Enlightenment in France*, Harvard University Press, Cambridge, Mass, 1968.

46 On Freemasonry in the Kingdom of the Two Sicilies, see Anna Maria Rao, *La Massoneria nel Regno di Napoli*, in Gian Mario Cazzaniga (edited), *La Masoneria. Storia d'Italia*, op. cit., pp. 513–542; Elvira Chiosi, *Lo spirito del secolo. Politica e religione a Napoli nell'età dell'illuminismo*, Giannini, Napoli, 1992, pp. 27–28, 30–31 and 52–53; Vincenzo Ferrone, *I profeti dell'illuminismo*, Laterza, Laterza, Rome-Bari, 2000, pp. 209–210, 250–258, 269–270, and 350–353.

aristocratic members were initiated, including Raimondo di Sangro, Prince of Sansevero and Gennaro Carafa, Prince of Rocella, who were already attending the Parisian lodge *Coustos-Villeroy* in 1737. However, a papal bull, *Providas Romanorum Pontificum*, published by Benedetto XIV on May 28, 1751, stated the reproach of Freemasonry. As a result, on July 2, King Carlo III published an edict against the Fraternity and began the first Neapolitan persecution, which caused the retraction of the Prince of Sansevero and the seizure of all masonic papers.

This first recoil, however, was not enough to extinguish the masonic light in Naples and in 1763, a new lodge called *Les Zélées* was signed from the Grand Lodge of Holland. The Neapolitan Freemasonry had been collecting the noble elite, endorsed by Queen Maria Carolina, who defied minister Tanucci.

In 1773, Francesco d'Aquino, Prince of Caramanico, established an independent national Grand Lodge, the first in Italy. However, lodges linked to foreign Obedience continued to exist, engendering a lively and diverse masonic mosaic with fertile ties all over the continent. The following years of prosperity saw the membership of prominent personalities from city *life* such as Domenico Forges Davanzati, Mario Pagano, Gaetano Filangieri, Felice Lioy, Antonio Jerocades, Francesco Longano and Francescantonio Grimaldi, who were members of the so called Antonio Genovesi's school.

Tanucci held an anti-Hispanic attitude and was worried by the rise of the Freemasons which he believed to be a Hapsburg attempt to infiltrate. Under pressure from Tanucci, Ferdinando IV promulgated a new anti-subversive edict on September 12, 1775. However, it was unheeded. In response, Tanucci arranged an ambush to catch a number of influential Freemasons who were jailed and referred to the State Council for the crime of lese majesty, which could result in the death penalty. This was protested from all over Europe where Masonry was present in the top ranks of many countries. One of the most prominent Brethen, the lawyer Lioy, evaded arrest and travelled to plead the case of the imprisoned Neapolitan Brothers and was warmly received in the illustrious Parisian lodge *La Candeur*.

Meanwhile in 1776, under mounting international pressure, Ferdinando IV dismissed Tanucci and freed the prisoners, allowing for a Masonic expansion throughout the Kingdom. This expansion was not only a political phenomenon allied to the Hapsburg interests of Maria Carolina, but it also gave rise to a lively cultural debate.

As mentioned, lodges were a place for diverse scholars—including Antonio Genovesi in middle of the century—to ponder the sort of features a modern society should have, the nature of trading and ways to perfect human beings. The fundamental issues Genovesi probed were virtue, education and happiness. However, these issues concealed a more subversive discourse on equality.

Freemasons, however, did not all share the same vision of virtue and equality. Although these were considered key values of the masonic universe, they were recognized as universal qualities the enlightened masons were supposed to share with all humankind. Neapolitan masonry shows the intricacy of the issue.[47] Francescantonio Grimaldi and Gaetano Filangieri, though both belonging to the Genovesi school, being part of the same circles and being both affiliated to the Freemasonry, developed two opposing theories. While the former tried to spread conservative theses and justified the political inequality of the Ancient Regime societies, the latter strongly reaffirmed the principles of equality, political and moral of all men.[48]

In *La vita di Diogene Cinico*,[49] Grimaldi claims that virtue is unselfish love. The text mentions a few important ideas including temperance, to pursue one's own wealth and charity, to get the wealth of others. Virtue, therefore, was defined as a principle of self-discipline to live free (from lust) and quiet in whole harmony.

In the *Riflessioni sopra l'ineguaglianza*,[50] Grimaldi not only denied the genetic character of virtue, but also claimed there was a lack of globally-accepted moral issues. Out of this absence, the Calabrian philosopher suggested there was moral inequality amid humans, which he believed explained political disparity.

---

47 Grimaldi and Filangieri were both Emulation Rite initiated. Cfr. Vincenzo Ferrone, *I profeti dell'Illuminismo*, op. cit., p. 250.

48 Vincenzo Ferrone, La società giusta ed equa: repubblicanesimo e diritti dell'uomo in Gaetano Filangieri, Laterza, Roma-Bari, 2005, pp. 90–99, 178.

49 *Life of Diogene Cinico* [translator's note]. Francescantonio Grimaldi, *La vita di Diogene Cinico*, Mazzola-Vocola, Napoli, 1777.

50 *Speculation upon inequality* [translator's note]. Francescantonio Grimaldi, Riflessioni sopra l'ineguaglianza, Mazzola Vocola, Napoli, 1779–1780.

Filangieri took the idea from Genovesi that a sense of virtue is a universal and natural seed equally present in all beings, therefore sprouting from passion, but only if they are well-nurtured. Filangieri developed the idea of a humanitarian and philanthropic virtue, completely reduced to a civil dimension and whose goal is welfare: a "virtù civile, che combina la volontà col dovere e che può sola costituire l'umana felicità".[51]

Filangieri shaped a new meaning of virtue, redefining it due to latomistic influences into one of the pillars bearing a new society, very diverse from the one he was in and where "eternare le virtù e la felicità del popolo".[52] It was that "società giusta ed equa"[53] already aimed by the master, but now shown as a solid alternative to the failed experience of enlightened despotism. This change was pursued as a radical reform in laws, public education and religion. These were facets the young prince set out to deal with in the never completed *La scienza della legislazione*,[54] touched by a vast European fortune.[55]

Since the first volume of his treatise, Filangieri had expressed his sense of virtue as "capacità di unire interessi privati co' pubblici",[56] defined not as self-denial but as a well-tempered lust for power, able to create charity and humanity. Ambition was, therefore, thought to be a positive trait; same as luxury, "un mezzo per azioni virtuose in nazioni dove alberga libertà e virtù"[57] and, conversely, ignition of further decadence in wicked nations.

---

51 "civil virtue, which matches the will with duty and alone can constitute human happiness" [translator's note]. Paolo Bianchini (edited), Gaetano Filangieri, *La scienza della legislazione. Libro IV* [1785], Centro di studi sull'Illuminismo europeo G. Stiffoni, Venice, 2004, V, p. 292.

52 "to eternal the virtues and the happiness of people" [translator's note]. Gerardo Tocchini (edited), Ivi, Libro V [1791], 2003, VI, p. 14. On the links between the thought of Filangieri and masonry, see Vincenzo Ferrone, *I profeti dell'Illuminismo*, op. cit., pp. 250–258, 350–353.

53 "unbiased and fair society" [translator's note].

54 *The science of laws* [translator's note].

55 Antonio Trampus (edited), *Diritti e costituzione. L'opera di Gaetano Filangieri e la sua fortuna europea*, Il Mulino, Bologna, 2005; on the relevance of this work in the frame of late Enlightenment, see also Vincenzo Ferrone, *Storia dei diritti dell'uomo*, op. cit., pp. 341–348.

56 "ability to unite singular with public interests" [translator's note]. Antonio Trampus (edited), Gaetano Filangieri, *La scienza della legislazione. Libro I* [1780], 2003, I, p. 129.

57 "a means for virtuous actions in nations where liberty and virtue dwells" [translator's

Being virtuous does not mean to suppress one's own flame—from "più forti passioni"[58] descend "le azioni più grandi"[59]—but to address the universal happiness which is achievable through three instruments: fair laws, "universale ma non uniforme"[60] state education and a "pure" religion. The outcome would have been a society rooted in virtue and merit, characterized by "una libertà soda, e durevole".[61]

Virtue and law were in a mutually beneficial bond to Filangieri: if just laws inspire virtue, the law was to ensure that virtue doesn't turn into weakness or even vice. This way, exemplary was the issue of "clemency" and the criticism toward the grace by the sovereign to the condemned, kept as an "ingiustizia commessa contro la società"[62] since "la virtù che si chiama con questo nome [clemenza] dee manifestarsi nella correzione delle leggi ingiuste, e feroci, e non nel privarle del loro rigore".[63] To Filangieri, virtue was not a mere abstract notion to refer to, but a real empirical principle: this is clear if we consider the attention he gave to the issue of state education, whose main purpose was precisely to lead passions toward virtue.

Educating to virtue was not a utopian dream or an empty political promise, but the precise aim of improving mankind, diminishing crimes and cultivating better citizens. He was not satisfied with seeing the elites educated, but he wished to extend this privilege to everyone, albeit with some differences:

> L'educazione pubblica finalmente, per essere universale, richiede, che tutte le classi, tutti gli ordini dello stato vi abbiano parte; ma non richiede, che tutti questi ordini, tutte queste classi, vi abbiano la parte istessa. In poche parole: essa dev'essere universale, ma non uniforme; pubblica, ma non comune.[64]

---

note]. Maria Teresa Silvestrini (edited), *Ivi, Libro II* [1780], 2004, II, p. 250.

58 "stronger passions" [translator's note].

59 "greater actions" [translator's note]. *Ivi, Libro IV*, p. 271.

60 "universal—but not flat" [translator's note].

61 "a firm and lasting freedom" [translator's note]. *Ivi, Libro I*, p. 122.

62 "injustice committed against society" [translator's note].

63 "the virtue called by this name [clemency] must be shown in the correction of unjust and fierce laws and not in depriving them of their rightness" [translator's note]. Gerardo Tocchini, Antonio Trampus (edited), *Ivi, Libro III, parte II* [1783], 2004, IV, pp. 333–334.

64 "Finally, public education, to be universal, requires that all classes, all the orders of the

Despite the huge gap in thought, a significant case of the cohesion of the Neapolitan masonic-intellectuals gathering around the school of Genovesi can be found in the *Elogio del marchese Francescantonio Grimaldi*[65] (1784) by Melchiorre Delfico. Written after Grimaldi's death, it described his life and thought while appeasing his pessimism. In the end, the author combined the *Riflessioni sull'ineguaglianza*[66] with the *Scienza della legislazione*,[67] affirming the two shared a common goal since both insisted on the need to enhance a new sense of virtue as action and guiding principle for political improvement.

1.6 Masonic, Cultural, and Political Networks: La Lira Focense

The Kingdom of Naples gave birth to the most distinguished masonic literary experience in Italian idiom during the eighteenth century. It was In the Parthenopean capital that Antonio Jerocades, the "bard of Freemasonry," created, diffused, and then published his poetic collection, *La Lira focense.*[68] Jerocades, first in Italy, moved in the direction of a poem whose purpose was the disclosure of freemasonry values. Jerocades is an interesting cultural mediator who, although moving in traditional framings such as Arcadia, set in verse the masonic message in the peculiar way of the Neapolitan scholars of Antonio Genovesi.[69] Jerocades—after having received a religious education at the Tropea seminary and having founded a school in the native village of Parghelia in Calabria—met Genovesi, who encouraged him to move to Naples and publish the *Saggio dell'umano sapere ad uso de' giovanetti di Paralia* (Naples 1768),[70] where the young priest

---

state be part of it; but it does not require that all these orders, all these classes, partake same way. Briefly: it must be universal, but not uniform; public, but not common" [translator's note]. *Ivi, Libro IV, p. 26.*

65 In praise of Marquis Francescantonio Grimaldi [translator's note].

66 See note n. 54.

67 See note n. 58.

68 Antonio Jerocades, *La lira focense*, Napoli, sold by Gennaro Fonzo, 1783.

69 For a referenced bibliography on Jerocades and his work, see Vincenzo Ferrone, *I profeti dell'illuminismo*, op. cit., pp. 210, 269–270, where comes out a match between the poetic language of Jerocades and that used in the literature by the members of the Neapolitan group.

70 *Essay on the human knowledge for the use of youngsters* [translator's note]. On the care to education that always qualified the action of Jerocades, who also raised a Project of civil catechism to Tanucci, see Pasquale Matarazzo, *I catechismi degli stati di vita alla fine del Settecento*, in Anna Maria Rao (edited), *Editoria e cultura*, op. cit., pp. 508–511.

postulated a pedagogy grounded in "uso del senso, della fantasia, e della ragione"[71] whose aim was "il compimento della virtù, senza di cui non si potrà esser felice".[72] In the essay, Jerocades also introduced his ideas on the tutorial duty of poetry—seen as a method of communication and possible dialogue amid people rather than as an artistic fact—as painted in the *Puerile rhymes* in the appendix. Taking over the myth of Orpheus, the author recalled the civilizing role of poetry able to render the truth pleasing, making use of imagination. Later, thanks to Genovesi, Jerocades obtained a chair at the college Tuziano in Sora, where, despite his mentor's advice, he gave free rein to the satirical vein painting Ferdinando IV under the guise of Pulcinella in a recital of students in 1770. As the scandal followed, Jerocades reacted by first repairing in Naples and then in Marseilles, where he had relatives. His first contact with masonry dates back to France. In Italy again, he spent a period of expiation in Sora and, in 1776, back to Naples, founded a private school, and tightened closely with Gaetano Filangieri, Francesco Mario Pagano, Domenico Cirillo, Donato Tommasi, Matteo Galdi , Saverio Mattei, and Francescantonio Grimaldi. In the Neapolitan years, Jerocades devoted himself to the verses, stating that "i poeti e gli storici"[73] had been "i primi maestri de' popoli".[74] *La Lira focense*, as the author himself explained, was born by merging poems yet widely known—"non sono stato avaro nel dispensarle, né tantomeno bel dire altrui l'aria per la musica; ma stanco oggi mai di farne più copie si è pensato di darle alle stampe"[75]—and had—in the eighteenth century—two other Neapolitan reprints (1785 and 1789).

Further confirming its diffusion in the Kingdom of Naples, it also kept the attention of the most conservative Catholic circles, being publicly refuted in the *Antilira focense* or *Dialoghi con cui si rende ravveduto un massone o libero muratore*[76] (Naples 1789) by Calabrian abbot Francesco Spadea, who charged the poet to be a "master of impiety." To the pamphlet, anonymously

---

71 "sense, fantasy, and reason" [translator's note].

72 "the fulfillment of virtue, without of which one can not be happy" [translator's note]. Antonio Jerocades, *Saggio dell'umano sapere ad uso de' giovanetti di Paralia*, stamperia Simoniana, Napoli, 1768, p. xvi.

73 "the poets and historians" [translator's note].

74 "the first tutors of folks" [translator's note]. Antonio Jerocades, *Parabole dell'Evangelio*, nella stamperia, Raimondiana, Napoli, 1782, p. 104.

75 "I was not stingy in dispensing them, nor even the air of music; but tired nowadays ever to deliver more copies, then the thought has been to print it" [translator's note].

76 Dialogues to repent a mason or freemason [translator's note].

published, Jerocades replied with the *Gigantomachia* (Naples 1789). It was not just a literary quarrel, but also a very ideological dispute. On one side, there was a will to spread the Masonic message, kept as a whole knowledge able to merge the cyclical-catastrophic envisioning of nature with the effort to a virtuous progress—a new golden age—where mankind would have lived in peace, fraternity, and freedom. Opposite to these, the strenuous defense of customary values—as religious as political—of Ancien Régime, sensed as subversive the new language of Jerocades. His answer was built as a series of letters to real recipients, such as the friend and Brother Saverio Mattei, seeded with poetic texts, where the criticisms raised against the Lira were addressed and refuted. The *Gigantomachia* was not, however, a simple apology, but a chance to reflect on his work. If the Lira embodied the virtuous man generically as "friend" and "Brother," in *Gigantomachia*, this figure was embodied by Gaetano Filangieri who, after his untimely death, had become a true symbol of virtue. As well known, the Masonic funeral of the young prince, in 1788, had been turned into a sort of secular sanctification by Jerocades himself and, then, by Francesco Mario Pagano, Domenico Cirillo, Donato Tommasi, and Matteo Galdi.[77] A year later the author, on a letter in Gigantomachia addressed to mason Luigi Rossi—a very young jurist-poet from Calabria disciple of Gregorio Aracri and future Republican patriot—still celebrated the "virtue" of Filangieri and recalled their close bonds:

> Era mio grande amico [...] e amico dell'uomo. Il suo libro sulla scienza della Legislazione, tradotto in molte lingue di Europa, e sparso per tutta la terra, fu in Roma proibito per opera di qualche Abate Spadea, o di qualche Frate Masdea. Ad esso lui piacevano tanto le mie canzonette, che è mi chiamava l'Orfeo, e voleva sempre ascoltarle con la moglie, e co' figli. Or cantiamo la canzone che si cantò nelle solenni esequie, dalla virtù vivente celebrate alla defunta virtù.[78]

---

77   Vincenzo Ferrone, *I profeti dell'Illuminismo*, op. cit., pp. 209–210.

78   "He was my great friend [...] and man's friend. His book on the science of law, translated into many idioms of Europe, and spread throughout the earth, was forbidden in Rome by the work of some Abbot Spadea, or some Friar Masdea. He liked my melody that much to call me Orpheus, and he always wanted to listen to them with his wife, and with his children. Let's sing the song sung in the solemn funeral rites, from the living virtue celebrated to the defunct virtue" [translator's note]. Antonio Jerocades, *La Gigantomachia*, op. cit., p. 127.

Still in the Gigantomachia, he made the funeral song follow the aforementioned letter, printing it for the very first time. In the poetic text, we witness the glorifying of Filangieri's philosophical, peaceful, and contemplative values, making him emerge as a sage who, on the trail of Orpheus, devoted himself to steadily enlighten mankind and thus becoming the "Great Hero of our age"—as unceasingly repeated at the end of each short stanza. Filangieri wasn't just destined to endless recognition in the "Temple of the Heroes", but to a real immortality as a model to be emulated. The song resumed what already declared in *La gloria del saggio*[79]—an epistle in verses—again celebrating Filangieri. The same purpose had the *epicedio* by Pagano, declaimed during the Masonic funeral and printed in 1788.[80] Pagano, after comparing his deceased friend to the civilizing heroes Prometheus and Hercules, set him amid the "Eccelsi Eroi, del Ciel prole ed imago"[81] whose task was "rimenar alla virtù smarrita / l'errante mondo [...] / come la stella del mattin lucente / sorge a schiarar la tenebrosa notte".[82] As in the elegy by Jerocades, the outcome was a stunning and dramatic depiction of Filangieri, martyring himself against "error" in pursuit of righteousness and happiness.

The Gigantomachia strongly reiterated the universe of Masonic values expressed in the Lira and, with other opuses in memory of Filangieri, made the young prince the "hero," outlining in "flash and blood" a renewed virtue reflecting Enlightenment and Masonry: the wise man who fought a peaceful struggle with the weapons of thought for the progress of humanity.

Why could *Lira focense* be considered subversive? What hid Jerocades under the easy-singing rhythms that outraged so much Spadea? Which principles did Jerocades whirl his personal poetic temple around? First of all, we must comprehend the verses of Jerocades were openly blamed since politically hazardous only after the capture of the Bastille. Following the French

---

79   *The luster of the sage. To Attorney D. Donato Tommasi, a letter by Antonio Jerocandes on the passing of Gentleman D. Gaetano Filangieri* [translator's note]. La gloria del saggio. All'avvocato D. Donato Tommasi epistola di Antonio Jerocades in morte del Cavalier D. Gaetano Filangieri, Raimondi, Napoli, 1788.

80   On the passing of Gentleman Gaetano Filangieri epicedio by Attorney and Royal Academician Francesco Mario Pagano translator's note]. In morte del Cavalier Gaetano Filangieri epicedio dell'avvocato e regio cattedratico Francesco Mario Pagano, Raimondi, Napoli, 1788, from which all the quotes are taken until otherwise reported.

81   "Sublime Heroes, of Heaven sons and mirrors" [translator's note].

82   "to lead to the lost virtue / the wandering world [...] / as the star of the shiny morning / rises to clear the dark night" [translator's note].

events, the topics of the Lira, originally framed into the Neapolitan reform-ism, were taken as revolutionary and disrespectful not only to religion, but first and foremost to the monarchical order.

About the subject, the poetry of Jerocades merged the epicurean-freema-sonic tradition embodied by Crudeli with Neapolitan suggestions from Vico to Genovesi up to Filangieri. Read in its entirety, the Lira reveals the unvarying words and key formulas: friendship, love, freedom, peace, piety, virtue, and the golden age.[83] And, it was precisely the return of the gold-en age the main theme of the collection: this return had nothing in com-mon with coeval expressions of escape from reality as the Arcadian poetry, but with the desired reform toward that "just and fair society" drawn by Genovesi and well outlined by Filangieri. It was a community—to Jero-cades—grounded in brotherhood and friendship, and without any distinc-tion apart from those based on merit. The boot camp to act and improve these changes was definitely the masonic lodge, but the ultimate recipient was the whole of humanity indeed.

The early reformist intent and the tenacity on the chance to educate both the king and the people, however, did not prevent the author himself from re-reading and re-framing his work in a Jacobin key, giving public reading of his texts in pro-French and pro-republicans milieu, such as meetings on the vessel of the French Admiral Latouche-Tréville,[84] held between 1792 and 1793, showing again the openness of masonic lodges to the contemporary political debate.

1.7 Hapsburg Lombardy: Milan, Cremona, Pavia

In Milan, then the center of Hapsburg Lombardy, around the 50s again, it's reported the presence of a lodge founded by a Calvinist watchmak-er, Pierre Georges Madiott.[85] The news we have derive from the papers of the trial brought in 1756 by the senator Gabriele Verri, father of Pietro

---

83 On the European success of the golden age myth, see Dan Edelstein, *The Terror of Natural Right: Republicanism, the Cult of Nature and the French Revolution*, University of Chicago Press, Chicago–London, 2009, pp. 11–14.

84 Giuseppe Giarrizzo, *Massoneria e illuminismo nell'Europa del Settecento*, Marsilio, Ve-nezia, 1994, pp. 391–392.

85 On Freemasonry in Lombardy, see Giuseppe Giarrizzo, *La massoneria lombarda dalle origini al periodo napoleonico*, in Gian Mario Cazzaniga (edited), *La Massoneria. Storia d'Italia*, op. cit., pp. 356–386.

and Alessandro. The lodge, a true example of cosmopolitanism and tolerance, with a singular mixture of urban (bourgeois and aristocratic) and
military members, united Brethen of various classes and creeds: craftsmen
like Madiott, clergymen like Abbot Pavesi and father Francesco Sormani,
aristocrats like the marquis Ottaviano Casnedi, the count Alari, the count
Giuseppe Castelbarco, the count Carlo Belgioioso and the knight Melzi,
imperial officers like General Joseph Esterhazi. The audit quitted unfruitful,
just inflicting pecuniary penalties and commanding open abjuration: the
commission, who came across influential citizens, had preferred to put the
story down as soon as possible. There was, however, an official condemnation, by the governor, the duke Francesco of Modena, in the edict issued on
May 6, 1757, in which Freemasonry was prohibited throughout Lombardy.
Even in Milan, as in Florence and Naples, there was an early confluence
between masonic and intellectual environments. And once again it's by the
life and work of a writer and poet, Giuseppe Cerretesi, these bonds become
known. Cerretesi, as seen, had attended the same masonic environments
as Crudeli in the Florence of the '30s and had been directly involved in the
trial of the Inquisition. However, he managed to escape arrest through a
lifelong vagrancy, also due to family conflicts.

The first statement of literary activity, after trial and exile in England and
Flanders, was the translation of Pope's *Epistles*, appeared in Milan in 1756
with dedication to the marquis Giorgio Clerici, condottiere and then imperial ambassador. The epistles of the English poet were defined as a "philosophical offering"[86] to the powerful Milanese patrician and to Maria Teresa
and provided the structure to the three *Idilli* dating back to the Milanese
period. In the first, *Il pregio dell'amicizia*[87] (1760), the poet reworked the
theme of friendship and the "social knot" introduced 20 years earlier by
Crudeli. The opus begins with a dedication to the governor Karl Joseph
von Firmian. Not without masonic echoes, friendship was raised to "the
first item of civil life" and to "the sublimated essence of virtue."

The interweaving virtue–friendship–happiness was resumed with ampli-
tude in the second idyll, *Il tempio della felicità*[88] (1760), dedicated to the

---

86   *Le quattro epistole morali del sig. Pope poeta inglese, esposte in versi sdruccioli da Giuseppe
      Cerretesi* [The four moral epistles of Mr. Pope English poet, exposed in slippery verses
      by Giuseppe Cerretesi], Nella stamperia Malatesta, Milano, 1756.

87   *The value of friendship* [translator's note].

88   *The temple of happiness* [translator's note].

Countess Teresa Simonetta Castelbarco, sister of freemason Count Joseph. Here, through the metaphor of the temple, Cerretesi sings on how happiness descend from virtue and observance of "quelle leggi naturali, che il Cielo / scolpì nel cuor d'ognun"[89] through which "l'uomo ami l'altr'uomo come se stesso".[90] The image of the temple, of Masonic derivation, clearly underlined the idea of a progressive construction of virtuous character and of happiness, appearing to be "rights" everyone could reach. It was the theme of equality—meant however more as an primordial state and moral attribute than as a political premise to undo the class system from the *Ancien Régime*—perhaps the very original part of this second text.

The last idyll was *Il tesoro della povertà* (1761), dedicated to Vittoria Serbelloni Ottoboni, in whose lively Milanese *salon* gathered the Verri brothers' group— which soon was going to found Il Caffè—and who hired as tutor for her children Giuseppe Parini. The poet, not missing biographical echoes—he was chronically in disgrace because of family arguments—claims the true virtue, and therefore happiness, consisted in being "del poco contento".[91]

As Cerretesi's work fairly shows, despite the trial brought by Gabriele Verri, in Lombardy, the masonic stimuli were not dormant and, around 1776, there was notice of a new lodge: the "San Paolo Celeste" in Cremona, founded by officers of the garrison and soon becoming a center of diffusion of the Enlightenment, and operative until 1785, when by imperial; will, it merged with "La Concordia" [*Concord*] of Milan. The cultural diversion of the lodge was due to the mastery of Giambattista Biffi. Educated in Pavia, he moved to Milan where he became a friend of Verri and Cesare Beccaria and partook in the Accademia dei Pugni. In 1762, however—yet keeping in touch with Beccaria—the family recalled him to Cremona. Biffi was an early devotee of English writers like Pope, Hume, Swift (read in the original idiom); however his culture "simile a quella degli altri membri dell'Accademia dei pugni [è] ispirata soprattutto ai francesi":[92] his library counted

---

89 "those natural laws, which Heaven / carved in the heart of each" [translator's note].

90 "the man loves other man as himself" [translator's note]. Giuseppe Cerretesi, *Il tempio della felicità*, Mazzucchelli, Milano, 1760.

91 "joyful with little" [translator's note]. Giuseppe Cerretesi, *Il tesoro della povertà*, Mazzucchelli, Milano, 1761.

92 "similar to that of the other members of the Accademia dei Pugni [is] inspired above all to the French" [translator's note]. Franco Venturi, *Un amico di Beccaria e Verri: Giambattista Biffi*, in "Giornale Storico della Letteratura Italiana", CXXXIV, 1957, n.1,

Montesquieu, Voltaire, Buffon, D'Alembert, Diderot, but above all Rousseau and Brother Hélvetius, whose *Esprit* translated. Amid the Brothers during his mastery, there were the writers Carlo Castone Rezzonico della Torre and Giovanni Pindemonte, and Lorenzo Manini, the Italian publisher of eminent members such as Francesco Algarotti and Benjamin Franklin.

Meanwhile, Giuseppe II, ascending to the imperial throne, assumed a markedly philo-masonic policy aimed at protecting "la corrente laica e razionalista della libera muratoria"[93] and culminated with an edict on December 11, 1785, where "Sua Maestà si era 'compiaciuta di graziosissimamente risolvere e ordinare che queste società si abbiano a prendere sotto la protezione e tutela dello stato', essendo i massoni 'tanti rispettabili uomini noti a Sua Maestà,' utili 'al prossimo e alle scienze.'"[94]

The Emperor's intent was clearly to use Freemasonry for his own political ends, foretasting Napoleon Bonaparte's strategy.[95] His policy, anyhow, encouraged a new flowering of the freemasonry also in Milan and since 1783, we account "La Concordia," which counted among its ranks diverse outstanding citizens, as well as artists as the painter Andrea Appiani and men of letters like Aurelio de' Giorgi Bertola and Adelmo Fugazza or scientist like Johann Peter Frank, professor of Medicine at the University of Pavia and Gregorio Fontana, professor of Calculus sublime in the same Institution. The University of Pavia seems to have been, under Josepeh II and Napoleon, an influential center of Masonic gathering, Brothers were indeed noteworthy professors such as Bertola, Frank, Fontana, Samuel August David Tissot (professor of clinical medicine) then Vincenzo Monti, Ugo Foscolo, Gian Domenico Romagnosi, and Lorenzo Mascheroni. Münter himself chose it as the end of his masonic voyage and in the same occasion

---

pp. 66–67: 44–45 (poi in Id., *Settecento riformatore. Da Muratori a Beccaria*, Einaudi, Torino, 1969).

93   "the secular and rationalist current of free masonry" [translator's note]. Carlo Francovich, *Storia della Massoneria in Italia*, op. cit., p. 355.

94   "His Majesty 'was pleased to resolve and order with dignity these companies have to take under the protection of the state', 'being the Masons many respectable men renown to His Majesty', profitable 'to mankind and knowledge'" [translator's note]. Here is the text of the decree, effective in all the imperial territories, as widespread in Trieste by the governor Pompeo Brigido—a mason—*Codice ossia Collezione sistematica di tutte le leggi e ordinanze emanate sotto il regno di S.M. Imperiale Giuseppe II* [*Codex or Systematic Collection of all the laws and ordinances issued under the reign of S.M. Imperial Giuseppe II*], Milano, 1789—Biblioteca Civica di Trieste, n. 13271.

95   Carlo Francovich, *Storia della Massoneria in Italia*, op. cit., p. 362.

he met, further to the aforementioned members, the group of Jansenists led by Pietro Tamburini and Giuseppe Zola. Yet, no lodge appears to have been operating in those years. About, only one letter remains from Brother Giovanni Viazzoli, a state official from "La Concordia"—written on October 28, 1784, to Antonio Reina, representative of the Milanese lodge at the Grand National Lodge of Vienna—where he expressed the will of founding a lodge in Pavia, endorsed by Brother Bertola. The outcome remains however unknown.

1.8 Masonic, Cultural, and Commercial Networks: The Free Port of Trieste

The garrison officer Walz, together with Matteo Hochkoffler and the lieutenant De Courten, built the first lodge in Trieste in 1773, with the distinctive title *Alla Concordia*. Members were the judge G. M. Stefani, the merchants Giuseppe Weber, Cesare Pellegrini, Anastasio Papaleca, Sebastiano Fels, Giovanni Blachenay, Ignazio Hagenauer, the officers Saint Eloi and Jacoviti. The Foundation Charter was then requested from the Prague Provincial Lodge, which granted it only in 1775, after the purge of Hochkoffler, Saint Eloi, and Jacoviti. The same governor of Trieste, Karl von Zinzendorf was a freemason, as was his successor, Pompeo Brigido.[96]

Scarce facts are known on the lodge in the next decade, until 1784, when venerable became François Emanuel Joseph Baraux and the lodge changed its name to *De l'harmonie et concorde universelle*. It joined the Eclectic Federation (*Eklektischer Bund*), built from the ashes of the Strict Obedience in Frankfurt, after the Wilhelmsbad conference. With personal protection granted by Giuseppe II to freemasonry—and appears indeed on the advice of Grand Master Francesco di Brunswick—the Trieste lodge passed to the Federation of Austrian Lodges (*Oesterreischischer Logenbund*). The news of the accession to the Austrian Federation was also reported in the *Journal für Freymauer.*[97]

The greatest advance of Freemasonry in Trieste happened in this period, mainly thanks to the efforts of the singular figure of Baraux, a merchant

---

96 On Zinzendorf and his relations with the Austrian and German Masonic context, see Pierre-Yves Beaurepaire, *L'espace des francs-maçons: une sociabilité européenne au 18e siècle*, Presses universitaires de Rennes, Rennes, 2003, pp. 151–179.

97 *Journal für Freymauer als Manuskript gedruckt für Brüder und Meister des Ordens—II Jahrgang, I. Vierteljahr—5875*, p. 218.

from Antwerp who came to Trieste in 1782 as a member of the Austrian East India Company. In 1789, he eventually became consul of the States General of the United Provinces for the Austrian Litoral. Baraux was a man of many engagements, witnessed by his library. He even developed his own line of thought, close to the ideas of Montesquieu for the criticism of excessive wealth, the praise of meritocracy, and esteem for the British monarchy. Baraux also compiled a charter *Del commercio e dell'industria*,[98] published in 1828 (but drafted already in 1816), where he outlines trading as the premise of civilization which "sviluppa il genio, infonde attività nello spirito, rende le nazioni sagge e colte, le fa inventare e perfezionare le arti";[99] commerce was also seen as an instrument of modernity and equality, being able to erase "quell'eccedente ineguaglianza, frutto dell'oppressione e del potere de' tempi feudali".[100] This way, then, Trieste, house of trades, was the ideal city for cultural and political development.

Overall, the eighteenth-century Italian lodges show how the masonic environment was conceived as innovative space of debate and dialogue in the *Ancien Régime*. On Trieste, these features emerge even more clearly. From the lists of the affiliates in span 1773–1793, it appears lodges were the communities where the ambition of the emerging bourgeois classes— traders and professionals—those of the intellectuals, the gentry, and the high cadres of the state concurred.[101] Thus, in Trieste, the distinctive trait of eighteenth-century Masonic sociability merged with the singularity of the free port, a crossroads of gatherings and exchanges and a place of authority deferment, where even the political power was constantly challenged in the name of commercial needs.

1.9 1805: The Birth of the Grand Orient of Italy

This brief overlook illustrates the diverse scenery of freemasonry in the eighteenth-century Italian states. As seen, masonry had a labored beginning, marked by complaints, trials and persecution which, however,

---

98   *On business and trade* [translator's note].

99   "develops genius, infuses activities in the spirit, makes nations wise and educated, he invented and perfected the arts" [translator's note].

100 "that redundant inequality, the result of oppression and the power of feudal times" [translator's note].

101 Attilio Tamaro, *Documenti di storia triestina del secolo XVIII*, in "Atti e memorie della società istriana di archeologia e storia patria", XLI, 1, 1929, pp. 191–192.

allowed it to seed and prosper. Another conventional feature amid various Italian masons is the strong bond established immediately with the intellectual class closer to those reformistic claims we today know as Enlightenment: Crudeli and Cerretesi in Florence, Goldoni in Venice, Biffi in Milan, Bertola in Pavia, Filangieri and Jerocades in Naples.

At the end of the century after the early struggles and persecutions, throughout the Peninsula freemasonry was a widespread body to which nobles, officials, intellectuals and bourgeois belonged; in short it was constant presence in the Italian social and cultural panorama. The revolutionary period marked a season of challenges: as already said, French freemasonry had even ruled out in the hardest years of the Terror, while in the Italian States began a new season of oppression and bans, due to anti-masonic propaganda, depicting masons as inspirers of the feared Jacobins.

In 1793, the Emperor Leopold promulgated an edict that banned Masonry again from the imperial lands. However, the scenario suddenly shifted when Napoleon descended a few years later. It was in 1805 that, along with the foundation of the Realm of Italy, the Grand Orient of Italy was born: thus, it is no surprise that it has been wittingly called "figlio dell'Europa francese".[102]

The new Obedience was born on March 16, 1805, as the Supreme Council of Sovereign Grand Inspectors General of the 33rd Degree; Eugenio de Beauharnais — viceroy of Italy, adopted son of Napoleon — mastered it. On March 20, it was rebuilt as an order, with the title of Grand Scottish General Lodge, and renamed again on June 20 to the Grand Orient of Italy. The birth of the Grand Orient and Napoleon's desire to exploit the network of masonic lodges for political purposes favored the wide diffusion of the latter throughout the Italian territory.

---

102 "offspring of French Europe" [translator's note]. Giuseppe Giarrizzo, *La massoneria lombarda*, op. cit., p. 384: "Il Grande Oriente d'Italia è figlio [...] dell'Europa francese". Gian Mario Cazzaniga, *Nascita del Grande Oriente d'Italia*, in Gian Mario Cazzaniga (edited), *La Massoneria, Storia d'Italia*, op. cit., pp. 545–558.

2. Italian Freemasonry from the Eighteenth Century to Unification
Protagonists, Metamorphoses, Interpretations

Luca G. Manenti

2.1 Intro

Historians wondering about when the Italian Risorgimento began give the earliest date as 1713, the year when the Treaty of Utrecht was signed and the Savoy dynasty acquired the royal title, and then 1748—the year of the Treaty of Aix-la-Chapelle—after which the Italian peninsula experienced a long interval of peace and of reforms grounded in the principles of the Enlightenment.[103] Others have attributed great importance to the arrival of Bonaparte's army in Italy in 1796.[104] In fact, the 21 years between Napoleon's arrival and Joachim Murat's failed attempt to unify the country in 1815 did indeed coincide with a period of modernization which fostered a desire for independence.[105] Conservative historiography claimed that a continuous line connected the French occupation of Italy with the unification process, viewed in an eschatological perspective as undeniable proof of evil Masonic influence. A host of conservatives blamed the French Revolution, the Napoleonic Wars and the Italian nationalist movement, all on the work of the brothers, proposing an unbroken continuum stretching from 1789 to the proclamation of the reign of Vittorio Emanuele II in 1861. In a series of anti-Risorgimento novels published in the first half of the nineteenth century, the Jesuit Antonio Bresciani described the Lutheran Reformation and the French Revolution as the greatest evils of mankind, and depicted Mazzini's *Giovine*

---

103 Luigi Salvatorelli, *Pensiero e azione del Risorgimento*, Einaudi, Torino, 1963, pp. 34–35. I would like to adpress my heartfelt thanks to Judith Moss for the inguistic revision of the English version of this essay.

104 Alberto Mario Banti, *Il Risorgimento italiano*, Laterza, Roma-Bari, 2005.

105 Antonino De Francesco, *Prima dell'Unità. Dalla Massoneria italiana alla Carboneria*, in Massimo Rizzardini, Andrea Vento (edited), *All'Oriente d'Italia. Le fondamenta segrete del rapporto fra Stato e Massoneria*, Rubbettino, Soveria Mannelli, 2013, pp. 15–30, here p. 16.

Italia (Young Italy) as a satanic, pseudo-Masonic sect, dominated by Protestants and Jews.[106]

Other historians argued that the unbroken timeline connecting 1789 and 1861 was interrupted by the disappearance of Freemasonry during the restoration and by the purely domestic origins of unification. They tended to exaggerate the glorious achievement of their homeland and minimize or deny any support from outside, although on one point, their theories were correct: while it was true that the ideology of revolution had provided the opportunity for the process of nation-building to begin, this process was founded nevertheless on a whole range of myths and memories taken from indigenous cultural traditions which had been developing in the Italian peninsula since the early modern age.[107]

In 1925, the same year in which the fascist laws against secret societies appeared, aimed in particular at the freemasons' lodges, Alessandro Luzio published *La massoneria e il Risorgimento italiano*,[108] theorizing the destruction of freemasonry during the Risorgimento and its replacement with the more militant Carboneria.[109] In the same year, Giuseppe Leti published an article, which, like Luzio's, was as well-documented as it was biased, but in the other direction. He tried to show that the Carboneria—together with all the other secret societies of the Risorgimento—had their origin in freemasonry, thereby enhancing the role of the Brotherhood in the process of unification: "D'altra parte i maggiori esponenti della *massoneria*, nella impossibilità d'ostacolare la reazione, piuttosto che traviarsi, si restrinsero nel chiuso de' *templi*, e diedero il *via* alle altre *società segrete* perché tenessero il campo, mentre quella si selezionò, si venne rinnovando e preparando a maggiori cimenti".[110] Taking the second half of the eighteenth century as

---

106 Paolo Orvieto, *Buoni e cattivi del risorgimento. I romanzi di Garibaldi e Bresciani a confronto*, Salerno Editrice, Roma, 2011.

107 Antonino De Francesco, *The Antiquity of the Italian Nation. The Cultural Origins of a Political Myth in Modern Italy, 1796–1943*, Oxford University Press, Oxford, 2013, p. 15.

108 *Masonry and the Italian Risorgimento* [translator's note].

109 Alessandro Luzio, *La massoneria e il Risorgimento italiano*, 2 vv., Zanichelli, Bologna, 1925.

110 "While the main exponents of freemasonry—finding themselves unable to stop the reaction, rather than betray their order, withdrew into their temples, and let other secret societies take their place, while they selected and renewed their ranks and prepared for further trials" [translator's note]. Giuseppi Leti, *Carboneria e massoneria nel*

the starting-point for our analysis, we shall examine the role played by Italian freemasonry up until unification, following its transformations along with the history of institutions and ideas, and analysing the genealogies and specific characteristics of the lodges and secret societies of the time, and the contributions and legacies which came from abroad.

2.2 From Enlightened Despotism to Napoleon

In 1952, Carlo Francovich summed up the divergent opinions of historians on the activity of eighteenth-century freemasons: according to some, they were both spiritually and politically extraneous to the Enlightenment, while for others, they were at the very forefront of the movement. He argued that these two theories were both right and wrong at the same time, and over fifty years later, his opinion can still be considered as having a certain validity.[111]

In the age of enlightened despotism, which was characterized by an alliance between sovereigns and intellectuals aimed at making the state's machinery more efficient and at procuring the greatest happiness for the greatest number of people, the role played by Italian freemasonry was more important in some geographical areas than in others. The reforms which were the fruit of the alliance described above were most successful in Lombardy and Tuscany, and arrived some time later in Naples and the Papal States; there was little room for them elsewhere and by 1775 they were beginning to fail, even before the end of the ancient regime.[112] In a context such as this, masonry was in turn an inspiration or a tool for rulers championing the cause of social restraint and secularization within their domains: it is not always easy to distinguish between *raison d'état* and sincere adherence to Masonic values. The common ground shared by freemasonry and the Enlightenment consisted on the one hand, in the primacy of reason as a means for the attainment of truth, and on the other, in the common aim of giving back to the people the knowledge taken from them by ecclesiastic and secular powers.[113]

---

risorgimento italiano, Res Gestae, Milano, 2016, p. 80.

111 Carlo Francovich, *Albori socialisti nel Risorgimento. Contributo allo studio delle società segrete (1776–1835)*, Le Monnier, Firenze, 1962, p. 1.

112 Stuart J. Woolf, *Il Risorgimento italiano*, Mondadori, Milano, 2010, pp. 140 and 154–162.

113 Giuseppe Giarrizzo, *Massoneria*, in *Enciclopedia delle Scienze Sociali*, v. 5, Treccani,

In the twenty years between 1770 and 1790, the Italian lodges had an aristocratic imprint, numbering prominent figures at court, military officers, university professors, and churchmen with Jansenist leanings.[114] Though not a theatre of actual war, the Italian peninsula was still a place where the great powers clashed, a situation reflected in the dynamics of inter-lodge relationships, with scenes of conflict between the pro-British and the pro-French, and between Hanoverian Protestants and Jacobite Catholics.[115] Most of the lodges were to be found in Turin and Naples, seats respectively of the Grand Priory of Italy, founded in 1775 and presided over by Count Gabriele Asinari of Bernezzo, and the Grand Lodge "Lo Zelo" [*The Fervour*], led by Francesco d'Aquino, prince of Caramanico and the favorite of Queen Maria Carolina.[116]

Asinari lived in a climate characterized by benevolent tolerance towards freemasonry, demonstrated by the renovation of the meeting hall in Turin's prestigious Academy of Sciences into a space where masonic symbols were interspersed with royal insignia.[117] This began to change in 1790 with the ministerial ban on masonic meetings, until in 1794, Vittorio Amedeo III definitively closed all the lodges in the kingdom.[118] In Naples, the prince of Caramanico had founded the Grand Lodge with the aim of making freemasons independent of London and associating them with the German Order of Strict Observance, which was linked to the Templar tradition and favoured a hierarchical model centred on figures called "unidentified superiors".[119] Coming into conflict with Minister Bernardo Tanucci, who had ordered the arrest of some low-ranking masons in order to bring the queen into disrepute, d'Aquino intervened in their favour with the help of influential European masonic dignitaries, having the prisoners freed and

---

Roma, 1996, pp. 551–559, here pp. 554–555.

114 Renato Soriga, *Le Società segrete, l'emigrazione politica e i primi moti per l'indipendenza, scritti raccolti e ordinati da Silio Manfredi*, Società Tipografica Modenese, Modena, 1942, p. 28.

115 Fabio Martelli, *Massoneria e Illuminismo*, in Santi Fedele, Giovanni Greco (edited), *Massoneria ed Europa. 300 anni di storia*, Bonanno, Acireale, 2017, pp. 35–53, here p. 44.

116 Renato Soriga, *Le Società segrete*, op. cit., pp. 28–29.

117 Federico Navire, *Torino come centro di sviluppo culturale. Un contributo agli studi della civiltà italiana*, Peter Lang, Frankfurt am Main, 2009, pp. 228–229.

118 Antonio Trampus, *La massoneria nell'età moderna*, Laterza, Roma-Bari, 2008, p. 116.

119 Giuseppe Giarrizzo, *Massoneria*, op. cit., p. 554.

strengthening ties with the most influential masonic circles on the continent.[120] Although we should not over-estimate the capacities for political intervention of the freemasonry movement in southern Italy, which never lost its marked profile as a place of socialization and mutual aid for its members, it undoubtedly played a more important cultural and ideological role than freemasonry in other parts of Italy, where the Brotherhood made its presence felt in various areas, helping to create consensus around the government or, on the other hand, destabilizing the ruling classes.[121]

In Lombardy, the movement was skilfully controlled by Giuseppe II,[122] son of the freemason Francesco Stefano di Lorena and a brother himself.[123] With his patent of December 11, 1785, the emperor reorganized the masonry in the territories of his realm, placing a limit on the number of lodges allowed in each region and ordering them to report the registers and dates of meetings to the authorities. This provision, in line with the re-organization of the Habsburg territories being carried out at the administrative and bureaucratic levels, gave substance to the concern that the lodges might exert a power parallel and potentially hostile to the governing one, as shown by the episode of the Illuminati of Bavaria and the excessive influence of the Strict Observance.[124] Giuseppe II's plan for reform had among its main proponents the Triestine Marquis Domenico Piatti, a member of the Viennese lodge "Alla Vera Concordia" [*To true Amity*], on whose behalf he travelled around Italy in the 1780s with the aim of creating a masonic confederation under the aegis of the Grand National Lodge of Vienna.[125] Passing through Venice, where he met the Venerable Michele Cessa, coordinator of the Rectified Scottish Rite between north and south;[126] he then went to

---

120 Antonello Scibilia, *Aquino, Francesco Maria Venanzio d', principe di Caramanico*, in *Dizionario Biografico degli Italiani*, v. 3, Treccani, Roma, 1961, pp. 664–672.

121 Vincenzo Ferrone, *I profeti dell'Illuminismo. Le metamorfosi della ragione nel tardo Settecento italiano*, Laterza, Roma-Bari, 1989, p. 247.

122 Antonio Trampus, *Prefazione*, in Joseph Lavallée, *Viaggio pittoresco e storico nell'Istria e nella Dalmazia*, Italo Svevo, Trieste, 2017, pp. I–VII, here p. III.

123 Fulvio Conti, *La massoneria*, in "Nuova informazione bibliografica", a. IV, n. 1, 2007, pp. 84–97, here p. 85.

124 Antonio Trampus, *La massoneria nell'età moderna*, Laterza, Roma-Bari, 2001, p. 123.

125 Carlo Francovich, *Storia della massoneria in Italia. Dalle origini alla Rivoluzione francese*, La Nuova Italia, Firenze,1974, pp. 378–379.

126 Renata Targhetta, *La massoneria veneta dalle origini alla chiusura delle logge (1729–1785)*, Del Bianco, Udine, 1988, p. 83.

Milan, Turin, and Naples, travelling with his son Antonio, and later paid the ultimate price for taking part in the Parthenopaean Republic of 1799, when he died at the hands of a Sanfedist.[127]

In 1790, Leopold II ascended the throne of Austria, to be succeeded two years later by Francis II, who suppressed freemasonry in all the territories of the Holy Roman Empire due to the prominent role it had presumably played in the French Revolution.[128] This is an understandable accusation, if we consider on the one hand, the high number of freemasons who played a leading role in that event, and on the other, that certain lodges were veritable breeding-grounds for those democratic principles summed up in the three words liberty, equality and fraternity.[129] A decade before the revolution, some lodges had turned themselves into terrorist cells, where members were taught how to organize a *coup d'état* and manipulate public opinion.[130] However, such a transformation only occurred in certain masonic circles, showing that it is impossible to provide blanket interpretations of the European freemasons' movement of the late eighteenth century. Although many masons had been victims of the Jacobin Terror, it's true that the political sectarianism of certain late century lodges had left a lasting ideological–organizational legacy, taken up by Babeuf as well as by the "patrioti 'anarchistes' del Triennio giacobino in Italia",[131] which finally came together in the subversive activities of the anti-system movements of the following century.

The French Revolution had a strong influence on the attitude of the sovereigns of the Italian peninsula, including Maria Carolina, who shifted from being a supporter of the freemasons to its opponent. When the wind changed, Italian freemasons were divided between those who were willing to get more involved in politics and those who chose to put an embarrass-

---

127 Elio Predonzani, *Domenico e Antonio Piatti, martiri triestini dell'epopea napoletana del 1799*, edited by Ufficio stampa e propaganda della Lega Nazionale, Trieste, 1948.

128 Paolo Gastaldi, *La Massoneria e l'emancipazione degli ebrei*, in "Hiram", n. 4, 2006, pp. 21–53, here p. 43.

129 Albert Soboul, *La Franc-maçonnerie et la Révolution française*, Société des Études Robespierristes, Paris, 1969.

130 Giuseppe Giarrizzo, *Massoneria e illuminismo nell'Europa del Settecento*, Marsilio, Venezia, 1994, pp. 214–215, 240–241, 315–316, 330–331.

131 "anarchic patriots of the Italian Jacobin triennium" [translator's note]. Eugenio Di Rienzo, *"Illuminismo politico"? Alcuni problemi di metodo sulla storiografia politica del Settecento*, in "Studi Storici", a. 36, n. 4, 1995, pp. 977–1010, here pp. 1009–1010.

ing past behind them.[132] Two Italian freemasons who had witnessed the revolution in Paris repudiated their former involvement: Vittorio Alfieri, with a biting satire on freemasonry,[133] and Ippolito Pindemonte, in a work entitled *Abaritte. Storia verissima*,[134] printed in 1791, which expressed his disillusionment with the impossibility of achieving human perfectibility, one of the guiding principles of rationalist-inspired freemasonry.[135] In hindsight, then, the European journey of the Veronese writer in the years 1788–1791 came to lose every positive attribute, ending up as a drastic "annullamento del valore iniziatico del 'viaggio' della tradizione massonica".[136]

The Revolution became the target of a host of reactionaries, who saw in it the hand of dangerous hidden agents. In his 1790 publication, *Reflections on the Revolution in France*, Edmund Burke put the blame on the literati, together with sovereigns and capitalists, for having planned the annihilation of Christianity. Among others, the Italian counter-revolutionary literature was represented by the Sicilian abbot Nicola Spedalieri, who in his 1791 article *De' diritti dell'uomo*[137] attacked both deism and revolution, deemed to be the result of the seditious project of the National Assembly, aimed at destroying Catholicism and overthrowing governments. In the German-speaking area, articles by the Viennese Leopold Alois Hoffman circulated in which he attacked enlightened freemasons. But it was Augustin Barruel who enjoyed the greatest success with his *Mémoires pour servir à l'histoire du jacobinisme*, published in five volumes between 1797 and 1799, which highlighted the contrast between the legitimist masonry before 1789 and the later one with Jacobin tendencies, responsible for the revolutionary cataclysm together with encyclopaedists, Jansenists, and the Illuminati of

---

132 Renato Soriga, *Le Società segrete*, op. cit., p. 41.

133 Vittorio Alfieri, *Satire e poesie minori*, Barbera, Bianchi e comp., Firenze, 1858, *Satira decimaquinta. Le imposture*, pp. 113–117.

134 *Abaritte. A completely true story* [translator's note].

135 Ivano Caliaro, Renzo Rabboni, "*A' tuoi verdi anni... ". Sui viaggi e le memorie di Pindemonte*, in Helmut Meter, Furio Brugnolo (edited), *Vie lombarde e venete. Circolazione e trasformazione dei saperi letterari nel Sette-Ottocento fra l'Italia settentrionale e l'Europa transalpina*, De Gruyter, Berlin-Boston, 2011, pp. 169–189, here pp. 174–175.

136 "cancelling out the initiatory value of the 'journey' of masonic tradition" [translator's note]. Eros Maria Luzzitelli, *Introduzione all'edizione dei diari dei viaggi d'Ippolito Pindemonte in Europa (1788–1791) ed in Italia (1795–1796)*, in "Memorie. Classe di scienze morali, lettere ed arti", v. 40, f. 4, 1987, p. 6 note 3.

137 *On Mankind's Law* [translator's note].

Weishaupt.[138] The existential journey of Joseph de Maistre, Count of Savoy, appeared to prove him right: in 1778, de Maistre had set up an occultist and alchemical lodge, which aimed to develop a spiritualist masonry led by Catholics able to reconcile Rome with Orthodox Christians. Distancing himself from the affairs of the lodge after the Revolution (which he saw as divine punishment), he continued to think his old plan was ethically laudable,[139] although the first papal condemnation dated back to 1738. In Barruel's opinion, the freemasons had foreseen and pre-arranged everything, so as then to sit back and enjoy the satanic spectacle of Jacobin violence.

The theory of the French Revolution as being an outcome of the subversive plan of radical secret societies near to or coinciding with the lodges, was applied to the Risorgimento by both Catholic conservatives[140] and for opposite reasons, by some freemasons, eager to give their order the credit for any supposedly progressive event. By following different cultural routes, then, was how the myth of the never-ending masonic plot behind the scenes of politics and finance took hold.[141] The Revolution had been observed with interest by the most restless fringes among the freemasons of southern Italy, who re-organized themselves in secret to look more like the clubs of Paris.[142] That events in France and the subsequent arrival of Napoleon in Italy had a profound effect on the way in which belonging to the freemasons was perceived is made clear by the example of the "Accademia Aletina" of Naples: some of its members had been loyal to the crown, but were destined to take a completely different stand during the time of the Neapolitan Republic of 1799: masons, reformers, revolutionaries and anti-revolutionaries first coexisted and then fought against each other.[143]

---

138 Zeffiro Ciuffoletti, *Il complotto massonico e la Rivoluzione francese*, Edizione Medicea, Firenze, 1989.

139 Massimo Introvigne, *La contro-rivoluzione di Joseph de Maistre*, in http://www.cesnur.org/2011/mi-mai.html.

140 Walter Maturi, *Interpretazioni del Risorgimento. Lezioni di storia della storiografia*, Einaudi, Torino, 1962, p. 332.

141 Luca G. Manenti, *Massoneria italiana, ebraismo e movimento dei Giovani Turchi*, in "Rassegna mensile di Israel", v. 78, n. 3, 2012, pp. 161–175, here p. 171.

142 Dario Ippolito, *Pagano, Francesco Mario*, in *Dizionario Biografico degli Italiani*, v. 80, Treccani, Roma, 2014, pp. 259–263.

143 Anna Lisa Sannino, *Costruire la controrivoluzione. L'associazionismo politico-culturale anti-democratico in Puglia e Basilicata alla fine del Settecento*, in Angelo Massafra (edited), *Patrioti e insorgenti in provincia: il 1799 in Terra di Bari e Basilicata*, Conference proceedings of Altamura-Matera (14–16 October 1999), Edipuglia, Bari, 2002, pp.

2.3 Bonapartism and Freemasonry

Napoleon's invasion of Italy in 1796 swept away the old order and threw the diverse world of Italian freemasonry into disarray. By 1799, the troops sent by the Directory had reached the furthest extent of territories occupied, when they were pushed back by the Austro-Russians. They came back in 1800, and by 1808 once again controlled the entire peninsula, with the exception of Sicily and Sardinia. Bonaparte pushed to the extreme the Enlightenment reforms begun by the overthrown sovereigns, reducing the power of the Church, promoting the social advancement of the bourgeoisie, and adopting a conciliatory approach with the aristocracy. The French alternated a rapacious attitude towards resources and works of art with an attempt to modernize public and economic institutions by introducing new laws and limiting class-based privileges. To bring about such far-reaching changes, they needed support on the ground, and the freemasons' lodges were perfectly suited to this purpose, containing men steeped in those values of freedom and equality which were the rallying cry of the Revolution, but were soon to be abandoned by the French for political motives. In the Grand Duchy of Tuscany, freemasonry had been opposed by the church and state authorities since its first appearance, but the persecution got much worse immediately following the Revolution, until the arrival of Napoleon's troops in June 1796 made it possible for the lodges to re-open.[144]

In that same year, a lodge called "Les Amis de l'Union Parfaite" (The Friends of the Perfect Union) was founded in Livorno, the offshoot of a lodge with the same name situated in Perpignan, which was itself the offshoot of a Parisian lodge. Having started life in 1796 as a military lodge composed of soldiers and officers from a local infantry brigade, it managed to detach itself from the military and become independent, but in 1800, when the Grand Duke returned, all its furnishings and fittings were seized.[145] On June 1, 1796, the *Armée d'Italie* entered a half-empty Verona, abandoned by its aristocracy who had thought it wiser to go elsewhere. Until not long before, the city had given refuge to the Count of Lille, brother of the beheaded king of France who had proclaimed himself Louis XVIII, and around whom the local nobility had gathered. The pro-revolutionaries

---

487–527, here pp. 497–498.

144 Carlo Francovich, *Albori socialisti nel Risorgimento*, op. cit., p. 89.

145 Ivi, pp. 90–91.

were either members of the bourgeoisie or enlightened aristocrats, such as Sebastiano and Leonardo Salimbeni, both officers in the Venetian army and both freemasons. Since the sovereignty of the Republic of Venice was still formally recognized, when some individuals were arrested in Verona in 1796 on suspicion of Jacobinism, the French turned a blind eye and allowed the trial to take place, leaving their former allies in the hands of the Venetian judges. Among these were the freemason Luigi Campagnola and the Polfranceschi brothers—of noble descent—the older of whom was an artillery lieutenant who was very probably a mason.[146]

The short-lived Neapolitan Republic of 1799, which was not above using religion to ingratiate itself with the local population—it kept the ceremony of the liquefaction of San Gennaro's blood, and had the French army's trees of freedom blessed by priests[147]—welcomed to its highest ranks masons like Carlo Lauberg, Grand Master of an order he himself had founded—"Le colonne della democrazia"[148] [*The pillars of democracy*]—, and Francesco Mario Pagano and Domenico Cirillo, both members of Armonia, an English-rite lodge where they had developed a keen interest in the Hermetic tradition.[149] Both of the latter were executed in October 1799 when the Bourbons returned to power. According to Benedetto Croce, the most prominent female figure to participate in those events, Eleonora de Fonseca Pimentel, who shared the fate of her comrades, was also "ascritta alle società massoniche, nelle quali, a Napoli e altrove, si gettarono i germi delle posteriori 'società patriottiche' e delle cospirazioni repubblicane".[150]

In the first republican period (1796-1799), freemasonry tended mostly to collaborate with the French, who supported the masons and were supported by them, but some sections rebelled against more foreign subjugation. Every aspiration for national independence on the part of Italian patriots

---

146 Gian Paolo Romagnani, *Dalle "Pasque veronesi" ai moti agrari del Piemonte*, in "Studi Storici", a. 39, n. 2, 1998, pp. 367–399, here pp. 381–384.

147 John Robertson, *Enlightenment and Revolution: Naples 1799*, in "Transactions of the Royal Historical Society", v. 10, 2000, pp. 17–44, here p. 23.

148 Renata De Lorenzo, *Lauberg (Laubert, Lambert), Carlo Giovanni*, in *Dizionario Biografico degli Italiani*, v. 62, Treccani, Roma, 2005, pp. 47–51.

149 John Robertson, *Enlightenment and Revolution: Naples 1799*, op. cit., pp. 33, 38.

150 "enrolled in the Masonic societies, in which, in Naples and elsewhere, the seeds of later 'patriotic societies' and Republican conspiracies were sown" [translator's note]. Benedetto Croce, *La Rivoluzione napoletana del 1799. Biografie, racconti, ricerche*, Laterza, Bari, 1912, p. 24.

was thwarted, fanning the flames of a discontent that went underground. Thus, secret anti-Bonapartist lodges appeared, along with other movements connected in various ways to the masonic universe. Despite what has been said, it seems highly unlikely that the "Società dei Raggi" [*Society of Spokes*] was a radical lodge;[151] it was, nevertheless, part of that network of groups and associations involved in political opposition to the French.[152] According to Carlo Botta, it was established in France in 1798 by Italians seeking emancipation, who wanted to "camminare con le proprie gambe, e por mano essi stessi a quello che per opera dei forestieri non potevano sperar di acquistare".[153] Its headquarters was in Bologna, "e siccome da Bologna, come da centro, queste adunanze si spandevano, a guisa di raggi, tutto all'intorno negli altri paesi d'Italia, così chiamarono questa loro intelligenza Società dei Raggi".[154]

This great improvement in the level of organization of Italian freemasonry coincided with the second and longer-lasting republican period. In 1805, the Grand Orient of Italy was founded in Milan, the capital of the Kingdom of Italy. The Grand Mastery was entrusted to Prince Eugene of Beauharnais, assisted by Pietro Calepio and a board of eight grand inspectors, including Daniele Felici and Giuseppe Lechi.[155] According to a dispatch from the Austrian police, Calepio (affiliated in his youth to the Bergamo lodge "L'Unione" [*The Union*], founded perhaps by the Count of Cagliostro) was, "l'alter ego del principe Eugenio nella Gran Maestranza".[156] As in France,

---

151 Derek Beales, Eugenio F. Biagini, *Il Risorgimento e l'unificazione italiana*, Il Mulino, Bologna, 2005, p. 42.

152 Antonino De Francesco, *L'Italia di Bonaparte. Politica, statualità e nazione nella penisola tra due rivoluzioni, 1796–1821*, Utet, Torino, 2011, pp. 157–158.

153 "stand on their own two feet, and obtain themselves what they could not expect the foreigners to obtain for them" [translator's note]. Carlo Botta, *Storia d'Italia dall'anno 1789 all'anno 1814*, with corrections and notes by Luigi Toccagni written for this edition, v. 3, Giovanni Silvestri, Milano, 1844, p. 50.

154 "and because these meetings spread out from Bologna, at the centre, like the spokes of a wheel, all around the other parts of Italy, for this reason they called this network the Society of Spokes" [translator's note]. Ivi, p. 51.

155 Franco Della Peruta, *Il mondo latomistico della Restaurazione*, in Giampietro Berti, Franco Della Peruta (edited), *La nascita della nazione. La Carboneria intrecci veneti, nazionali e internazionali*, Conference proceedings of XXVI Convegno di Studi Storici Crespino, Rovigo, Fratta Polesine 8–9–10 novembre 2002, Minelliana, Rovigo, 2004, pp. 9–29, here p. 10.

156 "Prince Eugene's alter ego in the Grand Mastery" [translator's note]. Carlo Capra, *Calepio (Caleppio), Pietro*, in *Dizionario Biografico degli Italiani*, v. 16, Roma, Treccani,

freemasonry in the newborn Kingdom of Italy became an obedient propaganda machine in the hands of Bonaparte, but from then on, there was a strong attachment to the idea of an Italian nation.

In order to achieve total control over the lodges, the Napoleonic regime confined them to areas which increasingly coincided with the borders of the state, in a manner similar to the policy adopted by Giuseppe II. In 1805, then, Italian freemasonry underwent a process of partial unification, thereby gaining semi-official status. Placed under the indirect control of Napoleon, the lodges became willing tools of imperial policy, a place where the Franco-Italian military and bureaucratic machinery came together, where a rising bourgeoisie could gather, hungry for favour and recognition. The lodges were attended by intendants, notables, intellectuals, artists, writers, and even churchmen—ignoring the Church of Rome's anathemas against freemasonry because of its secrecy and the oath of loyalty required of its members. Milan also saw the appearance of a Rite of Misraïm which claimed to be of Egyptian origin, the expression of a fascination with the east dating back to Cagliostro which had come back into fashion after Napoleon's Egyptian campaign, during which, according to testimony unsupported by written evidence, he himself had been initiated.[157]

Crowned King of Naples in 1806, Giuseppe Bonaparte, who since 1805 had been Grand Master of the Grand Orient and Knight Commander of the Supreme Council of France, was appointed Grand Master of the Grand Orient in Naples until 1808, when he was made King of Spain and replaced by Murat,[158] who put local prefects and commissioners in charge of the lodges to guard against possible anti-government leanings.[159] In the lodges situated in territories annexed by the Empire and coming under the jurisdiction of the Grand Orient of France—i.e. Piedmont, Liguria, Tuscany and the Papal States—the Scottish Philosophical Rite and the Modern Rite prevailed, while in the Kingdom of Italy the Ancient and Accepted Scottish Rite was more popular.[160]

1973, pp. 676–677, here p. 677.

157 Aldo Alessandro Mola (edited), François Covalleri, *Napoleone imperatore e massone*, Firenze, Nardini, 1986, pp. 85–87.

158 Renata De Lorenzo, *Murat*, Salerno Editore, Roma, 2011.

159 Zaffiro Ciuffoletti, *La massoneria napoleonica in Italia*, in Zeffiro Ciuffoletti, S. Moravia (edited), *La massoneria. La storia, gli uomini, le idee*, Mondadori, Milano, 2004, pp. 121–134, here pp. 129–130.

160 Ivi, p. 126.

In 1810–1811 (according to calculations which are probably an underestimate), the number of Italian freemasons belonging to the three Masonic communities of Milan, Naples, and Paris, was approximately 20,000, enrolled in 250 lodges.[161] As in the first republican period, during the second period of French occupation too, the freemasons were supported by satellite organizations characterized by the desire to destroy tyranny and defeat usurpers. Just think of the tradition—which started in the Neapolitan lodges from 1790 onwards and spread to the radical fringes of freemasonry—of swearing on a dagger placed on a copy of Fénelon's *Adventures of Telemachus*,[162] a proto-Illuminist text of 1699 which the brothers considered sacred, or later, of certain Carbonari rituals in which the opposing figures of Caesar, Herod, and Judah were used to represent the despots at the head of the restored governments.[163]

2.4 Brothers and Cousins

After the Congress of Vienna, freemasonry gained ground in the Netherlands, Denmark, Sweden, and Switzerland, but was harshly repressed in Spain and Italy.[164] In the latter, some of its branches remained loyal to Austria, mindful of the protection given to the masons by the rulers of Austria before the French Revolution. In Hapsburg Milan, a typical example of this is the magistrate and Venerable Member of the "Reale Loggia Gioseffina Antonio Salvotti",[165] who combined a strong feeling of Italian-ness with an unswerving loyalty to the emperor,[166] but this was an exception, and very much in contrast with the new political climate.

---

161 Luca G. Manenti, *Tra azione politica e cultura esoterica. Massoneria e società segrete nell'Italia dell'800*, in "Prometeo", a. 32, n. 127, 2014, pp. 92–101.

162 Gian Mario Cazzaniga, *Società segrete e massoneria nell'età della restaurazione e del risorgimento*, in Fulvio Conti, Marco Novarino (edited), *Massoneria e Unità d'Italia. La Libera Muratoria e la costruzione della nazione*, Il Mulino, Bologna, 2011, pp. 19–45, here p. 26.

163 R. John Rath, *The Carbonari: Their Origins, Initiation Rite, and Aims*, in "The American Historical Review", v. 69, n. 2, 1964, pp. 353–370, here p. 365.

164 Aldo Alessandro Mola, *Storia della Massoneria in Italia. Dal 1717 al 2018. Tre secoli di un Ordine iniziatico*, Bompiani, Milano, 2018, pp. 108–109.

165 *Royal Lodge Gioseffina Antonio Salvotti* [translator's note]. Alberto Cesare Ambesi, *Storia della Massoneria*, De Vecchi, Milano, 1971, pp. 197–198.

166 Stefan Malfèr, *Immagini dell'altro: austriaci e italiani*, in *Storia d'Italia. Annali*, v. 22, *Il Risorgimento*, Alberto Mario Banti and Paul Ginsborg (edited), Einaudi, Torino, 2007, pp. 825–856, here p. 844.

The restored governments in Italy prohibited freemasonry, forcing dissenting Brothers either to leave the country or hold clandestine meetings. The lodges were replaced by secret societies which indulged in intense conspiratorial practices, and it was not easy to clearly distinguish these societies from Masonic ones, because they used similar rituals, codes, organizational models, and sometimes even the same leaders. Groups appeared called Ermolaisti, Bersaglieri Americani, Figli di Marte, Fratelli difensori della patria, Pellegrini Bianchi, and Spilla Nera,[167] and they dreamt of liberty in the stifling climate of censorship imposed by the Austrians.[168] This ferment of radical associations was counterbalanced by the reactionary groups set up in support of the restored absolutism. In a climate imbued with a romantic taste for secrecy, a plethora of sects and counter-sects emerged.

Beales and Biagini have attempted to bring some order to the variegated universe of illegal groups existing in Italy in the period following the Congress of Vienna from the post-congress phase by dividing them into three categories: the followers of the mason Filippo Buonarroti, who had taken part in the Conspiracy of the Equals with Gracchus Babeuf and who was the undisputed leader—until his death in 1837—of a group of democratic extremists willing to partake in risky attempts at insurrection; the Carbonari with a moderate platform calling for the adoption of Cadiz constitution of 1812; and the very moderate Carbonari who advocated the adoption of the French constitution of 1814. This honeycomb of outfits with very different political aims (ranging from a republic to a parliamentary democracy, from a centralized stage to a federation) was so complicated at the time that Beales and Biagini's categories can only be accepted if we recognize their laudable intention to organize and simplify and give them some credit for it.

Despite the persecutions, in the Kingdom of the Two Sicilies, a few masonic lodges and splinter groups survived which had split away from the old Napoleonic lodges. In the five years between 1815 and 1819, the two lodges "Sapienza Trionfante" [*Triumphant Wisdom*] and the Palermo-based "Architettura Fiorita" [*Flourished Architecture*] were active. Since 1817, in the Terra d'Otranto, it was the Decisi [*Resolutes*] secret society that dominated, led by the priest Ciro Annicchiarico—who was described as a "massone e

---

167 The Ermolaists, the American Sharpshooters, the Sons of Mars, the Brethen Defenders of the Fatherland, the White Pilgrims, and the Black Brooch [translator's note].

168 Luca G. Manenti, *Tra azione politica e cultura esoterica*, op. cit., p. 94.

giacobino"[169]. He had the reputation of being a necromancer for the ease with which he avoided capture[170]—and he gave the band of brigands under his command a military air and a macabre array of symbolic trappings, including skulls, shin-bones, and tiaras split by thunderbolts.[171] Puglia and Salento had an impressive number of secret societies: Liberi Messapi, Liberi Dauni, Spartani della Peucezia, Cavalieri di Tebe, Seguaci di Coclite, Figli di Focione, Proseliti di Catone, Figli di Bruto.[172]

The English officer Richard Church, a lieutenant-general in the army of the King of Naples, wrote from his Lecce headquarters on January 13, 1818 to his commanding officer on January 13, 1818, giving a detailed description of the secret societies and political schemers it was his task to keep an eye on: "L'aumento del numero del partito chiamato carbonari coll'addizione di uomini dell'ultima classe del popolo, fu causa poi delle sue ramificazioni e della formazione di sette denominate Filadelfi, Patriotti, Liberi Europei, e per lo più in queste sette nuove furono aggregati generalmente travagliatori, artigiani e la plebe la più indigente delle campagne e delle città, insieme con molti giovani di cattiva educazione, oziosi ed ambiziosi di essere riconosciuti capi di sette misteriose. Furono pure arruolati con i medesimi un numero grande di assassini forestieri nel Regno, senza mezzi di vivere, e moltissimi de' corpi fucilieri reali, gendarmeria reale, e truppe locali di tutte le denominazioni. In queste società infami sono pure state arruolate moltissime persone dalla sola paura, intimorite dalle minaccie [sic] di assassini e capi malfattori".[173]

---

169 "mason and Jacobin" [translator's note]. Antonio Lucarelli, *Il brigantaggio politico del Mezzogiorno d'Italia dopo la seconda restaurazione borbonica (1815–1818). Gaetano Vardarelli e Ciro Annicchiarico*, Laterza, Bari, 1942, p. 108.

170 Charles William Heckethorn, *The Secret Societies of All Ages and Countries*, v. 2, George Redway, London, 1897, p. 181.

171 Piero Pieri, *Le società segrete ed i moti degli anni 1820–21 e 1831*, Vallardi, Milano, 1948, p. 77.

172 Free Messapi, Free Dauni, the Spartans of Peucezia, the Knights of Thebes, the Followers of Coclite, the Sons of Focione, the Proselytes of Cato, the Sons of Brutus [translator's note]. Luca G. Manenti, *Tra azione politica e cultura esoterica*, op. cit., p. 94.

173 "The increase in number of the party called Carbonari with the addition of men from the lowest class of people, was the cause of its branching out and of the formation of sects named Filadelfi, and Patriotti Liberi Europei, and for the most part in these new groups there were usually laborers, artisans and the most destitute peasants from the countryside and the cities, together with many uneducated youngsters, idle and eager to be recognized as leaders of secret societies. A large number of foreign assassins in the Kingdom who had no means of livelihood were also enlisted in these groups,

In the Papal States, there were the Concistoriali [*Consistorials*], supporters of an anti-Austrian version of temporal power; the Centurioni [*Centurions*], a sort of papal militia, and the members of the Costituzione latina [*Latin Constitution*], which had appeared in 1818 after the merging of the Carboneria with the Società Guelfa [*Guelph Society*].[174] When Pope Pius VII returned to Rome, the famous statue of Pasquino, on which the Romans used to attach satirical messages and complaints, was covered in scrolls linking the previous regime to masons and Jews.[175] In April 1815 in Viterbo, situated in the Patrimony of St. Peter—with Murat still active—the papal authorities uncovered an attempt to increase the number of members of the "Partenopea" [*Neapolitan*] lodge to include a priest, a curate, and a nun, whom, according to the inquisitors, had been seduced by one of the churchmen and converted "to Freemasonry".[176] In a confidential report to the police in 1817, the former conspirator Michele Mallio stated that, together with Carbonari and Guelphs, "molti Massoni, soprattutto in Roma, Perugia, Fermo, Ferrara, Bologna [plotted to overturn Italy], ma ora sono inoperosi e rimangono come un venerabile avanzo di antichità per i suoi ammiratori".[177]

On September 13, 1821, 14 months after the revolt in Naples started by a group of soldiers enrolled in the vendita[178] of Nola, Pius VII issued the Papal Bull *Ecclesiam a Jesu Christo*, officially excommunicating members of secret societies, accusing them of perverting mankind by leading peo-

---

together with many of the royal fusiliers, the royal gendarmerie, and local troops of all denominations. Countless people have been enlisted in these infamous societies just out of fear, frightened by the threats [sic] received from murderers and evil chiefs" [translator's note]. Richard Church, *Brigantaggio e società segrete nelle Puglie (1817–1828)*, G. Barbera, Firenze, 1899, p. 39.

174 Luca G. Manenti, *Tra azione politica e cultura esoterica*, op. cit., pp. 94–95.

175 Giuseppe Tambara, *La lirica politica del Risorgimento italiano (1815–1870)*, Dante Alighieri, Roma-Milano, 1909, p. 452.

176 Claudio Canonici, *Opposizione e coscienza politica nella Viterbo della Restaurazione*, in "Studi Storici", a. 33, n. 4, 1992, pp. 881–905, here p. 883.

177 "many freemasons, especially in Rome, Perugia, Fermo, Ferrara, Bologna [plotted to overturn Italy], but they are now inactive and remain like a venerable relic of antiquity for their admirers" [translator's note]. Domenico Spadoni, *Sette, cospirazioni e cospiratori nello Stato pontificio all'indomani della Restaurazione. L'occupazione napoletana la Restaurazione e le sette*, Casa editrice nazionale Roux e Viarengo, Torino-Roma, 1904, pp. CIII–CIV.

178 Vendita, literally trade-place: a cell, part of the Carboneria organisation [translator's note].

ple astray. The document was the result of longstanding pressure from Prince Metternich, the director of the Congress of Vienna, who hoped to defeat Carboneria by using the moral force of the church as well as Austrian military power, successfully deployed the previous year to put down the Neapolitan constitutionalists. Needing to find a crime of a spiritual and not just political nature in order to justify the papal sanction, the Bull denounced the blasphemous Carbonari rituals, which seemed to show extraordinary zeal for the Christian religion but mocked Jesus, calling him—using a term borrowed from Masonic usage—the grand master of their society.[179]

Then in 1825 came the condemnation of Leo XII with his *Quo graviora,* in which he claimed to know about "alcune società, ceti, adunanze, unioni, congreghe, o combriccole, comunemente dette *de' Liberi Muratori, o Francs-Maçons*",[180] who were making "progressi amplissimi"[181] and were in the habit of meeting in secret, just as delinquents do, because if they hadn't done evil, they would surely not hate "a sì alto segno la luce".[182] In November of that year, Angelo Targhini, head of a Carbonari vendita, was executed in Rome, together with Leonida Montanari, who—according to unconfirmed reports—shouted from the gallows: "Muoio innocente, frammassone, carbonaro e non pentito".[183] Freemasons played a central role in the riots which occurred in February 1831 in Bologna, part of the Papal Legations. According to police reports, 39 freemasons took part in the uprising, mostly notables belonging to the city's four lodges.[184]

---

179 Alan Reinerman, *Metternich and the Papal Condemnation of the* carbonari, *1821,* in "The Catholic Historical Review", v. 54, n. 1, 1968, pp. 55–69.

180 "some societies, classes, meetings, unions, congregations, or gangs, commonly called de 'Liberi Muratori, or Francs-Maçons" [translator's note].

181 "very great progress" [translator's note].

182 "the light to such a degree" [translator's note]. *Bolla del Sommo Pontefice Leone XII colla quale si condannano le Sette segrete e clandestine,* in *Collezione degli Atti emanati dopo la pubblicazione del Concordato 1818. Parte quarta,* Tipografia nella Pietà de' Turchini, Napoli, 1829, pp. 79–122, here pp. 81–82.

183 "I die innocent, a freemason, a Carbonaro and unrepentant" [translator's note]. Roberto de Mattei, *Le società segrete nella Rivoluzione Italiana,* in Massimo Viglione (edited) *La rivoluzione italiana. Storia critica del Risorgimento,* Il Minotauro, Roma, 2001, pp. 127–151, here p. 130.

184 Alessandro Boselli, *Massoneria e sette segrete a Bologna nel Risorgimento,* in Giovanni Greco (edited), *Bologna massonica. Le radici, il consolidamento, la trasformazione,* Clueb, Bologna, 2007, pp. 127–142, here pp. 134–135.

In Tuscany, masonry continued to have a modest presence. In Portoferraio, Lucca, Massa, and Carrara, the lodges did not completely disappear from city life, despite countless problems, while in Livorno, a lodge was established by Pietro Pensa in 1817, followed by a Carbonara vendita in 1818, and 15 years later, a family of Veri Italiani [*True Italians*], an organization promoted in Paris by Buonarroti, which espoused a radical social programme based on the ideas of Babeuf.[185] The general Statutes of the Società dei Veri Italiani abandoned the mystical trappings of freemasonry and Carboneria in favour of a clear statement of intentions, and welcomed the reform of the conspiratorial mechanisms promoted by *Giovine Italia*. However, they distanced themselves from Mazzini's association and insisted on the need to achieve a democratic government where there would be perfect equality among citizens: an equality not simply juridical, but real and absolute.[186]

Some secret societies adopted an ideological framework inherited from the Illuminati of Bavaria, a para-masonic group founded in Ingolstadt in 1776 by Adam Weishaupt. Represented in Italy by the Neapolitan Costanzo di Costanzo[187] and by the Bolognese Alessandro Savioli Corbelli—who had tried to sow the seed of Italian patriotism in Trento by putting pressure on the lodges[188]—the Illuminati of Bavaria promoted egalitarian ideas and Rousseauian naturalism, philosophical ideals that were supposed to be slowly assimilated by its followers through a series of revelations, according to a classic paradigm of transmission of knowledge typical of initiatory circles from the eighteenth century onwards.[189] The associations inspired by Buonarroti, too, began at the lowest level by contemplating agrarian law, and then taught the republican ideal at the intermediate level; only in the end, did they exalt tyrannicide and the common ownership of goods. Scattered cells with connections to the Illuminati managed to survive the Napoleonic experience, and constituted the basis for the Filadelfi, endowed with a rich ideological legacy based on the idea of rebellion. Their name came from one of the seven Asian Churches of the Apocalypse, considered

---

185 Carlo Francovich, *Albori socialisti nel Risorgimento*, op. cit., pp. 139–140.

186 Ivi, p. 124.

187 Gianluca Paolucci, *Illuminismo segreto. Storia culturale degli Illuminati*, Bonanno, Roma, 2016, p. 157.

188 Furio Bacchini, *La vita rocambolesca del conte Alessandro Savioli Corbelli (1742–1811)*, Pendragon, Bologna, 2011, pp. 216–223.

189 Luca G. Manenti, *Tra azione politica e cultura esoterica*, op. cit., p. 95.

by Saint Bonaventure to be a sign of new times to come and interpreted in millenarian tones by a long line of heretics. Reappearing in the revolutionary England of the seventeenth century, the term "Filadelfi" was then taken in 1780 by a French occultist and Rosicrucian lodge, and eventually came to refer to a branch of the frenzied world of Risorgimento associationism.[190]

Filadelfia merged with Adelfia, promoted in Italy by Luigi Angeloni[191] and led, among others, by the mason Alessandro de Rege, Count of Gifflenga.[192] Adelfia then merged with the Sublimi Maestri Perfetti [*Sublime Perfect Masters*], which at a congress held in Alessandria in 1818 had proposed itself as the central point of reference for all the secret societies which had sprung up in Italy. The same congress in Alessandria witnessed the birth of the Federati, which, according to an anonymous dispatch delivered to the Imperial Royal Government of Lombardy in April 1821—aimed to create an Italian federation divided into three interconnected kingdoms. Federico Confalonieri, who had previously belonged to the Italici Puri [*Pure Italians*], was a Federati; he had been initiated as a mason in England in 1818 on the invitation of the Duke of Sussex, brother of King George III.[193] The Sublimi Maestri Perfetti were organized into synods and lower churches connected to masonic lodges which served as recruiting centres. Referring back to a Gran Firmamento [*Vast Firmament*] with headquarters in Paris and Geneva, led in Italy by Michele Gastone and Gaspare Grandi,[194] they recruited those who had reached the highest levels in freemasonry or Carboneria, whose symbolic and liturgical debts to the lodges were unquestionable, though located in a sober narrative framework of a Christological nature.[195]

---

190 Giorgio Galli, *Introduzione*, in *Esoterismo e rivoluzione (1789–1870)*, Edizioni Della Lisca, Milano, 1992, pp. 7–13, here pp. 8–9.

191 Armando Saitta, *Momenti e figure della civiltà europea. Saggi storici e storiografici*, v. 2, Edizioni di Storia e Letteratura, Roma, 1991, p. 899.

192 Piero Crociani, *Gifflenga, Alessandro de Rege conte di*, in *Dizionario Biografico degli Italiani*, v. 54, Treccani, Roma, 2000, pp. 637–640.

193 Franco Molinari, Il "fratello" Federico Confalonieri e il "buon cugino" Pellico, in Aldo Alessandro Mola (edited), *Sentieri della libertà e della fratellanza ai tempi di Silvio Pellico*, Bastogi, Foggia, 1994, pp. 89–99, here p. 94.

194 Cesare Spellanzon, *Storia del Risorgimento e dell'Unità d'Italia*, v. 2, *Da dopo i moti del 1820–21 alla elezione di Papa Pio IX (1846)*, Rizzoli, Milano, 1934, p. 220.

195 Carolina Castellano, *Segreto e società segrete*, in *Atlante culturale del Risorgimento. Lessico del linguaggio politico dal Settecento all'Unità*, Alberto Mario Banti, Antonio Chiavistelli, Luca Mannori, Marco Meriggi (edited), Laterza, Roma-Bari, 2011, pp.

The sense of spiritual attachment to Italy, which during the Napoleonic era had found an ideal place for its development in the masonic lodges, was subsequently embraced by men belonging to the Carboneria, whose true origins remain veiled in a mist made denser by various myths of foundation: created in ancient times by Philip of Macedonia, in the Middle Ages in Germany or France, in the British Isles by Scottish freemasons; the most generally accepted legend associates the society with the figure of St. Theobald, who is supposed to have founded it in Switzerland in order to aid travellers and pilgrims.[196] A historiographical line of interpretation (which not everyone agrees with) sees in the early Carboneria, which opposed Napoleonic Caesarism, the *longa manus* of the Anglo-Bourbons in their plotting to subvert the dominion of the French, a goal they both tried to attain by using the weapon of banditry.[197] After the fall of the French, Carboneria would establish itself as the main proponent of a constitutionalism that ranged between the two opposite poles of democratic republic and liberal monarchy.

The thesis of the Bourbon origins of Carboneria was supported by Giuseppe Pecchio, alias Androfilo Filoteo, in a *Catechismo Italiano*[198] published in 1830 in the fake city of Philadelphia, in reality Lugano. The text, which placed the House of Savoy at the head of the unification movement, took the form of a dialogue. When asked if the constitution was the work "dei carbonari, i quali si sa che sono ribelli, atei e quasi quasi filosofi e filantropi",[199] the interlocutor replies that they "vennero alla luce verso il 1807 in Sicilia ed ebbero per padrini una Regina ed un Cardinale".[200] The reference was to Maria Carolina of Habsburg Lorraine, the wife of Ferdinand IV—ousted by the Neapolitan Jacobins in 1799—and to Cardinal Fabrizio Ruffo, who put down the Republic with the help of the army of the Santafede. The Carbonari—the text went on to say—encouraged by the English to fight the French, "furono nemici di Giuseppe Bonaparte e di Gioachino Murat quando sedevano sul

---

176–186, here p. 180.

196 R. John Rath, *The carbonari*, op. cit., pp. 353–354.

197 Angela Valente, *Gioacchino Murat e l'Italia Meridionale*, Einaudi, Torino, 1965, pp. 107–128.

198 *Italian Catechism* [translator's note].

199 "carbonari, who are known to be rebels, atheists and you might almost say, philosophers and philanthropists" [translator's note].

200 "first appeared around 1807 in Sicily and had a Queen and a Cardinal for godparents" [translator's note].

trono di Napoli, come professano di essere nemici di qualunque straniera potenza che pretenda signoreggiare l'Italia".[201]

In a text dating back to 1848, and subsequently rewritten and republished countless times with additions and corrections,[202] Atto Vannucci described how the identity of Italian Carboneria changed from being anti-French to being anti-Bourbon, constantly in search of forms of liberty which were abused by those in power: "Napoleone che poteva renderci grandi e felici, preferì di avere in noi sudditi malcontenti, anziché amici devoti. [...] Gli amatori di repubblica odiando qualunque dominazione straniera, si ritirarono sui monti dell'Abruzzo e delle Calabrie, ed ivi intenti a cospirare contro i re dettero principio alla setta dei Carbonari, la quale presto divenne potentissima";[203] so powerful as to be viewed with increasing sympathy by the opponents of the French: "Gl'Inglesi che stavano in Sicilia a difesa di Ferdinando Borbone si rallegrarono appena ebber sentore della mala contentezza che in ogni parte del regno di Napoli nasceva contro i Francesi. Si rallegrarono dei sentimenti che animavano la setta dei carbonari, e con essi fecero pratiche, e promisero loro una costituzione, se si adoprassero a distruggere i presenti ordini, e a richiamare il re antico".[204] As soon as they had regained the throne, "i Borbone non che dar sostegno e favore a chi avea cooperato al loro ritorno e alla rovina dei loro nemici, non che dare la

---

201 "were the enemies of Giuseppe Bonaparte and Gioacchino Murat when they were sitting on the throne of Naples, just as they profess to be the enemies of any foreign power that claims to rule Italy" [translator's note]. Androfilo Filoteo, *Catechismo italiano ad uso delle scuole, dei caffè, delle botteghe, taverne, bettole e bettolini ad anche del casino dei nobili e semminarj*, Filadelfia, 1830, reprinted in Paolo Bernardelli (edited) *Giuseppe Pecchio, Scritti politici*, Istituto per la Storia del Risorgimento Italiano, Roma, 1978, pp. 545–566, here p. 560.

202 Fulvio Conti, *Italia immaginata. Sentimenti, memorie e politica fra Otto e Novecento*, Pacini, Ospedaletto, 2017, pp. 66–79.

203 "Napoleon, who could have made us great and happy, preferred to make discontented subjects of us, instead of devoted friends. [...] The lovers of the republic, hating any foreign domination, withdrew to the mountains of Abruzzo and Calabria, and there, intent on conspiring against kings, established the sect of the Carbonari, which soon became very powerful" [translator's note].

204 "The English, who were in Sicily to defend Ferdinando Borbone, were delighted as soon as they heard of the discontentment with the French which was felt everywhere in the Kingdom of Naples. They were pleased with the sentiments that moved the Carbonari sect, and they worked together with them, and promised them a constitution, if they did their best to destroy the present order, and bring back the previous king" [translator's note]. Atto Vannucci, *I martiri della libertà italiana dal 1794 al 1848*, Le Monnier, Firenze, 1860, pp. 138–139.

Costituzione promessa, si mostrarono pronti a punire chi di libertà parlasse o pensasse. I carbonari allora cominciarono a cospirare contro i Borboni di Napoli, come contro gli altri principi cospiravano negli altri stati d'Italia".[205]

If, as is claimed by one historiographical tradition, Carboneria descends from the English lodges backed by the Illuminati present in southern Italy, a second interpretation in line with Luzio's sees a clear passing of the baton between a masonry in decline and a Carboneria on the rise, while a third school of historiography sees the Carboneria as an offshoot of the French army stationed in southern Italy. The mastermind behind this grafting onto southern sociability is supposed to have been the ex-Jacobin freemason Pierre Joseph Briot, who, in disagreement with his emperor, was in favour of the unification of Italy.[206] Though the French origin of the sect is just one of the plausible hypotheses, Briot's role is indicative of how fluid the relationship was between freemasonry and Carboneria, to the extent that freemasons were co-opted to the Carboneria by a simple vote, without the trials which ordinary candidates had to undergo. An intermingling which was confirmed in 1942—but placed in a framework of upside-down relationships between political power and initiatory societies—by Ettore Fabietti, who claimed that the minutes from the committee set up in 1806 by Giuseppe Bonaparte to prevent reactionary revolt in Naples—preserved in the Cosenza archives—which bore the signatures of its members, were sometimes followed by the three triangle-like points of the masons, and sometimes by the aligned points of the carbonari.[207]

Felice Foresti, who had been a good cousin[208] since 1817, claimed in the course of an interrogation he underwent three years later that the Carboneria was "una riforma della Massoneria, originata in Napoli in epoca molto

205 "the Bourbons, instead of giving support and favour to those who had helped them return and bring about the ruin of their enemies, instead of giving the promised Constitution, they proved themselves willing to punish anyone who spoke or thought about liberty. And so the Carbonari began to conspire against the Bourbons of Naples, just like they were conspiring against the other princes in the other states of Italy" [translator's note]. Ivi, p. 140.

206 Francesco Mastroberti, *Mimetismo o conversione? Pierre Joseph Briot da giacobino a funzionario napoleonico*, in Luigi Mascilli Migliorini (edited), *Nelle Province dell'Impero. Colloquio internazionale in occasione del bicentenario della nascita di Victor Hugo*, Centro di Ricerca Guido Dorso, Annali 2000–2002 (VIII), Edizioni del centro G. Dorso, Avellino, 2007, pp. 133–151.

207 Ettore Fabietti, *I carbonari*, Ispi, Milano, 1942, p. 43.

208 Cousin was an appellative used by the Carbonari to addressed each other.

remota",[209] while in his *Ricordi*,[210] he described the social make-up of the vendite: "nobili, moltissimi del ceto medio (cittadini), cioè medici, legali, preti, ingegneri e proprietari; mercadanti e preti formavano la minorità. Fra gli ufficiali della dispersa armata di Napoleone vi erano migliaia di carbonari... E la massima parte era di soldati graduati".[211] Those who have insisted on the native roots of Italian Carboneria traced its origins back to the associations of charcoal makers from Calabria and Abruzzi, or to a semi-masonic sect of the eighteenth century created by the Pignatelli family, or—again—promoted by Queen Maria Carolina to sabotage the French rule in Naples.[212]

The nineteenth-century legal sources emphasized repeatedly the links between freemasonry and Carboneria. During a trial held in Macerata in 1817 against a group of seditious individuals, Luigi Domenico Valentini (unable to deny his involvement) stated—pressed by the magistrates—that the two organizations shared a common goal "nella distruzione di tutti i sovrani, nell'annientamento della religione cattolica, e nella distruzione del pretismo".[213] Valentini was boasting, but such statements heightened the fears of the established powers, so much so that in 1824, Francesco IV of Modena issued a decree, which was deemed "un vero capolavoro"[214] by the Jesuit journal "Civiltà Cattolica",[215] expressing firm condemnation of the numerous newly founded societies, which were, despite their various names and minor differences, considered to be expressions of a single re-founded freemasonry movement: "Che tutte queste sette non sono che

---

209 "A reform of Freemasonry, originating in Naples in very remote times" [translator's note].

210 *Recollections* [translator's note].

211 "nobles, many of the middle class (citizens), i.e. doctors, lawyers, priests, engineers and landowners; merchants and priests were in the minority. Among the officers of Napoleon's scattered army there were thousands of Carbonari ... But the largest proportion of all were non-commissioned officers" [translator's note]. Dino Felisati, *I dannati dello Spielberg. Un'analisi storico-sanitaria*, FrancoAngeli, Milano, 2011, p. 21.

212 R. John Rath, *The carbonari*, op. cit., p. 355.

213 "consisting of the destruction of all sovereigns, the annihilation of the Catholic religion, and the destruction of clericalism" [translator's note].

214 "a true masterpiece" [translator's note].

215 "La Civiltà Cattolica", v. X of the fifth series, 1861, *Rivista della stampa italiana, I. Documenti riguardanti il Governo degli Austro-estensi in Modena dal 1814 al 1859, pubblicati per ordine del (Dottor Luigi Farini) Dittatore delle Provincie modenesi—Modena 1860*, vol. 2 in 8°, pp. 194–212, here p. 202.

emanazioni della preesistente setta dei Franchi Massoni, o liberi Muratori, la quale giudicando che il mondo fosse abbastanza imbevuto del veleno anti-cristiano, e anti-sociale, che essa da tanto tempo andava insinuando di nascosto negli animi, credette giunto il momento di poter finalmente compiere il suo gran progetto di rovesciare ogni Autorità Ecclesiastica e secolare; ed immaginò a tal fine di dare diversi nomi, diversi segni, diversi emblemi a quelli fra i suoi rami subalterni, che destinava ad una attività che poteva compromettere il segreto; affinché se taluno di essi, mal riuscendo nell'intento, provocasse contro di sé la severità delle leggi e l'indegnazione [sic] delle oneste persone, l'effetto se ne limitasse al solo ramo colpito, e non si propagasse alla gran radice, ascosa tra le più dense tenebre amiche sempre dell'inganno e del delitto".[216]

In spite of their similarities and their constantly being mentioned together in the sources (and in people's general perception, an idea neatly expressed in 1838 by Gioacchino Belli with these lines: "Chiameli allibberali, o fframmassoni, / O ccarbonari, è ssempre una pappina: / È ssempre canajjaccia ggiacubbina"[217]), masonry and Carboneria were not the same thing: the former was a cultural laboratory which assumed different forms in time and space, while the latter was an instrument for political intervention with a precise geographical and chronological location.[218] The issue of who belonged to the Carboneria has divided historians: some have described it as "l'embrionale organizzazione politica della borghesia cos-

---

216 "That all these sects are nothing but emanations of the pre-existing sect of the Franc-Masons, or free Masons, which, having decided that the world was sufficiently imbued with the anti-Christian and anti-social poison which they have for so long been secretly instilling into souls, thought the time had come to finally accomplish its grand design of overthrowing every Ecclesiastical and secular Authority; and for this purpose, it decided to give different names, different signs, and different emblems to those of its various sub-branches assigned to activities that might reveal the secret; so that if some of these, having failed in their intent, happened to bring the severity of the law down upon them and the indignation [sic] of honest folk, the effect would be limited solely to the branch involved, and would not reach the great trunk hidden in those darkest of shadows which are always the friend of deception and crime" [translator's note]. Ivi, p. 203.

217 "Call them liberals, or freemasons, / Or carbonari, it's the same old thing: / They're still filthy Jacobin dogs" [translator's note]. Giorgio Vigolo (edited), *Giuseppe Gioachino Belli, Sonetti*, A. Mondadori, Milano, 1994, p. 554.

218 Anna Maria Isastia, *Massoneria e Carboneria*, in Giampietro Berti e Franco Della Peruta (edited), *La nascita della nazione. La Carboneria intrecci veneti, nazionali e internazionali*, op.cit., pp. 35–50, here p. 35.

tituzionale meridionale",[219] which "pur subendo il fascino del rituale massonico, fu cosa diversa dalla Massoneria";[220] for others, it was a Masonic
offshoot aimed at welcoming members of the working classes previously
excluded from the lodges.[221]

Leaving aside these discussions, it is clear that the influence of Freemasonry within the national movement and its importance in that tangled web of
sects, vendite and secret societies which Italy was teeming with, was to a
large extent indirect, but fundamental all the same, and it found expression
at three different levels. Firstly, the rituals: from the ceremonial aspect, the
Carboneria was considered quite rightly to be a sort of revisited masonry,
aimed at catering to the tastes of the Catholic masses with an emphasis on
the figure of Christ, the great architect of the universe.[222] A re-elaboration,
then (not a new invention) of the cultural movement of esoteric Christianity which had always been part of Masonic tradition.[223] Secondly, the
organizational approach: these were single Masonic elements which were
passed on to a generation of new men who came to politics through the
symbolic tools and devices elaborated by those who had been active in the
lodges. Thirdly, social training: as well as the signs, codes, and terms of reference, some of the masons themselves left associations which were failing
and joined new forms of conspiracy, producing complicated situations of
successive—and sometimes even contemporary—membership.[224]

Despite the weakness of their situation, the surviving lodges still fuelled
the fears of the counter-revolutionaries. In order to root out Carboneria
and freemasonry from the Kingdom of the Two Sicilies, the Prince of Ca-
nosa, who was Ferdinando I di Borbone's Minister of Police, a firm believer

219 "The embryonic political organization of the pro-constitutional bourgeoisie of the
south" [translator's note].

220 "even though it was fascinated by masonic ritual, was a different thing from Freemasonry" [translator's note]. Franco Della Peruta, *La Massoneria in Italia dal Risorgimento alla
Grande Guerra (1859–1915). Dalla Restaurazione all'Unità*, in Aldo Alessandro Mola
(edited), *La Massoneria nella storia d'Italia*, Atanòr, Roma,1981, pp. 61–67, here p. 63.

221 Gian Mario Cazzaniga, *Origini ed evoluzioni dei rituali carbonari italiani*, in *Storia
d'Italia. Annali*, v. XXI: *La Massoneria*, edited by himself, Torino, Einaudi, 2006, pp.
565–566.

222 R. John Rath, *The carbonari*, op. cit., pp. 359, 365.

223 Gian Mario Cazzaniga, *La religione dei moderni*, Ets, Pisa, 1999, p. 236.

224 Vincenzo Francia, *Il mito dell'empietà. Chiesa e Massoneria*, Tip. Forense, Napoli, 1946;
Antonio Celotti, *La massoneria in Friuli. Prime ricerche sulla sua esistenza e influenza*,
Del Bianco, Udine, 2006.

in a theocratic society and a convinced anti-mason,[225] founded the Società dei Calderari [Stokers Society], which was legitimist and conservative, and was called "the counterweight" being determined to resist the presence of liberal societies. Made up of veteran Sanfedisti, it was responsible for acts of such harsh repression that the ambassadors of Austria and Russia demanded that it be closed down. Comprising three ranks of knight, prince, and grand prince, its emblem was a cauldron burning coal, an explicit reference to the grim struggle against Carboneria.[226] In 1821, the democrat Orazio De Attellis pointed to Sicily as the place of origin of the society "denominata de' calderaj, che tra lor chiamavansi Cavalieri, ed i quali facean subire agl'iniziandi la filantropica pruova di pugnalar la carne fresca di un animale, e di mangiarne un pezzettino, simboleggiando la virtuosa carneficina a farsi de' carbonari e de' massoni".[227]

2.5 In Riots and Revolutions

B etween 1819 and 1820, the languishing freemasonry movement was the subject of a failed attempt at reform by a group of liberals led by Francesco Saverio Salfi, one of Murat's former councillors, a university professor in Paris, and author of a book, published by the Grand Orient of Italy in the Masonic year 5811 (actually 1811) entitled *Della utilità della Franca Massoneria sotto il rapporto filantropico e morale*.[228] The plan was to trim the institution of the plethora of decorations and bombastic formulas which weighed down its structure, and give it a national identity and a leading role in the struggle to achieve unification in a monarchical-constitutional system.[229]

The confused picture of Italian sectarianism was dramatically transformed in 1831 thanks to Giuseppe Mazzini, who founded Giovine Italia and gave

---

225 Nicola Del Corno, *Italia reazionaria. Uomini e idee dell'antirisorgimento*, Bruno Mondadori, Milano, 2017, pp. 24–45.

226 Piero Pieri, *Le società segrete ed i moti degli anni 1820–21 e 1831*, op. cit., p. 75.

227 "called *de 'calderaj*, who called themselves Knights, and who made their new members undergo an initiation involving the magnanimous test of stabbing the raw flesh of an animal and eating a piece of it, thus symbolizing the virtuous act of massacre to be performed on Carbonari and masons" [translator's note].

228 *On the utility of Free Masonry from a philanthropic and moral perspective* [translator's note].

229 Franco Della Peruta, *Francesco Saverio Salfi e un progetto di riforma della massoneria italiana nei primi anni della restaurazione*, in *Storia della massoneria, testi e studi 2*, Edi. Ma., Torino, s.d., pp. 61–73.

it the features of a modern democratic–republican political party, with a public programme and a well-organized territorial network, going beyond the failed models of Carboneria and Jacobinism.[230] Reflecting on the negative experiences of the uprisings of 1820–1821 and 1831, which were strictly elitist in nature, Mazzini came to the conclusion that the common people—won over to the struggle for national liberation by the promise of their material needs being satisfied—needed to be guided towards political and social redemption by the bourgeoisie, whose task it was to relinquish its privileges so as to favour the blending of the different classes. When recounting details of his life, he described having been made a freemason rather sloppily and without his having asked for it, by Francesco Antonio Passano in the course of an encounter in a Savona prison in 1830. An irregular initiation, therefore, devoid of any validity.[231] However, Mazzini, the son of a freemason,[232] gave speeches at the *Freemason's Tavern* in London and accepted all the titles conferred upon him *ad honorem* by the Italian lodges,[233] despite refusing to take on any position of responsibility.[234] Luzio's belief in "uno stacco completo, un incolmabile abisso tra la M.[assoneria] e Giuseppe Mazzini",[235] would appear therefore to have been dictated by prejudice, and a profound distaste for the Brotherhood.

In truth, many of Mazzini's followers were masons; he had theosophical sympathies, and he was a man of heterodox philosophical interests.[236] Giovine Italia managed to answer the needs of various social strata, from the middle classes to the peasants, by providing a model for competing associations. Among these, was the Figliuoli della Giovane Italia [*Sons of Giovane Italia*] of Benedetto Musolino, which—though disowned by Mazzini for its atheism and the communistic flavor of its catechisms—represented a

---

230 Giovanni Belardelli, *Mazzini*, Il Mulino, Bologna, 2010.

231 Fulvio Conti, *Mazzini massone? Costruzione e fortuna di un mito*, in "Memoria e Ricerca", n. 21, 2006, pp. 157–175.

232 Augusto Comba, *L'influenza di Giuseppe Mazzini nella massoneria italiana*, in "L'Ipotenusa", fifth series, n. 24, 2011, pp. 3–11.

233 Franco Della Peruta, *I democratici e la rivoluzione italiana*, Milano, Feltrinelli, 1974, p. 262.

234 Aldo Alessandro Mola, *Storia della Massoneria in Italia*, op. cit., p. 151.

235 "a complete separation, an unbridgeable gulf between M.[asonry] and Giuseppe Mazzini" [translator's note]. Alessandro Luzio, *La Massoneria sotto il Regno Italico e la Restaurazione austriaca*, Cogliati, Milano, 1918, p. 40.

236 Cesare Vetter, Andrea Stefanel, *Giuseppe Mazzini. Felicità, reincarnazionismo e sacralizzazione della politica*, in "Contemporanea", a. XIV, n. 1, 2011, pp. 5–32.

spurious version of both the Carboneria, from whom it borrowed the symbolic imagery, including the skulls and black banners, and of Giovine Italia,
espousing its ambition to obtain freedom without foreign assistance.[237]

Nicola Fabrizi's Legione Italica [*Italian Legion*] established in Malta in
1838 and describing itself as the military headquarters of Giovine Italia,
made direct reference to the Mazzinian experience, but Mazzini snubbed
it because of its propensity to concentrate men and efforts in the south
rather than in the north, and in particular in Sicily, which was seen as offering more fertile revolutionary terrain.[238] In the wake of Mazzini's teaching, came the Bandiera brothers, who in 1840 founded Esperia, which was
pro-unity and republican, open to the idea of a monarchy, reluctant to allow common people to join and pervaded by a religious idea of politics.[239]
In Giovine Italia, the key figures among the Apofasimeni came together.
First founded in Belgium in the 1820s by the tireless Buonarroti, these
societies sprang up all over the Italian peninsula thanks to Carlo Bianco
of Saint-Jorioz: they demanded a united, independent, and republican
Italy, and shared precisely the same political aims as Mazzini, who was
welcomed into their ranks with the name of Trasea Peto and the rank of
centurion, given that the organization was based on the military structure
of Ancient Rome.[240]

There were significant differences of opinion, however, between Buonarroti and Mazzini, who, in line with his mystical-religious idea of the people
as a single entity, rejected the notion of class warfare, even though Giovine
Italia included militants such as Bianco and La Cecilia, both believers in
egalitarianism. The former had written a seminal article in 1830 entitled
Della guerra nazionale d'insurrezione per bande applicata all'Italia;[241] he was
a member of the central committee of Giovine Italia under the pseudonym
Ghino di Tacco and one of the first signatories, three years later of the statute of Giovine Europa: according to Mazzini, he was a clear-minded "ter-

---

237 Christopher Duggan, *La forza del destino. Storia d'Italia dal 1796 a oggi*, Laterza, Roma-Bari, 2008, p. 159.

238 Franco Della Peruta, *Mazzini e i rivoluzionari italiani. Il "partito d'azione" 1830–1845*,
Feltrinelli, Milano, 1974, pp. 278–314.

239 Ivi, pp. 371–372.

240 Giorgio Candeloro, *Storia dell'Italia moderna*, v. 2, *Dalla restaurazione alla Rivoluzione
nazionale*, Feltrinelli, Milano, 1958, p. 200.

241 *On the national war of insurrection operated by bands applied to Italy* [translator's note].

rorist",[242] who took part in many uprisings before committing suicide in Brussels in 1843.[243]

Other lodges which were part of the pre-unification network of associations included the "Peucezia" lodge in Bari, the Verona Arena, the "Liberati" [*Freed*] in Occhiobello, "Stella folgorante" [*Dazzling* Star] in Venice,[244] and "Fermezza" [*Firmness*] in Perugia. However, what was missing in the masonic universe was an organized network, while the patriots in exile were often welcomed in foreign Orients, in Europe or America. Mid-century, there was a large number of Italian masons in Lima, affiliated to the Grand Lodge of Peru. Garibaldi himself had been initiated in Montevideo in 1844, in a lodge called L'Asil de la Vertud, and was then regularized at Les Amis de la Patrie under the auspices of the Grand Orient of Paris. After joining Giovine Europa in 1835, Garibaldi would then distance himself from Mazzini and turn towards the utopian idea of humanitarian socialism. Before returning to Italy in 1854, Garibaldi frequented the mason Antonio Meucci in New York, with whom he visited the Tompkins lodge on Staten Island. In London, he made contact with the revolutionaries Herzen, Kossuth, and Pulzsky, and with the French anti-Bonapartist exiles.

In Italy, Garibaldi had a brilliant masonic career: he reached the high levels of the Scottish Rite and Egyptian masonry; he was honoured with the high-sounding title (created especially for him and never again awarded) of "primo libero muratore italiano";[245] in 1862, he was elected Grand Master of the Supreme Council of the Scottish rite in Palermo, and when he was put in command of the Grand Orient of Italy in 1864, the Hero of the Two Worlds saw freemasonry as a way of bringing together the separate currents of the Italian democratic movement, as a source of inspiration for the struggle for independence of oppressed nations, for the setting-up of boards of arbitration for the peaceful settlement of disputes among states, for general disarmament, and for universal brotherhood.[246] Mazzini and Garibaldi are

---

242 Cesare Vetter, *Dittatura rivoluzionaria e dittatura risorgimentale nell'Ottocento italiano: Carlo Bianco di Saint-Jorioz e Benedetto Musolino*, in "Il Risorgimento", a. XLIX, n. 1–2, 1997, pp. 5–51, here p. 15.

243 Franco Della Peruta, *Bianco, Carlo Angelo, conte di Saint-Jorioz*, in *Dizionario Biografico degli Italiani*, v. 10, Treccani, Roma, 1968, pp. 226–229.

244 Rosario Francesco Esposito, *La massoneria e l'Italia dal 1800 ai nostri giorni*, Paoline, Roma, 1969, p. 106.

245 "the first Italian freemason" [translator's note].

246 Fulvio Conti, *Il Garibaldi dei massoni. La libera muratoria e il mito dell'eroe (1860–*

only the most well-known examples of patriots who spent part of their lives abroad, members of a network of exiles who—laden with experience—enlivened the debates on Italian independence and the creation of a liberal ideology not at all dominated by international models.[247]

After the failure of the anti-Bourbon uprising of Gerace in 1847, in which Calabrian Mazzinian and masonic patriots participated,[248] Italy saw a revival of freemasonry in 1848, when more than one Brother climbed onto the barricades. On January 8, four days before the revolt in Palermo, the mason Rosario Bagnasco handed out leaflets proclaiming that the revolution would begin on the birthday of Ferdinand II. Significantly, on the very same day, a Grand National Lodge of Sicily called "I Rigeneratori del 12 gennaio 1848" [*The Restorers of January 12, 1848*] saw the light, together with a Neapolitan lodge called "I Partenopei Risorti" [*The Resurrected Neapolitans*]—a name which, by referring to the resurrection of Neapolitan freemasonry, bore witness to its earlier disappearance.[249]

Among the masons who took up arms in August 1848 to defend Bologna from the Austrians was Gioacchino Napoleone Pepoli, commander of the Civic Guard which defeated the troops of General Welden.[250] The government formed by Pius IX on March 10, 1849, saw the presence of the initiate Giuseppe Galletti as minister, and later as president of the Consituent Assembly of the Roman Republic.[251] In *Storia della rivoluzione di Roma*, written between 1868 and 1870, the pro-clerical Giuseppe Spada blamed the 1848 revolt on a plot of gigantic proportions involving "gli illuminati di Germania, i filosofi di Francia ed i liberi muratori di tutto il mondo"[252] together with "i carbonari d'Italia sorti nel secolo presente"[253] and the English

1926), in "Contemporanea", v. 11, n. 3, 2008, pp. 359–395.

247 Maurizio Isabella, *Risorgimento in esilio. L'internazionale liberale e l'età delle rivoluzioni*, Laterza, Roma-Bari, 2011.

248 Santi Fedele, *La massoneria italiana tra Otto e Novecento*, Bastogi, Foggia, 2011, pp. 30–31.

249 Rosario Francesco Esposito, *La massoneria e l'Italia dal 1800 ai nostri giorni*, op. cit., p. 103.

250 Alessandro Boselli, *Massoneria e sette segrete a Bologna nel Risorgimento*, op. cit., p. 137.

251 Rosario Francesco Esposito, *La massoneria e l'Italia dal 1800 ai nostri giorni*, op. cit., p. 101.

252 "the Illuminati of Germany, the philosophers of France and the freemasons of the whole world" [translator's note].

253 "the Carbonari of Italy who appeared in the present century" [translator's note].

Protestants, without forgetting "i deisti, i razionalisti, gli atei, sparsi su tutta la superficie del globo".[254]

The Roman experience was a harbinger of passionate reflections about the project of unification for an enlarged peninsula, including the Istrian coast. In 1849, the Cremonese supporter of Mazzini, Marcello Cerioli, who belonged to a family of liberal and Masonic tradition, published *Il Nuovo Misogallo, sogno di ventiquattro ore*,[255] inspired by the desperate resistance by the Republicans to the French soldiers besieging the city. Here, the Italian identity of Gorizia and Istria was asserted on the basis of some verses by Dante, which would in future become a *topos* of irredentist propaganda.[256] Once the 1848 earthquake was over, the rulers made freemasonry illegal once again, but the Masonic tradition did not die out completely, as the 1850s saw the founding of the lodges Trionfo Ligure [*Ligurian Triumph*] in Genoa and Amici Veri Virtuosi [*True Virtuous Friends*] in Livorno.[257]

The right moment for the re-establishment of a headquarters for Italian freemasonry came at the end of the decade. With the purpose of setting up a Masonic body fit for a unified Italy under Vittorio Emanuele II, on October 8, 1859, between the Second War of Independence and the Expedition of the Thousand, seven Turin freemasons established the Ausonia lodge. Once Felice Govean had joined too, on December 20, the group founded the Italian Grand Orient.

Once unification had been achieved and with freemasonry by now well-established throughout the country, there was no shortage of discussion by both Brothers and laymen about the role the movement had played in the past. These opinions were indicative of how freemasonry was perceived in the liberal period and to a lesser extent, of what the lodges actually did in the Risorgimento. In 1869, an irritated Luigi Stallo, whose works had the honour of being on the shelves of Garibaldi's bookcase in Caprera,[258]

---

254 "the deists, the rationalists, the atheists, scattered all over the surface of the globe" [translator's note]. Quoted in Nicola Del Corno, *L'ossessione continua. Rivoluzione e Risorgimento fra sette e complotti, in Risorgimento. Studi e riflessioni storiografiche*, Zeffiro Ciuffoletti, Simone Visciola (edited), Centro Editoriale Toscano, Firenze, 2011, pp. 105–129, here p. 115.

255 *The New Misogallo, a dream of twenty-four hours* [translator's note].

256 Arianna Arisi Rota, *I piccoli cospiratori. Politica ed emozioni nei primi mazziniani*, Il Mulino, Bologna, 2010, pp. 56–57, 163–172.

257 Luca G. Manenti, *Tra azione politica e cultura esoterica*, op. cit., p. 99.

258 Tiziana Olivari (edited), *La biblioteca di Garibaldi a Caprera*, foreword by Giorgio

attacked those who kept repeating that, given "le conquiste del progresso umano operate per mezzo della sacra istituzione massonica",[259] there was no longer any reason for it to continue to exist, nor could it bring any further advantages to the nation, while according to Stallo, there was still a lot for it to do, and before anything else, liberate Rome, where "[continuavano] a gozzovigliare i preti ed il Papa".[260]

Thirty-eight years later, the irredentist Domenico Lovisato addressed his friend and fellow-mason Eugenio Popovic: "Sono amico di molti massoni del tuo stampo e di quello del povero Gigi Castellazzo, ma sono nemico acerrimo dei nuovi, perché sono canaglie: quella massoneria d'un tempo sotto i governi stranieri, tirannici, ecc. era compatibile, ma quella d'oggi che tutto sfrutta, tutto corrompe, no!".[261] The masonic brotherhood was therefore recognized as having played anything but a marginal role in the struggle for independence, and this role was not called into question by affiliates or by detractors, who if anything tended to disagree about whether there was a need for it to continue to exist in the young Italian state.

2.6 Conclusions

Now that we have recreated the mosaic pattern of Italian freemasonry in the eighteenth and early nineteenth century, what conclusions can be drawn? The scientific debates are still ongoing. In a long review of Fulvio Conti's 2003 *Storia della massoneria italiana*,[262] Francesco Benigno challenged the thesis that the freemasons' organization in Italy was weak in the years from the Congress of Vienna to 1859, since such an argument provides no easy answer to the question posed by Nello Rosselli: if the lodges' contribution to the struggle for unification was indeed non-existent, how was it that as soon as unification came about, the freemasons emerged as

---

Montecchi, FrancoAngeli, Milano, 2014, p. 32.

259 "the conquests of human progress made through the sacred Masonic institution" [translator's note].

260 "the priests and the Pope kept on stuffing themselves" [translator's note].

261 "I am a friend of many masons of your ilk and poor Gigi Castellazzo's, but I am a sworn enemy of the new breed because they are scoundrels: the masonry that used to exist under foreign and tyrannical governments, and so on, was acceptable, but today's masonry, that exploits everything, corrupts everything, no!" [translator's note]. Luca G. Manenti, *Massoneria e irredentismo. Geografia dell'associazionismo patriottico in Italia tra Otto e Novecento*, Isrml FVG, Trieste, 2015, pp. 232–233.

262 *History of Italian Freemasonry* [translator's note].

being one of the very few associations with branches all over the country, and the only one able to bring together the different ideological tendencies of the patriotic movement?[263]

The criticism was correct, although Conti had expressed himself elsewhere on the matter in a more nuanced way. Using the effective formula "rifondazione nella continuità",[264] he recognized on the one hand, that in 1859 there was an effective reconstitution of the order in Italy and on the other that, however weak they may have been, some Masonic currents remained intact all the way from restoration to unification.[265] This is quite true, and some further comments are in order here.

In the second half of the eighteenth century and during the Napoleonic era, freemasonry played a visible role in Italian society. It had connections with foreign interlocutors and was politically multifaceted; it reflected the tormented gestation in the Italian peninsula of an ideal of independence, preparing the ground for the phase of unification. The Congress of Vienna was a watershed. Between 1815 and 1859, masonry disappeared from the Italian scene, but the Brothers themselves did not. When the legitimate sovereigns returned, and the French presence was replaced by the Austrian one, masonry was shattered into a thousand different secret societies and combined with various intervention groups: it was no longer what it had been, some of its branches withered, while others bore new fruit. It no longer existed as a centre organized out in the open; it became dispersed in countless separate currents, and changed to such an extent that it would be absurd to say it survived at the institutional level; instead, it endured in symbolic trappings and became a channel for ideological contagion, shaping the associations that came after it as well as the lives of individuals fascinated by its air of mystery.

Thanks to a lengthy masonic apprenticeship, the Brothers were able to provide the new patriots (forced to resort to conspiracy) with the ritual apparatus with which to create that sense of solidarity which was essential to give some shape to unstable secret societies, always at risk of breaking up because of the difficult situations they had to work in. Masons also took part in person, often at the highest level, and moved over, for example, from

---

263 Francesco Benigno, *Massoni per caso*, in "Meridiana", n. 47–48, 2003, pp. 329–330.

264 "refoundation in continuity" [translator's note].

265 Fulvio Conti, *Laicismo e democrazia. La massoneria in Toscana dopo l'Unità (1860–1900)*, Centro Editoriale Toscano, Firenze, 1990, p. 26.

masonry to Carboneria, shifting from one or another of the countless secret societies that had sprung up. Although the maze of Risorgimento cults
and clubs grew continuously and some of them had nothing to do with
freemasonry, the latter was not completely eradicated. It adapted and it survived, vanishing at times, then reappearing furtively, losing cohesion but
preserving a legacy of values which the supporters of unification absorbed
and made fresh use of.

Its supposedly almost unlimited power during the Risorgimento was an
invention of sovereigns, clergymen, supporters of the old order and counter-revolutionary authors—afraid of a danger they themselves exaggerated.
In 1860, Giuseppe Garibaldi, a mason, led the Expedition of the Thousand
having adopted the motto "Italia e Vittorio Emanuele". After conquering
Sicily, he landed in Calabria with the help of the Sprovieri brothers, who
were masons, and in September he entered Naples escorted by Liborio Romano, a mason. Mazzini was not an initiate, and neither was Cavour; nor,
would it appear, was the king. Freemasonry did not guide the process of
Italian independence, but it played a key role in helping it along.

3. From the Rebirth of Freemasonry to the Grand Mastery of Adriano Lemmi (1859–1896)

Demetrio Xoccato

3.1 Intro

With the fall of Napoleon and the following restoration of monarchs to their thrones, Masonry knew a long span of silence and apparent oblivion. Since many Brethren consorted with the French regime, the Restoration led to a ban and subsequent persecution of the organization, which was seen as seditious.

The masonic awakening was slow and late, with its core in the Kingdom of Sardinia. The only realm to keep the monarchic-constitutional asset established in 1848, it didn't host lodges until 1856, when the "Trionfo Ligure" arose in Genoa. This one, anyway—considering the customary relations between Liguria and Southern France—subdued to the Grand Orient of France, disdaining any initiative of giving birth to a subalpine Obedience.[266]

Shortly after, the "Oriente Ligure" was established in Chiavari. Following the same modus operandi, its members even joined the Grand Orient of Perù.[267]

So even though the Albertine Statute had granted the right of association, it was not enough to bring new blood to the masonic movement. The representatives of the liberal universe would have felt a need for an instrument for organizing and coordinating just before the Italian unification.

It's from this viewpoint that the "Ausonia" lodge's foundation in fall 1859 must be judged. The Second Italian Independence War had ended two

---

266 Luigi Polo Friz, Giovanni Anania, *Rispettabile Madre Loggia Capitolare "Trionfo Ligure" all'Oriente di Genova. Uno sguardo alla Massoneria ligure dall'Unità ad oggi*, Associazione Culturale Trionfo Ligure, Genova, 2004.

267 "Bollettino officiale del Grande Oriente Italiano", n. 10, 1863, pp. 147–148.

months earlier, bringing the annexation of Lombardy to the Kingdom of Sardinia. While there were negotiations about the pro-Piedmont provisional governments controlling the states in the Po valley (Parma, Modena, and Romagna) and in Tuscany, there took shape what would later be known as the Expedition of the Thousand.

In the narrow range of existing lodges at the end of the fifties, the "Ausonia" diverged in its national focus. From the first meeting, the Brethren based in Turin aimed to build a masonic body in an Italy unified by the Savoy dynasty as soon as possible.[268]

Similarly, the choice of the name "Ausonia", Greek for "Italy," highlighted this clear will to support the unification process.

This initiative gained the endorsement by Count Camillo Benso di Cavour, whom collaborators—as explained below—enrolled in this lodge, transforming Turin into a site of meeting for the future Italian Freemasonry.

This process met two specific requirements. First of all, there was a widespread wish to join the same community from the different masonic components spread over the Italian territory. Secondly, this was a perfect way to address the needs of the subalpine moderate elite: removing republicans and democrats from this project and, following the example of Napoleon III, setting a group of trusted men as leaders. As a matter of fact, Prince Lucien Murat, the Emperor's cousin and follower, was the Grand Master of the Grand Orient of France from 1852.[269]

So, from a proposal by journalist Felice Govean—editor of the newspaper called "Gazzetta del Popolo" and a renowned writer—on December 20, 1859, the Italian Grand Orient was born. Its members decided to adopt a rather vague "Rito Francese". It's unclear what they referred to, surely neither the namesake Rite, consisting of seven degrees and developed in 1786, nor the whole of the transalpine rituals. Maybe they referred to the French Obedience as an organizational structure, composed of lodges giving the first three degrees and gathered in a national body—named

---

268 Marco Novarino, *Nel nome del grande statista. Le Logge Cavour di Torino dall'Unità d'Italia ai giorni nostri*, Sottosopra, Torino, 2011, p. 1.

269 Fulvio Conti, *La rinascita della massoneria: dalla loggia Ausonia al Grande Oriente d'Italia*, in Fulvio Conti, Marco Novarino (edited), *Massoneria e Unità d'Italia. La Libera Muratoria e la costruzione della nazione*, Il Mulino, Bologna, 2011, p. 127.

Grand Orient—led by a Grand Master and a Federal Council appointed by a national assembly.[270]

3.2 The Italian Grand Orient: The Early Years

By early 1860, many prominent characters belonging to the local political and cultural milieu joined the project. Among these there were Count Livio Zambeccari—who, as Giuseppe Garibaldi, fought in Latin America—the mentioned Govean, and some leading politicians such as Giuseppe La Farina—founder of Società Nazionale, a society gathering all the men backing the Savoy dynasty and its action for the national unification—Michele Coppino, Pier Carlo Boggio, David Levi, Filippo Cordova, Costantino Nigra— ambassador in Paris—and Giuseppe Toscanelli.

To this original group there joined, on December 3, 1861, two other distinguished individuals: Pietro Francesco La Chenal—Counselor of the Appellate Court in Cagliari—and Carlo Michele Buscalioni—henchman of La Farina in Società Nazionale and editor of the newspaper "L'Espero".[271]

Based on the shared background of many of these members, the newborn organization bore an ideology that combined Cavour and Società Nazionale prospects: in its action, it embodied a collective uncommitted neither to conservatives nor to republicans and Mazzini-subjects.

Almost all those initiated went through a hurried ritual, and often rose to mastery all at once. This happened to La Chenal and Achille Pagano, endorsed to establish lodges, respectively, in Cagliari and Milan. This procedure is not uncommon in Italian Masonic history. Prominent people rose quickly, showing this decision was prone to material than initiatory and esoteric choices.[272]

Thanks to these prestigious men, at the beginning of 1861 proselytism was prized by the multiplication of lodges and initiations of many Risorgimento

---

270 Marco Novarino, Giuseppe M. Vatri, *Uomini e logge nella Torino capitale. Dalla fondazione della loggia «Ausonia» alla rinascita del Grande Oriente Italiano (1859–1862)*, L'Età dell'Acquario, Torino, 2009, p. 23.

271 Vittorio Mirano, *Ad memoriam. Discorsi tenuti dal fratello Filippo Delpino, venerabile della rispettabile loggia Ausonia all'Oriente di Torino e gran maestro ad interim del Grande Oriente Italiano*, Tip. Dell'Espero, Torino,1862; Archivio Storico del Grande Oriente d'Italia (henceforth ASGOI), *Verbale* del 3 dicembre 1861.

272 Fulvio Conti, *Storia della massoneria italiana. Dal Risorgimento al fascismo*, Il Mulino, Bologna, 2003, p. 32.

activists belonging to the constitutional government of Vittorio Emanuele II. Furthermore, the lodges in upper Italy were attracted by Turin, leading to improvement of the organization.

In the span of two years then, in Turin "Progresso" and "Cavour" raised, while in the rest of the peninsula a range of new lodges adhered, including "Concordia Umanitaria" in Boulogne, "Concordia", "Unione" and "Garibaldi" in Leghorn, "Azione e Fede" in Pisa, "Concordia" from Florence, "Argillana" from Ascoli, "Valle di Potenza" in Macerata, "Rigenerazione" from Genoa, "Insubria" in Milan, "Fratellanza" in Mondovi, "Vittoria" from Cagliari, and "Lume e verità" from Messina.

Alongside these were four lodges in the Mediterranean (one in Tunis, two in Alessandria of Egypt, one in Cairo), plus one in Rome, named "Fabio Massimo" which was clandestine.[273]

To give steadiness to the young body, a monthly tuition of one lira was delivered to the Italian Grand Orient. This is a very modest amount if compared to the sum needed to enroll in a club, not just in Piedmont but across the whole peninsula.[274]

In the meantime, proclaimed the Kingdom of Italy (March 14, 1861), the young Masonry felt the need to find an authoritative leader, especially since a threatening competitor loomed on the horizon.

Unhappy with the flourishing Masonry that was distinctly biased by Cavour and filo-Savoy discourse, republicans, along with Mazzini and Garibaldi rooters—giving a solid contribution to Risorgimento—longed to manage differently. Thus, in 1860 a Supreme Council of Ancient and Accepted Scottish Rite was founded in Palermo, in straight opposition to Turin.

In January 1861, Francesco Crispi, a prominent figure in Sicilian life and one of the personalities that marked Italian politics at the end of the nineteenth century, was admitted. A year after, as representative of the Sicilian structure, he was commissioned to recruit new affiliates in central-

---

273 Fulvio Conti, *Massoneria e sfera pubblica nell'Italia liberale, 1859–1914*, in Gian Mario Cazzaniga (edited), *Storia d'Italia. Annali. La massoneria*, vol. XXI, Einaudi, Torino, 2006, p. 581.

274 For the Turin setting, see Anthony Cardoza, *Tra casta e classe. Clubs maschili dell'elite torinese, 1840–1914*, in "Quaderni Storici", n. 2, 1991, pp. 357–382. For the Neapolitan situation, instead, refer Daniela L. Caglioti, *Associazionismo e sociabilità d'élite a Napoli nel XIX secolo*, Liguori, Napoli, 1996.

northern Italy, while also trying to draw in the displeased within the adversary Obedience.[275]

In the meantime, Cavour supporters—comforted by the election outcome in the first Italian Parliament—cherished the idea of offering the Grand Mastery to the statesman, but unfortunately, this didn't happen: on June 6, 1861, he died out unexpectedly, creating a void.[276]

With Cavour dead, the leadership of the Italian Grand Orient considered who could assume its summit, the criterions were many: first, a regularly initiated mason; then, a strictly moderate member; and, finally a an internationally renowned man able to gain esteem within the Masonic lines. The election had to happen soon, since the increase in affiliates and the rivalry from Palermo required a national board that was firm and cohesive.[277]

The only person able to accomplish all this was Costantino Nigra, Italian ambassador in France and close friend of the Emperor. Saying yes to the duty, he wrote a manifesto claiming a straight inner protocol, the building of an inward asset, the acknowledgment by foreign Obediences, and the foundation of lodges in Rome and other unredeemed lands.[278]

Nigra's changes, strongly endorsed by Govean, wasn't actually painless: some lodges expressed bafflement at the nomination, refused to conform to a governmental plot. These arguments made the diplomatic gain a solid but not smashing majority. "Azione e Fede" from Pisa and "Amicizia" in Leghorn began a campaign to call a constituent assembly to discuss, broadly, issues such as programs, constitutions, and election rules.[279]

The congress took place in Turin between December 26, 1861, and January 1, 1862—the very founding moment of Italian Grand Orient. There, 23

---

275 Museo Centrale del Risorgimento di Roma (henceforth MCRR), Fondo Crispi, box 660, in. 14, missives of January 4 and April 7, 1862.

276 Adolfo Colombo, *Per la storia della Massoneria nel Risorgimento italiano*, in «Rassegna storica del Risorgimento», fasc. I, 1914, p. 69.

277 Marco Novarino, *Felice Govean. Dalla "Gazzetta del popolo" al Grande Oriente italiano*, in Fulvio Conti, Marco Novarino (edited), *Massoneria e Unità d'Italia. La Libera Muratoria e la costruzione della nazione*, Il Mulino, Bologna, 2011, p. 195.

278 Pietro Buscalioni, *La loggia Ausonia ed il primo Grande Oriente italiano*, Brenner, Cosenza, 2001, p. 129.

279 MCRR, Raccolta Nelson Gay, cass. 721, file 21 and 22, missives of October 30, November 12 and 22, 1861.

lodges of the Obedience drew up the first masonic charter in Italian Masonic history. It was the statement of independence and brotherhood among nations, of charity and equality of religious cults, as well as of the "moral and material" progress of the commoners.[280]

Other basal principles, approved during the summit, were the belief in a supreme being (the Great Architect of the Universe), the polling of offices, the fierce rejection of Rites to interfere in the organization routine, and the obedience to state laws. Further, every lodge had to donate 50 liras to the executives, while every member had to deposit one lira.[281]

Another element was Nigra's confirmation, since he resigned not long before the summit. The reasons for this were twofold: the defamatory campaign by clergy press and the worrying signs coming from French Freemasonry.

The harsh attacks in the headlines were compromising his diplomatic career, while the French situation—where the Grand Mastery shifted from Gerolamo Bonaparte to Murat, himself replaced by marshal Magnan in January 1862—demonstrated how uncomfortable that assignment could be.

Thus, he reaffirmed his quitting though the confirmation.[282]

With Nigra's retirement, the leadership was charged to Filippo Cordova, eminent Sicilian liberal and—at the time—minister of Agriculture. In March 1862, he gained the election as Effective Grand Master, prevailing 15 to 13 against Giuseppe Garibaldi.[283]

The scarce majority showed how the "democratic lodges" were widening alarmingly. Garibaldi's appointment was a clear sign.

Soured by the defeat, the General decided to surrender to the Supreme Council of Palermo, which for a long time pressed him to accept the

---

280 *Costituzioni della Massoneria italiana discusse e votate dalla prima assemblea costituente massonica italiana nelle tenute delli 27, 28, 29, 30, and 31 dicembre 1861*, Valle di Torino, s.e., 5861.

281 *Lux. Sunto del protocollo dei lavori della prima costituente massonica italiana*, Valle di Torino, s.e., 5861.

282 Adolfo Colombo, *Per la storia della Massoneria nel Risorgimento italiano*, op. cit., pp. 73–74.

283 Pietro Buscalioni, *La loggia Ausonia ed il primo Grande Oriente italiano*, op. cit., pp. 190–196.

supreme leadership: in just one session, he received all the degrees from 4° to 33°, and so was nominated Sovereign Grand Commander. March ending, thus, the two Obediences had in chief two pivotal figures in the social and political country scene.

With solid management in place, the masonic body in Piedmont founded a magazine representing the official mouthpiece of the Obedience: the "Bollettino officiale del Grande Oriente Italiano". Despite some ups and downs and headline changes, it was the first masonic press in Italian.

The Italian Grand Orient then looked abroad. Cordova tried to settle the institution down internationally, getting in touch with other masonic associations in Europe and the Americas. The outcomes were hugely satisfying, since most of them favored the fresh institution. Positive replies came from the Grand Orients of France, Belgium, Portugal, the Grand Lodges of Ireland, the Greek and Swiss Masonry, as well as from Chile, Peru, and Uruguay.[284]

The Grand Lodge of Hamburg instead, after an early disposability, cut off all ties. The greatest blow came from the United Grand Lodge of England: the most illustrious masonic body, on behalf of its officer William G. Clark, just took note of the situation and expressed a lively closeness without, however, securing any brotherhood.

The Italian Grand Orient, however, could still boast a stable international presence, thus granting a prestige echoing home as a boost to local territories.

3.3 A Diverse Masonic Panorama

In 1863, just three years after the birth of "Ausonia," the Obedience could account for 68 lodges, showing an indubitable vitality. Amid these, 58 were scattered across the whole territory (10 in Piedmont, 5 in Liguria, 4 in Lombardy, 6 in Emilia-Romagna, 13 in Tuscany, 5 in Umbria, 4 in Marche, 2 in Lazio, 2 in Campania, 1 in Apulia, Basilicata, and Sardinia, 4 in Sicily), while the remaining 10 were abroad (Egypt, Ottoman Empire, Greece, Tunisia, Peru).[285]

---

284 Marco Novarino, *All'Oriente di Torino. La rinascita della massoneria italiana tra moderatismo cavouriano e rivoluzionarismo garibaldino*, Chiari, Firenze, 2003, pp. 136–140.

285 *Protocollo dei lavori della terza assemblea costituente mass. italiana tenuta in Firenze li 1, 2, 3, 4, 5, 6, del 6. mese dell'anno 5863 della V. L.*, Tip. dei Franco–Muratori, Torino, 5863.

The data suggests a clear prevalence in center-northern lands and a modest penetration in the south. Here, again, the Italian Grand Orient had to face the lumbering presence of the Supreme Council of Palermo.

The statistics on this organization show in 1862, it had, depending on it, 21 lodges: the most in Sicily—17 indeed—while 3 were in Campania and 1 in Piedmont.[286]

The latter was "Dante Alighieri," which arose in February 1862 in Turin, and soon become a center for those collecting against Cavour. It had a tricky existence, shown in its field choices. Although tied early to the Turin Obedience, it detached—in pursuit of Crispi—and merged with Palermo. Made by democratically-oriented Brethren—though it included a flourishing group of exiles from Poland and Hungary[287]—experienced an inner crisis, first leading to a schism from the Palermitans and then, in October 1862, a reconnection to the Italian Grand Orient. It would drift apart again in May 1863 to then rejoin definitively.[288]

Although these articulate facts, the "Dante Alighieri" lodge represented one of the important masonic figureheads of the time. Here, many MPs and political key players from the Historical Left were initiated, giving a solid contribution to the national scenario: Aurelio Saffi, Antonio Mordini, Agostino Depretis, Giuseppe Zanardelli, Mattia Montecchi, and Francesco De Luca.[289]

Amid its members, in December 1862, Lodovico Frapolli—Colonel of Garibaldi, gifted in charisma and executive talent—was welcomed, contributing to the growth of the democratic trend on moderates. As proof of his skills, by January 10, 1863, he was unanimously elected Worshipful Master of "Dante Alighieri."

---

286 Giuseppe Colosi, *A tutti i massoni dell'uno e dell'altro emisfero. Il S. C. G. O. d'Italia e sue dipendenze di rito scozz. ant. ed. acc., sedente in Palermo*, Palermo, s.e., s.d.

287 On relations between Hungarian emigration and Italian Freemasonry, refer to Luigi Polo Friz, *Lodovico frapolli, la loggia massonica Dante Alighieri e l'emigrazione ungherese*, in "Rivista di Studi Ungheresi", fasc. n. 13, 1998, pp. 103–116.

288 For a detailed setting of the activity of the "Dante Alighieri" lodge see Luigi Polo Friz, *La massoneria italiana nel decennio post unitario. Ludovico Frapolli*, FrancoAngeli, Milano, 1998.

289 Pietro Buscalioni, *La loggia Ausonia ed il primo Grande Oriente italiano*, op. cit., pp. 186–188.

Returning to the Supreme Council, during the span of 1862–1869, it succeeded in having 126 ateliers, mostly in the south but numbering a crucial presence in Liguria and Tuscany. However this narrowed in 1870: only 23 were effective; of the remaining, 79 were inactive or independent and 24 were about to be demolished or expelled.[290]

To complicate the frame, other Obediences sprouted up, either locally endorsed or joined to charismatic figures.

In Sicily, there was a body called the Grand Consistory or Supreme Central Council of Sicily, referred to by Romualdo Trigona-Gravina, Prince of Sant'Elia. Consisting of very scarce members, in 1867—after some dealings—the group merged into G.O.I.

The Grand Orient of Naples was populate and meaningful. It was led by former archpriest Domenico Angherà from Calabria, who, after being compromised in the insurrection of 1847 and being initiated in Sicily, went to Malta as an exile. Returning home, he founded "Sebezia" in 1861, transforming it into a nucleus attracting dispersed and disaffected Brothers. In 1864, the new institution numbered 23 lodges: 17 in Campania, 5 in Apulia, 1 in Calabria.[291]

Up to 1878—when it ceased—the Grand Orient of Naples represented a flourishing organization able to gather, despite some ambiguities, more than 50 lodges—even abroad—and wedging in the Italian community of Egypt (with 7 lodges).[292] Here it unsuccessfully attempted to found an Egyptian Grand Orient.

Its end is linked to the fate of Angherà, who was charged with profiting on initiations and patents, and so was subject to a masonic trial. During the debate, it was found that in 1864–1877, he collected roughly 140,000 liras from licenses and promotions. Facing the evidence, Angherà was expelled and all the Neapolitan officers condemned, causing its end.[293]

---

290 *Le logge della comunione scozzese ed il Supremo Consiglio di Palermo*, in "L'Umanitario", April 30, 1870.

291 Domenico Angherà, *Memoria storico–critica sulla società dei FF ∴ ∴ liberi muratori del Grande Oriente Napolitano*, Stamperia del Fibreno, Napoli,1864, p. 164.

292 Luigi Polo Friz, *Logge in Italia dal 1815 al 1870*, in "Massoneria Oggi", fasc. 4, 1998, p. 35.

293 *Processo e sentenza contro Angherà Domenico, ex 33 ed ex Presidente del Supremo Consiglio del Grande Oriente Napoletano*, Napoli, s.e., 1878.

This high number of groups and factions was a frequently discussed issue, and many voices called for a reunification of an articulate masonic galaxy. As some comprehended—Cordova, Govean, and Buscalioni—it was a hard duty to accomplish.

The first issue was on the ritual aspect. The Supreme Council of Palermo, the Supreme Central Council of Sicily, and the Grand Orient of Naples adhered to the Ancient and Accepted Scottish Rite, whereas the Italian Grand Orient recognized only up to the third degree.

These diverse choices were directly tied to the second element of contradiction: the political visions in the Obediences. The Scottish Rite, qualified by a rigid hierarchy and giving to the initiate—according to degree—a different involvement, fully satisfied the need of a the framework which could be a potential headquarter to handle republican conspiratorial initiatives.

In the same way, the three degrees embraced by the moderates were suitable to the Cavour intent to make Freemasonry more "horizontal," a sort of "buffer" where the spare political orientations could produce a synthesis in accordance with the young state institutions.[294]

While the Cavour-prone leadership was about to find a solution to this intricacy, the 1863–1864 gatherings deeply modified the inner sense of the Obedience based in Turin.

3.4 From the Italian Grand Orient to the Grand Orient of Italy

The third and fourth assemblies defined the handover between moderates and democrats. Called in Florence, a few months before it became the new kingdom's capitol, these marked a true turning point.

First of all, in August 1863, the moderates held in a weak position. The bulk of Federal Council members (from Cordova to Govean and Buscalioni) indeed resigned a few months before the meeting to calm the hearts and regain consensus amid members.

More, the agenda focused solely on how to merge the various masonic families.

---

294 Marco Novarino, *Progresso e Tradizione Libero Muratoria. Storia del Rito Simbolico Italiano (1859–1925)*, Pontecorboli, Firenze, 2009, p. 16.

With these premises, the assemblies were marked by harsh quarrels bringing an institutional confusion: members from Piedmont were confirmed in the executive duties; at the same time, a council of Tuscan Brethren (Giacomo Alvisi, Giuseppe Dolfi, Neri Fortini, Cesare Lunel, and Ettore Papini) was established to survey and arrange a brand new Constituent Assembly to host representatives from lodges of any Rite.[295]

This peculiar share-out of faculties provoked a conflict for control of the Obedience between Florentines and Turineses, led by Buscalioni.

The latter double-acted: on one side he started a procedural and methodological audit of decisions taken in the gathering, hoping to discredit the Tuscans; on the other, he worked to widen his consensus, including the Supreme Council of Palermo plus those not comfortable with Frapolli's activity in "Dante Alighieri." In this frame, the birth of "Tempio di Vesta" lodge has to be mentioned: it arose to collect all the opponents to the Colonel.[296]

Distinctive is the initiation of Celestino Bianchi, a close accomplice of the former Prime Minister Bettino Ricasoli, which should have been the first step in co-opting the Florentine politician and running him for the Grand Mastery.[297]

The moderate leadership also made attempts to gain ground using the common anti-clergy sensibility. In January 1864, to mention, the Federal Council decided to endorse the lobbying promoted by "Azione e Fede" (Pisa) and "Fede e Lavoro" (Perugia) to ratify an act to suppress religious bodies.[298]

This laic rush was a qualifying issue of Italian Masonry, regardless of visions. As a matter of fact, "Insubria" from Milan—a lodge numbering amid its emeritus members of the city prefect, Marquise Salvatore Pes di Villamarina[299]—set up a competition (with a prize of 150 liras) to release a leaflet to sensitize the profanes.

---

295 Carlo E. Patrucco, *Documenti su Garibaldi e la Massoneria nell'ultimo periodo del Risorgimento italiano*, in "Bollettino storico–bibliografico subalpino", n. III, 1914, pp. 41–43.

296 Marco Novarino, *Progresso e Tradizione Libero Muratoria*, op. cit., pp. 20–21.

297 *Relazione alla giunta eletta*, in "Bollettino officiale del Grande Oriente Italiano", n. 17–18, 1864, pp. 251–255.

298 ASGOI, *Minute*, January 19, 1864.

299 ASGOI, *Minute*, February 3, 1863.

The plenary that took place from May 21–24, 1864, saw the partaking of representatives from most lodges belonging to the Obedience, the Grand Orient of Naples, plus the group led by Frapolli. Among the delegates, there were a number of outstanding people embodying all the range of political positions inside Freemasonry. Mikhail Bakunin, the Russian revolutionary who had recently been living in the city, participated in the session in an attempt to fold Masonry into an instrument for his subversive and counter-religious propaganda.[300] His aim, although short lasting, shows the passion and curiosity around the masonic world of those years and the entities involved in exploiting its activities.

The Florentine congress closed with many accomplishments. The first was the end of the Italian Grand Orient and its transformation in the Grand Orient of Italy. To this new subject went the executive duties and international deals, while the dogmatic and ritual matters were left for the two ceremonial authorities: the Symbolic Rite and the Ancient and Accepted Scottish Rite.

The assembly called Garibaldi to cover the Grand Mastery with a unanimous ballot outcome: 45–50. He obtained the charge only for a few months, since the Supreme Council of Palermo expressed its disappointment and asked the general to make a choice between the two organizations.[301] Facing the contrasts, on August 8, he resigned the office and regent Francesco De Luca succeeded, representative of southern Left and, as already stated, initiated in "Dante Alighieri" shortly before.

The change was largely the result of the labor by Worshipful Master Frapolli, able not just to bind main relations with the Florentine commission, but also ready to give important inputs in management and theory.[302]

He developed a project to reform Masonry, providing firm bases in ideology, protocol, and ritual. This draft—then published—proponed the adoption, in all the lodges, of a "simplified" Scottish Rite consisting of just seven degrees and the establishment of two different authorities—an

---

300 Luigi Polo Friz, *Michele Bakunin e la massoneria italiana*, in "Rassegna storica del Risorgimento", n. 1, 1989, pp. 41–56.

301 MCRR, Fondo Garibaldi, box 51, file 4, *missive* June 18, 1864.

302 Aldo Alessandro Mola, Luigi Polo Friz, *I primi vent'anni di Giuseppe Garibaldi in Massoneria*, in "Nuova Antologia", fasc. 2143, 1982, pp. 369–370.

admin and a dogmatic one. The first office, elective, was to manage the daily duties of Masonic life. The second focused on founding new lodges and promoting Brethren on the initiation ladder.[303]

This program had a wide echo, not only in subalpine lands, and represented the first attempt to give coherence and practicality to the composite masonic world in Italy.

The very first obstacle De Luca faced, as regent, was a schism, as a fair consequence of Florence assets. A group of lodges, professing only the three degrees, convened around rationalist philosopher Ausonio Franchi (alias of father Cristoforo Bonavino), enlivening, in July 1864, the Milanese Symbolic Rite.

This organization proposed a charter of reforms in both social and political fields to improve the commoners' situation. From this stance, Franchi envisioned the Masonic temples open to the popular classes with the narrowing of yearly tolls.[304] Furthermore, he supported the redrafting of symbolism and masonic rituality—seen as anachronistic—and a greater internal democracy. To better disseminate its message, the Masonic body released a bulletin, which was widespread in 1865–1868.[305]

Despite Franchi's involvement, De Luca contained the hemorrhaging numbers. As a result, the new Obedience remained substantially confined to the Padan Plain. Although there were 20 lodges, they were continuously carved up by inner conflicts. The outcomes moved the secessionists to a milder behavior, leading to them merging again with the G.O.I. in 1869.[306]

3.5 The Administrative and Structural Reinforcement

The first official public outings of regent De Luca appeared to underline the de-politicizing of the Order. Facing the riots hitting Turin in September 1864, a result of the city losing its status as the capital in favor of Florence, he released a document denying the claim by catholic headlines

---

303 Lodovico Frapolli, *Una voce—Une voix*, Tip. Vercellino, Torino, 1864.

304 *Discorso letto alla L∴ Insubria nella tenuta del 30 maggio 1864 dal F∴ V∴ Ausonio Franchi*, Milano, s.e., 1864, p. 14.

305 Its name was "Bollettino officiale del Gran Consiglio Massoneria Italiana al Rito Simbolico Valle di Milano".

306 Carlo Montalbetti, Luigi Polo Friz, *Ausonio Franchi e la massoneria. Il rito simbolico di Milano*, in "Il Risorgimento", fasc. 2, 1984, pp. 161–194.

that Masonry had been involved in the Italian–French treaty from which this decision originated.[307]

Even when some lodges—between 1864 and 1865—called a petition with the G.O.I. for the abolition of the death penalty and a campaign for abolishing Religious Corporations, the regent decided to lay low. He gave consent to the initiative, but asked for both local and profane management, without any national masonic involvement.[308]

Then, the Genoa congress took place (May 28–30, 1865). There, De Luca was officially confirmed as leader of the body, gaining the office of Grand Master, while Garibaldi was entitled Honorary Grand Master.

Secure in his role, De Luca emphasized his institution's detachment from politics. On September 10, namely, while approaching the ballots, he confirmed the separation of Freemasonry from factions, inviting the Brethren to choose candidates struggling for the "betterment of humankind", looking beyond small-minded interests.[309]

The GM, together with Frapolli and Garibaldi, decided to resume the negotiation with the Supreme Council of Palermo and all the other dissenters. Unifying all the Brothers in a sole entity was a main priority for the democratic leadership. Waiting for the Neapolitan session in 1867, the Hero of Two Worlds expressed his hope the Sicilian protestors would merge into the G.O.I. The defiant opposition from Gian Luigi Bozzoni and Zaccaria Dominici—who set openly unachievable requirements, such as the supremacy of the Scottish Rite—enraged the general. Thus in July (after the congress), he resigned all the titles awarded by the southern Obedience.

After he quit, the hard-pressed Supreme Council tried to find another outstanding public personality. The supreme position was offered to Carlo Cattaneo and Giuseppe Mazzini—profanes—but they both refused. Noticeable was the instance of the Genoese patriot. After receiving a 33rd degree patent and an oath formula to return signed, he replied that he had

307 *Decreti e disposizioni del Gran Consiglio*, in «Bollettino del Grande Oriente della massoneria in Italia», vol. 1, Tip. Vercellino, Torino, 1864, pp. 53–54.

308 Fulvio Conti, *Storia della massoneria italiana*, op. cit., p. 62.

309 *Decreti e disposizioni del Grande Oriente*, in "Bollettino del Grande Oriente della massoneria in Italia", fasc. X–XI–XII, 1865, pp. 344–346.

made a single promise in life: the establishment of the Republic.[310] The back-turn fell on republican Federico Campanella.[311] He, close to Mazzini, assented on July 20.

Campanella faced dramatic circumstances: amid 126 lodges officially enrolled to the Obedience, only 23 were fully operating.[312]

During the G.O.I. summit of 1867 very specific civil and political topics were handled, which showed how some themes were particularly prevalent in the community. Several lodges reissued the campaign to abolish death penalty and religious corporations, while others expressed the wish to celebrate Risorgimento and its heroes by raising monuments and epigraphs.[313]

With regards to the Obedience's organization structure, in the face of the five-year lapse of the Grand Mastery office, the members of Federal Council were narrowed from 40 to 24. The two Deputy Grand Masters would be elected by the General Assembly, thus becoming independent from the supreme leadership's influence.[314]

Another issue occurred with women entering Freemasonry. The female presence in France and other continental European countries, including Italy, had been significant throughout the eighteenth century. The "fair sex" was held in so-called "lodges of adoption," linked to male ones, and their

---

310 Alessandro Luzio, *La massoneria e il risorgimento italiano. Saggio storico–critico*, vol. II, Zanichelli, Bologna, 1925, p. 34.

311 Federico Campanella (1804–1884). Graduated in law in 1829, he approached Mazzini, becoming a man of trust. In 1833, forced to leave the kingdom of Sardinia, he refuged first in Marseilles and, after, in Geneva. During this exile, he undertook the rearrangement of Mazzinian movement and was amid the volunteers supporting Milan in 1848. The year after, he partook in the failed uprising of Genoa and the defense of Rome. After the Expedition of the Thousands alongside Giuseppe Garibaldi to Southern Italy, he was elected deputy (1861–1865). Departed Mazzini, he was—with Maurizio Quadrio and Aurelio Saffi—an essential representative of the democratic movement.

312 *Le logge della comunione scozzese ed il Supremo Consiglio di Palermo*, in "L'Umanitario", April 30, 1870.

313 On the role of Italian Freemasonry within the abolitionist movement, see Mario Da Passano, *La pena di morte nel Regno d'Italia, 1859–1889*, in Sergio Vinciguerra (edited), *I codici preunitari e il codice Zanardelli: diritto penale dell'Ottocento*, Cedam, Padova,1993, pp. 579–649.

314 *Atti dell'assemblea massonica legislativa e costituente tenutasi in Napoli nel 1867*, in "Bollettino del Grande Oriente della massoneria in Italia", n. 2, 1867, pp. 7–62.

main task was charity. In France, these had been operating during the whole Second Empire, and became a place for developing independence and autonomy requests, quickly reaching more profane fields such as the civil rights movements.[315] De Luca's approach was negative: women were still entrapped in catholic culture, thus an opening of ranks would have been self-defeating. However, he agreed to establish a committee investigating the issue and ponder a definitive decision. This board delivered its outcomes in 1869, confirming the former refusal.[316]

After all this, the renewal of the Council took place. Surprisingly, one final short performance by moderates made Cordoba Grand Master again. It was a short-term victory: the elderly statesman lacked in health and the temper required to accomplish the duty. The first Deputy Grand Master Frapolli then replaced him.

In this position, he moved on various perspectives. As the first, in October 1867 he printed a volume collecting statutes and regulations to apply to the Order, largely reprising his leaflet made in 1864.[317] This publication gave Masonry, for the very first time, a corpus for finding criterions of admission, members' rights and duties, the powers of the general assembly and Federal Council—including Grand Master. Regarding this last point, charters drew a pyramidal system where the bulk of functions were in the collegial body assisting the Grand Master and in the plenary assembly (now able to set the fundamental choices), rather than in the supreme leadership of the Obedience.

At the Florence gathering in June 1869, it became the official text for the Brethren belonging to the G.O.I., and remained the basic reference for a long time.

1867 was characterized by the Geneva congress, which saw the birth of the democratic trend inside the pacifist party, embodied by the *Ligue international de la paix et de la liberté*. The G.O.I. sent a delegation to the international forum, which acclaimed Garibaldi as Honorary Chairman. Though the results of the conference had been quite controversial, Italian

---

315 Beatrice Bisogni, *Le donne e la massoneria*, in Claudio Castellacci (edited), *La libera muratoria. Massoneria per problemi*, SugarCo, Milano,1978, pp. 119–125.

316 Ulisse Bacci, *Il libro del massone italiano*, Vita Nova, Roma, 1922, p. 297.

317 *Statuti generali dell'ordine massonico per l'Italia e le sue colonie pubblicati dal G∴ O∴ della Massoneria in Italia*, Tip. Nazionale del G∴ O∴, Firenze, 1867.

Freemasons also intervened in the following one taking place in Bern
(1868) absorbing in their cultural background the proposal to create
supranational bodies to solve states' controversies.[318]

Frapolli came to Florence with positive results during the two years of his
temporary leadership. He could boast an increase in the number of lodges
(150) and a firmness very different from the constant precariousness of
previous Italian masonic life: in 1869, amid 77 effective lodges in 1864, just
15 were still operating.[319]

During the summit, another delicate issue was handled, the abrogation
of the traditional invocation "to the glory of the Great Architect of the
Universe".[320] In 1877, the French brought in the removal of any religious
reference in official papers. The "Goffredo Mameli" lodge in Sassari
proposed to replace this plea with a more materialist and positivist
invocation: "in nome della patria universale e del progresso infinito".[321]
The overwhelming majority of lodges (63 to 5) refused firmly, confirming
that the Masonic anti-clerical attitude was not equal to irreligiosity, or to
a denial of the sacred. This stance was often reaffirmed, marking a neat
difference towards the Grand Orients of France and Belgium.[322]

The 1869 meeting closed by proclaiming Frapolli Grand Master. He
dismissed the role of acting regent and was now the fully-fledged leader of
the community.

In the meanwhile, the Catholic Church, through Pius IX, called for an
Ecumenical council, provoking immediate reactions from the laic world.
Neapolitan Giuseppe Ricciardi promoted an anti-council taking place
on the same days in Naples, launching a plea to make all the anti-clerical

---

318 On the Masonic commitment to pacifism, see Marco Novarino, *La solidarietà al di là
dei confini: l'impegno della massoneria a favore della pace e per la libertà e l'emancipazione
dei popoli*, in "Il Laboratorio", n. 23, 1996, pp. 23–32; Fulvio Conti, *De Genève à la
Piave. La franc-maçonnerie italienne et le pacifisme démocratique (1867–1915)*, in Marta
Petricioli, Donatella Cherubini, Alessandra Anteghini (eds), *Les Etats–Unis d'Europe.
Un project pacifiste*, Peter Lang, 2003, pp. 231–240.

319 Fulvio Conti, *Storia della massoneria italiana*, op. cit., p. 78.

320 *Ivi*.

321 "In the name of the universal homeland and the endless progress" [translator's note].

322 On Belgium, see John Bartier, *Laïcité et Franc-maçonnerie*, Edition de l'université de
Bruxelles, Bruxelles,1981; on France André Combes, *Histoire de la Franc-Maçonnerie
au XIXe siècle*, vol. II, Éditions du Rocher, Monaco, 1999, pp. 138–142.

forces to intervene. In the end, many associations, plus a number of lodges bound to the Supreme Council of Palermo, attended.[323] From the G.O.I., the welcoming was very cold. Frapolli pressed the Brethren to avoid the summit, receiving several critiques.

Coherently with these watchful guidelines, in 1870, when the Franco-Prussian War broke out, he stated that promoting the peace was the Freemasonry's duty, instead of backing one of the sides. The development of the conflict up to the resounding defeat of Sedan, however, had diverse consequences in the Masonic field.

As the first, in August 1870 Napoleon III was forced to retire his imperial troops from Rome, opening the way for Italian unification. As a matter of fact, the Italian government gave birth to a commission, made by Agostino Bertani, Benedetto Cairoli, Crispi, Nicola Fabrizi, and Urbano Rattazzi, whose job was planning the conquer and annexation of the Eternal City.

The Grand Orient of Italy, in "Rivista della Massoneria Italiana"—an upgrade of the bulletin of the Italian Grand Orient, mentioned above and strongly desired by GM—openly supported this "necessary" operation marking the end of Pope's secular power.[324]

The second outcome of the conflict, a few days after September 20 (the day Rome was kept), directly involved Frapolli. Making a grand gesture, he retracted his own thesis, resigning the office, and went to France as a volunteer among Garibaldi's lines to defend the Republic that had arisen from the Second Empire's ashes.

3.6 Toward the Merger of Italian Freemasonry

This decision deeply troubled the G.O.I., who were suddenly without a leader and hugely embarrassed for a purely political choice that compromised the whole institution. The Federal Council, then, hurried to accept his resignation, and published a missive by Frapolli where the former GM pointed out that his choice had been strictly personal—in no way linked to the Italian Masonry. This was the first step in the colonel's

---

323 *L'anticoncilio*, in "L'Umanitario", December 8, 1869, idem, January 28, 1870; *Elenco delle officine massoniche aderenti e rappresentate all'Anticoncilio*, in "L'Umanitario", February 10, 1870.

324 Luigi Polo Friz, *La massoneria italiana nel decennio post unitario. Ludovico Frapolli*, op. cit., p. 203.

distancing from the Obedience: later he was quite critical to the body he once led.[325]

Very shortly after, MP Giuseppe Mazzoni arose to the leadership, thus normalizing the scenario.

Like his precursor, he came from the democratic Left and, in 1849 he had been part of the triumvirate—with Francesco Domenico Guerrazzi and Giuseppe Montanelli—supervising Tuscany after the expulsion of Leopold II of Lorena. His ideological imprint, not dogmatic yet open to dialogue, and his patriotic past cooled down those still reeling from Frapolli's traumatic departure, and lay the foundations for a new dialogue with the dispersed masonic voices.

On May 29, 1871, the representatives from 97 lodges hosted an assembly in Florence proclaiming him Grand Master, thus finally closing the brief lapse of regency. Among the topics on the agenda were the transference of the Order's headquarters to Rome and a resuming of the negotiations with masonic groups still independent of the G.O.I.[326]

A commission was named to get in touch with the dissident groups and to summon a convention the following year in Rome to address, definitely, this matter. The preconditions for the participating lodges were: a year of activity, having a legitimate charter, and a list of members.[327]

On April 28, 1872, one of the most definitive meetings in recent years started in the Teatro Argentina of Rome.

After the return of the group led by Prince of Sant'Elia (1867) and the lodges under the Symbolic Rite of Franchi (1868), there was a concrete chance to merge the Supreme Council of Palermo with the G.O.I.. Its main leaders, whose authority was crumbling, knew all the obstacles dividing the Obediences had been smashed out. Thus, ending in 1870, Campanella expressed his willingness to join a convention to resolve the conflict.[328]

Also, a few weeks before this event, Mazzini died. The Brethren gave him impressive funeral tributes, not just in his hometown of Genoa, but also in

---

325 Alessandro Luzio, *La massoneria e il risorgimento italiano*, op. cit., vol. II, pp. 113–121.

326 Ulisse Bacci, *Il libro del massone italiano*, op. cit., p. 308.

327 Fulvio Conti, *Storia della massoneria italiana*, op. cit., p. 88.

328 Federico Campanella, *A tutte le logge e corpi massonici italiani a qualunque rito appartengano*, in "L'Umanitario", December 24, 1870.

the whole Italian territory. Mazzoni and Campanella gathered the Italian Freemasons, at first to celebrate the illustrious departed in seven consecutive sessions, and then to participate in a ceremony showing off—for the very first time—the masonic vessels in the city hosting the Pope for ages.[329] The impact was so great that the heads decided to transform the day of Mazzini's death (March 10), into a recurrence for commemorating the dead.

Then on this blast of excitement, the conference took place. From April 28 to May 2, Brethren representing 153 lodges convened on the theater, embodying almost all the Italian Freemasonry.[330]

Facing the public after years of discord, the Supreme Council of Palermo stated it would disband and merge in the Grand Orient of Italy. In that moment, the internal divisions in the Masonic galaxy were ending and all the dispersed masonic forces were virtually living in the same Obedience.

The second fundamental issue was the complete freedom for lodges to choose their Rites. Morover, Franchi's group had joined thanks to the statement of equality amid Scottish and Symbolic Rites. In parallel, lodges obtained the permission to exchange letters without former approval by the G.O.I. leadership. The strengthening of the general assembly was another accomplishment. It obtained the right to elect the Grand Master and all the supporting figures in the Federal Council (Grand Secretary, Grand Treasurer, *etc.*), and the capacity to dissolve lodges.[331]

Ballots showed Mazzoni winning over his direct competitor Campanella (69 to 48), thus retained as Honorary Grand Master, while Luigi Castellazzo and Luigi Pianciani became secretary and treasurer. Depretis was one of the outstanding defeated, since the former minister of finance—and upcoming premier—could not gain the office of Deputy GM.

These results highlighted the high rate of politicization distinguishing the Council: of 28 members, 15 were MPs and 3 were about to become so (the cited Castellazzo, Camillo Finocchiaro Aprile, and Corrado Tommasi Crudeli).[332]

---

329 ASGOI, *Minute*, March 15, 1872; *Funerali massonici*, in "L'Umanitario", April 24, 1872.

330 *Processi verbali dell'assemblea massonica costituente tenutasi nella valle del Tevere all'Oriente di Roma nei giorni 28, 29, 30 aprile, 1 e 2 maggio 1872*, Tip. Richiedei, Roma, 1872.

331 Fulvio Conti, *Storia della massoneria italiana*, op. cit., pp. 92–93.

332 *Ivi*, p. 94.

The close connection with politics was the third meaningful issue addressed in 1872 calling: this situation enshrined the beginning of the liaison between Freemasonry and the Italian democratic Left. The civil and political reforms proposed by progressive forces were part of the G.O.I. legacy and implied osmosis among initiates and profanes, with endless exchanges of ideas, plots, and men.

The Masonic renewed unity apparently helped the fast widening of the Obedience. In March 1873, 171 lodges were operating, 15 of which were abroad. The regions with a massive presence were Sicily and Tuscany, while Umbria, Lazio, Abruzzi, and Molise had low penetration.[333]

The records show however an impromptu growth, since the turnover of members was elevated and lodges had a precarious existence with constant demolition and re-foundation. Castellazzo, during the general assembly in May 1874, pointed out that just the previous year, the G.O.I. had suspended 70 lodges for inactivity.[334]

Over the course of that year, a proper makeover expelled defaulters, surveyed the regular members, and consolidated the overall financial stability. The executive in charge of this was Ulisse Bacci,[335] archivist and head of "Rivista della Massoneria Italiana".

The forum held in 1874 approved a new charter recalling the guidelines of 1872 about the different Rites followed by each lodge. The Obedience finally wrote down the total equality and independence of each improvement path according to the formula "freedom of Rites, unity of government".[336]

In contrast to the common practice of most European countries, each lodge could choose freely to follow the Symbolic Rite or the Ancient and Accepted Scottish Rite. The appointed authority managed its ritual, administrative, and judicial life. Only in 1920, under Grand Master Ettore Ferrari, a reform was approved—never actually operational, then resumed in the post-war period— in which lodges' control was severed from ritual organisms and advocated to the Grand Orient of Italy.

---

333 *Elenco generale delle logge e corpi massonici appartenenti alla comunione nazionale italiana*, in "Rivista della Massoneria Italiana" (henceforth RMI), n. 6, 1873, pp. 3–7.

334 *Bollettino ufficiale del Grande Oriente d'Italia*, vol. n. 1, Tip. Militare, Roma, 1875, p. 14.

335 Ulisse Bacci (1846–1935). Journalist of Republican and Mazzinian ideas, in 1872, he achieved the direction of "Rivista della Massoneria Italiana", a post he held until 1926, when the publications were suspended by order of authority.

336 *Bollettino ufficiale del Grande Oriente d'Italia*, op. cit., n. 1, p. 60.

Despite these steps forward in strengthening the institutional stability during the following 15 years, the G.O.I. did not make significant improvements from a statistical standpoint. The balance between suppressed lodges and new establishments kept substantially stable, while the average number of entries was between 400 and 500 a year.[337]

The 1874 meeting was also fundamental regarding the cremationist movement and its connections with the Italian Masonic world.

The idea of burning corpses, in fact, had arisen in positivist-inspired medical circles and, among its roughly declared aims, there was depriving the Catholic Church—in the name of progress and science—of one of the fundamental moments of an individual's life. During the gathering, therefore, this topic was addressed and from the ensuing debate the Obedience committed itself to legalize the crematory practice. The expectation was to turn cemeteries into places welcoming everyone, regardless of religion and the ceremony they followed.[338]

This close osmosis between the cremationist movement and Freemasonry is clear not just by seeing the backers of this practice in Italy (figures such as Amerigo Borgiotti, Gaetano Pini, and Malachia De Cristoforis[339]), but also by checking how many Brethren were cremated. Amid more than 20,000 people who, between 1876 (the year of the first official cremation) and the 1920s, chose this method were several Masons, including the future Grand Master Adriano Lemmi and Andrea Costa, the first socialist deputy in Italy.[340]

---

337 Fulvio Conti, *Massoneria e sfera pubblica nell'Italia liberale*, op. cit., p. 595.

338 *Bollettino ufficiale del Grande Oriente d'Italia*, op. cit., n. 1, pp. 49–50.

339 Malachia De Cristoforis (1832–1915). Belonging to a noble Milanese family, he graduated in medicine at the University of Pavia in 1856. Working in the Maggiore hospital of Milan, he became a patriot, participating as a volunteer among the troops of Garibaldi (in 1859 and 1866). Appointed in Parliament in 1895, he sided with Felice Cavallotti and the radical party, being confirmed until 1904. The following year he was elected senator. From 1889 to 1904, he was city council member of Milan, working hard in favor of educational institutions.

340 For a story of the connections between Masonry and cremation, please refer to Anna Maria Isastia, *La laicizzazione della morte a Roma: cremazionisti e massoni tra Ottocento e Novecento*, in "Dimensioni e problemi della ricerca storica", fasc. 2, 1998, pp. 55–96; Eadem, *La massoneria e il progetto di "fare gli italiani,"* in Fulvio Conti, Anna M. Isastia, Fiorenza Tarozzi (edited), *La morte laica. Storia della cremazione in Italia (1880-1920)*, vol. I, Scriptorium, Torino, 1998, pp. 179–271; Fulvio Conti, *Aspetti culturali e dimensione associativa*, pp. 1–105.

After 1874, Mazzoni focused on the last Masonic groups that still remained independent, such as the Supreme Council of Catania, which professed the Egyptian Rite of Memphis, or the Supreme Scottish Council of Turin. The outcomes were contradictory: if the first was successfully co-opted into the G.O.I.—so that, in 1881, Garibaldi accepted the office of Grand Hierophant—relations with the latter were considerably more tricky. In 1875, the two main supporters of this organism, the Garibaldinian of Polish origin Alessandro De Milbitz and the physician Timoteo Riboli, agreed to merge with the Obedience. The following year, however, when the transfer of the headquarters in Rome was raised, tangles and qualms by Turin executives took over, leading to the agreement collapsing.[341]

Among Mazzoni's ventures should also be underlined the birth, around the mid-70s, of a lodge specifically designed to accommodate politicians, civil servants, and cultural figures to ensure them a certain discretion. Already at the time of the Italian Grand Orient, the "Osiride" lodge, under the direction of Buscalioni, had been founded to host the Obedience's summits and key players belonging to the Cavourian faction. Later, in 1867, Frapolli created the "Universe" lodge, with the purpose of collecting in one place MPs and influential personalities of the Kingdom. Mazzoni decided the role of the "Universe" would be played by the "Propaganda": this lodge, therefore, became one of the clearinghouses of the Italian political and economic elite during the liberal age and it responded directly to the Grand Master.[342]

It was here, in June 1877, Lemmi was initiated: a mighty and wealthy man— nicknamed the "banker of the revolution"—who had been a close associate of Mazzini, repeatedly lending him financial backing for his enterprises.[343] The economic wealth he built over the years, thanks to the trades with the East, the railway constructions, and tobacco, flanked by a political career in the Italian democratic Left, made him a leading figure in the Masonic world of the capital. No wonder, then, his climb to the top was so quick. Despite the purging of 1874, the Grand Orient of Italy still suffered from precariousness and a chronic lack of funds.

The plenary assembly of 1877—shortly before the arrival of Lemmi— imposed an extraordinary tribute of 20 liras per lodge to handle the issue.

---

341 MCRR, Fondo Garibaldi, box 933, in. 7, missive, February 12, 1877.

342 Marco Novarino, *Grande Oriente d'Italia. Due secoli di presenza liberomuratoria*, Erasmo, Roma, 2006, pp. 35–36.

343 ASGOI, *Verbale* June 13, 1877.

Co-opted in the financial commission, he didn't hesitate to bear the debts the Brethren had towards the Obedience, gaining the leaders' recognition. Afterwards he was rewarded, being co-opted in the Council of the Order and designated as Treasurer, a position he held until 1885.[344]

The long-lasting administrative issues led the G.O.I. to retrace its steps, and reinforce the Grand Master's powers, giving him back some of the prerogatives subtracted in 1872.

This occurred in the constituent of 1879 where, moreover, an approved motion settled the need for larger Masonic involvement in favor of laborers and the fight against poverty.[345]

In these years the question of the relations with the raising socialist movement—offering alternative remedies to redeem the working classes—also emerged, especially since it had much in common with Masonic ideologies and values. It should not be forgotten that some of the early socialists were members of the Grand Orient of Italy. The attitude of the institution was, therefore, ambivalent: facing lodges' requests for the compatibility between membership of the International and Masonic affiliation, the leadership just reiterated the Order welcomed all honest men, regardless of their religious or political orientations.[346]

Significantly clearer was the choice of supporting the Risorgimentos celebration by installing many monuments around Italy. A clear example of this Masonic activity was the monument erected in Mentana in 1877, in memory of the ruinous Garibaldinian expedition for the conquest of Rome, or the one unveiled three years later in Milan to celebrate the same fact.[347]

Masonry thus ended up carving out a leading role in the nation-building process, based on the construction of the Risorgimento myth and a patriotic liturgy whose ultimate goal was to legitimize the fragile national state by strengthening its consensus amid the middle and popular classes.[348]

---

344 Ulisse Bacci, *Il libro del massone italiano*, op. cit., pp. 358–359.

345 *Riassunto dell'assemblea*, in "Rivista della Massoneria Italiana", n. 8, 1879, p. 122.

346 ASGOI, *Verbale* December 8, 1878.

347 Fulvio Conti, *Storia della massoneria italiana*, op. cit., p. 105.

348 Fulvio Conti, *La massoneria e il mito del Risorgimento*, in "Il Risorgimento", fasc. 3, 2000, pp. 503–519.

Of the decade marked by Mazzoni's direction, it's possible to have a reliable sociological and historical picture about the membership structure, thanks to a file dating back to 1874. This list offers a snapshot of 45 lodges (out of the 134 overall) with the names of about 1,900 Brothers.[349]

Its analysis shows how the Italian Freemasonry was essentially a bourgeois organization: 40.5% of the affiliates were employees, teachers, traders, and pensioners, with 2.4% being accountants, surveyors, veterinarians, opticians, and land surveyors. After this fairly plain group, liberal professions (13.9%) and owners (13.6%) followed, almost equally.

Public officials (1.7%), great entrepreneurs, and financiers (1.4%) stood out for their small presence.[350]

On the contrary, the presence of manual workers—craftsmen, workers, and service workers—reached about 20% of the total. This gross element, if added to 2.6% of maritime officers, shows how Freemasonry had quite an appeal towards social classes kept economically on the edge of the Italian life. Another fact of undoubted interest is the membership of a small but significant bulk of servicemen and artists (3.2%).

On May 11, 1880, after a brief and violent illness, Mazzoni died. To succeed him, the senior patriot—and conspirator—Giuseppe Petroni was called. Adherent of the Carbonari secret society, he then became a follower of Mazzini, spending 17 years in the prisons of the Papal State (1853–1870).

Under his direction, G.O.I. the accomplished the rearrangement process begun in 1874. Lodges and Brethren neither active nor paying were definitively expelled. In this way the ranks were closed, cutting out those elements limiting its ability to act and influence. Another contribution to the financial recovery was the decision—also wanted by Lemmi—to raise the membership fee to 100 liras (at the time on a voluntary basis). It was introduced on July 20, 1880, shortly after the appointment of Mazzoni to Grand Mastery, proving how precarious the financial conditions of the Order remained.[351]

---

349 Archivio Centrale dello Stato di Roma, *Fondo massoneria*, registro 1874.

350 Jean–pierre Viallet, *Anatomie d'une obédience maçonnique: le Grand Orient d'Italie (1870–1890 circa)*, in "Mélanges de l'Ecole française de Rome. Moyen—Age, Temps modernes", vol. 90, fasc. 1, 1978, pp. 171–237.

351 *Circolare n. 14*, in "Rivista della Massoneria Italiana", n. 14–15, 1880, pp. 230–231.

The implementation of this provision had prompt results on the coffers of the Grand Orient of Italy, and persuaded the top executives that there were new chances for acting on the country's socio-economic network: the organization could now take a leading role in the national scene.

During the 1882 general elections, the first with extended suffrage (the voters were more than 2 million compared to the previous 620,000), the G.O.I. pronounced itself decisively. At first, it invited its members to survey the electoral machine, fearing the increase of voters and the new system of scrutiny would cause frauds and corruption. In essence, Masonry would have been the guarantor of smooth running of voting.

Secondly, Mazzoni removed the ambiguities of the past by publicly coming out and giving precise indications to members: Brethren could choose only democratic and progressive candidates while opposing the "transformist" Left led by Depretis.[352]

This endorsement was grounded on the premise that electoral success of the progressive forces would lead to the improvement of civil society. Notably, he imagined a gradual strengthening of social bases of the State thanks to the involvement of classes so far kept on the fringes in the unitary process. In order to rejuvenate the country, fight the lack of education, and spread a sense of belonging to Italy, in the annual meeting of 1881 there were discussions about founding female lodges of adoption. According to the advocates of this project, once again rejected, women would have finally been freed from the tradition and they would have become modern wives, mothers, and citizens.[353]

The Catholic Church immediately noticed the Masonic change of pace and its improved capacity to affect society. No coincidence, then, on April 20, 1884, Pope Leo XIII issued the encyclical Humanum Genus. He reminded the faithful—for the umpteenth time—the illegitimate action that destroyed the Church's secular power by putting the blame on the Masonic "sect." The emerging perception of Freemasonry was therefore that of an obscure and diabolical conventicle, guilty of all wickedness ("Satan's synagogue" was one of the definitions used).[354]

---

352 *Circolare n. 6*, in "Rivista della Massoneria Italiana", n. 18–19, 1882, pp. 296–297.

353 *Congresso massonico di Milano*, in "Rivista della Massoneria Italiana", n. 4, 1882, p. 52.

354 Aldo Alessandro Mola, *Adriano Lemmi. Gran Maestro della nuova Italia (1885–1896)*, Erasmo, Roma, 1985, p. XXV.

This document gave way to an intense anti-masonic activity that saw the spread of numerous pamphlets, often written by former masons and characterized by sensational and the terrifying themes. French Gabriel-Antoine Jogand Pagés—nom de plume Léo Taxil—was the main exponent of this trend, even if Italian authors abounded (Domenico Margiotta, just to mention).

All of them produced successful works describing the lodges as places of depravity where immoral satanic rites were performed. The impact this had on the audience was significant since it helped to secure the stereotypical image of the mason: a powerful dissolute man, driven by anti-national social and economic interests.[355]

The phenomenon reached its peak in September 1896 when an anti-masonic convention (with over 1,500 people among clergymen, journalists, and members of the Antimasonic League) was held in Trento. The Vatican fully supported the rally and there were many appreciations: 242 cardinals and bishops and over 1,000 associations sent their greetings. In this poisoned climate, the experience of Petroni as Grand Master ended: the assembly held in Rome on January 16, 1885—where Crispi obtained a place in the Council of the Order—ratified the handover to Lemmi, after approving some changes that further strengthened the Grand Master's authority. Now, in fact, he could manage, at his own unquestionable judgment, the relations with foreign Obediences and the financial assets.[356]

3.7 The Era of Lemmi

Since the first circular (January 26), the new head of the G.O.I. clearly expressed what would have been one of the milestones of his policy: strengthening the authority of the highest office of the Order.[357]

To him, this concentration of power was essential to stop all the unorganized and disobedient acts of Brethren and lodges that, over the years, tarnished the public image of Italian Freemasonry. Cleaning masonry of its "harmful and useless" elements would have restored its former glory.[358] All this

---

355 For a story of the anti-masonic movement, see Luigi Pruneti, *La Sinagoga di Satana. Storia dell'antimassoneria (1725–2002)*, Laterza, Roma–Bari, 2002.

356 *Assemblea costituente*, in "Rivista della Massoneria Italiana", n. 1–2, 1885, pp. 1–13.

357 MCRR, Fondo Crispi, box 660, file 15, circular, January 26, 1885.

358 Ibidem.

implied a meaningful change of course and the definitive halt of the previous preference for increasing member numbers as much as possible. What urged the Grand Master was transforming the Grand Orient of Italy into a meeting place for the most influential and culturally relevant Italian elite. It's not surprising, therefore, in 1887, that Lemmi got the 100 liras tuition—previously only spontaneous—approved by the national assembly for each new member who entered the institution: in this way it could obtain a first patrimonial bulk that allowed the financing of activities. As stated above, the fund was supervised and managed directly by him.[359]

The decision to impose this disbursement, although paid in installments, had a further consequence. The removal of popular elements still in G.O.I. Masonry made it become more socially homogeneous and cohesive: a bourgeois organization, formed in the cult of the Risorgimento, anti-clerical, and confident in the secularization of Italian society.[360]

In the Grand Master's view, the G.O.I. increasingly assumed the profile of a lobby. With this perspective, he sent a questionnaire to all lodges in February 1886 to gather information on local Catholic organizations and how the latter related to local authorities and influenced the political and administrative ballots. Using this data, he decided to create models to replicate for a greater Masonic commitment in the "profane" area. Two years later, he ordered each lodge to be equipped with five permanent commissions with specific tasks: to audit charity institutions, legislative elections, mayors' actions, primary schools, and, finally, to know what facilities were lacking in urban centers.[361]

In accordance with the new way, during the 1886 round of elections, he dissociated from his forerunner by not siding with the extreme left, but backed the Historical Left, leaving the choice of which candidates to support to the Worshipful Masters.[362]

Lemmi gained a new personal success in February 1887, when he managed to solve the long-standing split tearing the Scottish Rite apart,

---

359 *Costituzioni generali del Grande Oriente d'Italia discusse ed approvate dall'assemblea co-stituente del 1887*, Civelli, Roma, 1887.

360 Marco Novarino, *Progresso e Tradizione Libero Muratoria*, op. cit., pp. 85–86.

361 *Circolare n. 10*, in "Rivista della Massoneria Italiana", n. 1–2, 1888, p. 3.

362 *Notizie della Comunione*, in "Rivista della Massoneria Italiana", n. 1–2, 1886, pp. 9–10.

thus obtaining unification of the Supreme Councils of Turin and Rome. The direct consequence of this accomplishment was his appointment as Sovereign Grand Commander for nine years.[363] It was the first time a man held both responsibilities at the same time, and this helped to perceive the action of the banker from Leghorn as a further step towards the control of all the Masonic vital nerve centers.

His steadiness caused discontents that erupted in 1886. Within Masonry, the first to openly express their dissent were—once again—the Lombard Brethren, who were very sensitive to social matters and hosting within their ranks petit-bourgeoisie and commoners.

In their opinion, the mandatory tuition led to a complete shift in the members' selection by shifting the focus from merit and quality to mere pecuniary disposal.[364] Moreover, the protestors highlighted one of the main defects of the general assemblies held in Rome: most of the lodges were unable to attend the meetings and, therefore, they had to appoint local representatives who were often closely linked to the summits of Obedience. Another irritating element was the renewed prohibition of the lodges communicating among themselves without explicit approval by the Council.[365]

The last decision detonating the conflict was the refusal to distribute a leaflet inviting the lodges to create anti-clerical commissions. Lemmi, while sharing the spirit of the initiative, recognized this project did not take into account the complex Italian situation because there were areas where the work of "laic apostolate" was extremely difficult and self-defeating.[366]

In response, a significant number of members from the lodges "La Ragione" and "La Cisalpina" in Milan issued an agenda that openly criticized the Grand Master and his work. This clash between the two sides clearly resulted in a split. The dissidents coming from the Milanese lodges were then joined by "Scienza e Lavoro" in Florence, "Cairoli" in Arezzo, "Felice Orsini", and "Il Dovere" from Leghorn as well as "Carlo Valle" in Alessandria. This last was a clear example of how the whole conflict was more linked to political–ideological positions than to organizational issues: it had already

---

363 MCRR, Fondo Crispi, box 660, file 15, circular February 12, 1887.

364 *Ragioni dell'ultimo movimento massonico milanese*, in "Humanitas", n. 1, 1886, p. 2.

365 Marco Novarino, *Progresso e Tradizione Libero Muratoria*, op. cit., pp. 86–87.

366 ASGOI, Missive, September 13, 1885.

been expelled by the G.O.I. since its dignitaries refused to swear using the formula of the Great Architect of Universe.[367]

Very shortly after, eight other lodges were built to welcome further rebels. In December 1886, the "G.B. Prandina" arose with a peculiar profile: according to Demetrio Prada it was "la prima loggia italiana veramente operaia"[368] since it would have also accepted popular classes so far unrelated to the Masonic family because they were considered intellectually and culturally deficient.[369]

Ahead of this split, the Grand Orient of Italy established, unlike other events, to completely ignore the group and to avoid any news about it.[370]

Meanwhile, Lemmi's project underwent a further step forward. Crispi, confirmed in May 1887 as Council member of the G.O.I., assumed the office of Prime Minister in July. The fact that a Brother was now guiding the country suggested a quickening of the social reforms cherished by many Freemasons: as a matter of fact, Lemmi really wanted to put pressure on this topic.

In domestic policy, some of the Sicilian statesman's actions seemed to confirm these expectations. In January 1888, for instance, he dismissed the mayor of Rome, Leopoldo Torlonia for having sent, on behalf of citizens, his best wishes to the Pope.[371]

On the foreign policy level, however, the scenery was completely different. Crispi was a staunch supporter of the Triple Alliance, in contrast to the pro-French sentiment shared by the vast majority of members in the Order. The competition for colonies between France and Italy—exacerbated by the French occupation of Tunisia—increased with his leadership and, in 1888, the two countries were on the verge of a war. In the face of such a possible outcome, the extreme left and the democratic newspapers promoted many rallies.

Lemmi, worried about possible coups led by Brethren, issued a circular forbidding attendance of these parades, and generated discontent in

---

367 *La Loggia Carlo A. Valle*, in "Rivista della Massoneria Italiana", n. 6–7, 1886, pp. 52–53.

368 "The first truly workers' Italian lodge" [translator's note].

369 *Parole del fr∴ D∴ Prada*, in "Humanitas", n. 6, 1886, p. 3.

370 *Tolleranza Mass∴*, in "Humanitas", n. 1, 1886, p. 6.

371 Fulvio Conti, *Storia della massoneria italiana*, op. cit., pp. 123–124.

several lodges, which was addressed by the most influential members of the Council of the Order. In December 1888, the leaders of the Symbolic Rite sent a communication to all their lodges trying to calm things down.[372]

A further element of tension was the enthusiastic reception of Emperor William II. During his visit to Rome in October, the G.O.I. exhibited its vessels on the façade of headquarters and delivered a circular emphasizing the alliance linking the kingdom of Italy to the German Empire.[373]

Lemmi, aware of the voices against his uncritical support to Crispi's action, decided to get ahead by convening a plebiscite to let the Brethren judge his work. The definite success of this initiative toughened its position and let him continue the strategy of making Masonry the main drive of "modernization" and secularization. Within this project, a relevant place belonged to the cult of Risorgimento and its heroes.

The search for "laic saints," however, was not limited to these patriots, but it went further back in time, identifying in the distant past some emblematic and heretical figures. Among all of them, the philosopher Giordano Bruno was the most known and significant. The Grand Orient of Italy organized an impressive event to honor the installment of the monument celebrating him in Campo de 'Fiori in Rome. On June 9, 1889, more than 3,000 Brethren arrived from all over Italy, and paraded with their own flags while heading toward the square. It was a resounding exhibition of strength displaying the vigor of Italian Freemasonry, while also launching a challenge to the Vatican.[374]

The belief of a Masonic activity to undermine (if not destroy) the pillar of Christian values shared by the Church institutions was confirmed by the commitment—by individual lodges and then by the G.O.I.—in favor of divorce and the preeminence of civil marriage over religious one. The climax was at the beginning of the 90s and saw as key players—in the public debate—two masons, the lawyer Giuseppe Ceneri and the former minister Tommaso Villa.[375]

---

372 *Notizie massoniche della Comunione*, in "Rivista della Massoneria Italiana", n. 17–18, 1888, pp. 283–284.

373 *Notizie massoniche della Comunione*, in "Rivista della Massoneria Italiana", n. 14–15–16, 1888, pp. 248–249.

374 Fulvio Conti, *Storia della massoneria italiana*, op. cit., pp. 127–128.

375 Tommaso Villa (1832–1915). Graduated in law, the young Piedmontese partook in several newspapers linked to local Left. Deputy in 1865, he fought for the revocation

The masonic community supported this bill, raising funds and promoting pamphlets and committees to increase awareness on the issue. All this effort, however, did not succeed due to several Catholic initiatives backing the indissolubility of marriage (in 1892, the Committee for the Defense of Marriage was established). Both attempts made that year in Parliament by Villa (March 12 and December 7) were rejected, confirming that the issue was not felt by the vast majority of country.[376]

Masonry, during Lemmi's Grand Mastery had, thanks to greater visibility, a remarkable organizational consolidation. The number of Italian lodges had a sharp increase, ascending from 107 in 1885 to 136 in 1897. Though those located abroad decreased (with the exception of Argentina and Egypt), in Italy there was greater uniformity in geographical location.

Many of the new establishments were born in areas until then not included by Masonic penetration. The situation saw 33% of lodges in the North, 29.4% in the Center, 19.99% in the South, and the remaining 17.7% in the islands. Finally, the average of new members in the last decade of the nineteenth century was around a thousand per year, proving the charm and attraction exerted on the urban classes.[377]

3.8 The Fall of Lemmi

T he celebration of the monument to Giordano Bruno was the moment of maximum glory for Lemmi. From that moment on, a delicate phase began for the supreme head of the G.O.I. Targeted by traditionalist Catholic newspapers for his past—covered below—, beginning in 1889 he was marked by some serious scandals undermining his prestige.

The first was that he had earned 340,000 liras on the backs of taxpayers due to a speculation on a supply of tobacco for the state monopoly. Thanks to Crispi, in fact, the American company he represented received an order

---

of Mazzini's proscription and Garibaldi's release after his failed attempt to occupy Rome. Tied to Benedetto Cairoli, he was called to serve as Minister of the Inner Affairs and then as Minister of Grace and Justice (1879–1881). President of the Chamber in 1895–1897 and in 1900–1902, he became a senator in 1909.

376 Silvano Montaldo, *Il divorzio: famiglia e nation building nell'Italia liberale*, in "Il Risorgimento", n. 1, 2000, pp. 5–57.

377 Fulvio Conti, *Storia della massoneria italiana*, op. cit., pp. 136–140; Marco Novarino, *Progresso e Tradizione Libero Muratoria*, op. cit., pp. 124–125.

that, after some trafficking, was paid by the Italian government at a higher price than normal.[378]

The story, a matter for parliamentary question, had a wide impact on the newspapers and cast a shadow over the Grand Orient, since the belief was that Lemmi had used his masonic connections to hide the crime (besides Crispi, the executive had five ministers and an undersecretary belonging to the Order).[379]

However, the news that mainly harmed his reputation was his involvement in the Roman Bank affair.

This credit institution was one of the six, nationwide, qualified to issue money. Compromised in real estate speculation in Rome and major Italian cities between 1889 and 1893, it was in a serious economic trouble. To overcome this excessive credit supply, the bank produced 65 million liras over the legal limit, duplicating serial numbers. Successively, from this amount of money, 40 million was loaned to deputies and ministers of the Italian government, including Crispi and Giovanni Giolitti (in 1892 a fresh premier). The outcome of the inquiry committee was made public in December 1892, raising a huge fuss, and was then followed by a judicial investigation that led to a major bust.[380]

Questioned for his morality, Lemmi tried to run for cover and regain consensus. Thus, he tried to revamp and strengthen the Order. The constitutions ratified in 1893 changed the GM election procedure, attributing to all Worshipful Masters the right to vote. The designation of the supreme guide of the G.O.I. thus became a democratic choice, guaranteeing him a new and scarcely opposable legitimacy.[381]

To assist the Grand Master a new body was established, the Executive Council, made up of a small number of Brethren, which became the real core of the Obedience.

Lemmi's stand was difficult but the coup de grace came from the man who,

---

378 Ferdinando Cordova, *Massoneria e Politica in Italia (1892–1908)*, Laterza, Roma–Bari, 1985, pp. 13–15.

379 *Ivi*, p. 45.

380 Enzo Magrì, *I ladri di Roma. 1893 lo scandalo della Banca Romana: politici, giornalisti, eroi del Risorgimento all'assalto del denaro pubblico*, Mondadori, Milano, 1993.

381 *Costituzioni generali della massoneria in Italia. Discusse ed approvate dall'assemblea costituente del 1893*, Tip. Civelli, Roma, 1893.

more than anyone, had been a close associate: Crispi. After the opening of the government towards reforms, the Prime Minister—back to his office after a brief interlude—followed an authoritarian path favorable to reconciliation with the Vatican.

The repression of Fasci Siciliani represented a key moment in this parable. Starting in 1891, Sicily had been overwhelmed by the urban proletariat and farm laborers protesting against the dominance of the landowners and the absence of the State. Unification had not indeed significantly changed the socio-economic conditions of these classes, and land redistribution remained a particularly sensitive issue.

The pressure aggravated in the autumn of 1893, when the movement organized strikes throughout the island and attempted a general insurrection. Following the resignation of Giolitti government, Crispi— once again premier—took care of the matter using repression. He authorized a military intervention, which, between December 1893 and January 1984, led to mass executions and arrests.

The radical-democratic wing, intolerant of how the workers on strike were repressed, communicated its strenuous dissent, forcing the Grand Master to intervene. In the very first days of February 1894, Lemmi claimed to have "full confidence" in Brother and "friend" Crispi, just as the southern statesman was radically changing his vision and assuming unpredictable positions.[382]

Thus, in September, the Premier made a famed speech in Naples, in which he highlighted the common fight that the civil and religious authority (i.e. the Vatican) had to promote against anarchism. To do this both institutions needed a mutual agreement: this way the popular masses, tempted by these destabilizing calls, would be brought back onto the right track.[383]

Lemmi and his close friends experienced this move as a real betrayal that opened a deep wound within the Masonic community. To many indeed, the words pronounced by Crispi were an open defiance of the whole Risorgimento experience.

---

382 *Governo Crispi sotto tutela di Adriano Lemmi*, in "La Lega Lombarda", February 1–2, 1894.

383 *L'inaugurazione di una lapide a Napoli*, in "La Lega Lombarda", September 11–12, 1894.

The Grand Master was accused of being too tied up with the political fortune of Crispi, thus making the Grand Orient of Italy a sort of fifth column enslaved to the interests of a faction. Moreover, Order authority had abdicated those inspiring principles which would have been the foundation of all its action in the "profane" society: civil liberties and a secular state.

The Grand Master was now wondering how to react to these new perspectives in Italian politics. The Milanese lodges asked Lemmi to clarify the situation in an attempt to push the G.O.I. to openly blame the illustrious Brother.

This request had a "profane" implication, crossing the limited masonic circle and reaching out to the national press. Not only did the clerical newspapers—traditionally very attentive—follow the affair with interest, so did the democratic and anti-Crispi medias, such as "Il Secolo" and "La Tribuna".

Just "Il Secolo", which was intensifying its campaign against the Prime Minister, emphasized the correspondence between the parties, underlining how the Grand Master's response had been unsatisfactory and hesitant: the lodges were ready for the schism.[384]

While the events were happening very quickly, the national congress (held in Milan on September 20) arrived. The supreme head of Italian Freemasonry, aware of the difficult times, attempted to shift the attention to financial issues (extension of sharecropping, parceling of uncultivated lands, progressive taxation) or laic matters (abolition of Church guarantees, suppression of religious corporations, extension of government control over religious bodies). Nevertheless, there were some unpleasant incidents during the plenary assembly, condensed in the shout «down to Crispi».[385]

At the end of the congress, the Grand Orient of Italy was clearly split: on one side, those who, despite faltering, still supported the Sicilian statesman; on the other, those who completely rejected his administration and whished the G.O.I had a specific commitment against him. Among the latter stood lawyer Onorato Barbetta, who, during the debate, painted Crispi as a Machiavellian man willing to do anything for his own benefit.[386]

---

384 *La massoneria contro Crispi*, in "Il Secolo", September 13–14, 1894.

385 *Il Congresso massonico italiano*, in "Il Secolo", September 22–23, 1894.

386 *Il Congresso massonico e il rapporto tra Stato e Chiesa*, in "La Sera", September 26, 1894.

The following month two events further disturbed the spirits: on October 28, socialist associations were dismissed by the government and—few days later—the new archbishop of Milan, Andrea Carlo Ferrari, was welcomed with all the honors by the city extraordinary commissioner, who accompanied him through the streets.[387]

On December 9, during the Council meeting, attended by the Grand Master and 25 councilors, new divisions emerged. If the democratic and radical opposition—embodied by Giuseppe Mussi, Federico Rebessi, and Felice Massano—was pressing to give up all ties and bonds of solidarity with the government, in the pro-Crispi front two different positions appeared. If Giovanni Bovio and Salvatore Barzilai[388], despite supporting the head of State, acknowledged the reasons and the restlessness the Brethren had, others figures, such as Alberto Fortis, fiercely defended Crispi and were ready for a split.[389]

Once again, Lemmi managed to prevail and in the approved agenda—with only one defection—no reference to Crispi was made, though it reiterated the need to fight Vatican interference for a complete secularization of the State.[390]

It was a pretty fragile result, all the more because the newspapers fueled tensions. "L'Italia del Popolo", for example, speaking of this controversy, said Masonry had a duty to defend its members but it should not have supported them when they were wrong.[391]

The administrative elections held in Milan in February 1895 were a testing ground for the breakthrough the Sicilian politician had. The conservative-liberals and the moderates, following Crispi's input, build a list also including Catholics, which defeated the democratic bloc (radicals,

---

387 Fulvio Conti, *Storia della massoneria italiana*, op. cit., p. 144; Marco Novarino, *Progresso e Tradizione Libero Muratoria*, op. cit., p. 120.

388 Salvatore Barzilai (1860–1939). Born in Trieste, city under the Hapsburg Empire, given his commitment to the unity cause, he was forced to leave and go to Italy. Other than being an editor for the magazine "Tribuna", he distinguished himself as a criminal lawyer. He entered Parliament in 1890 and remained in the republican party until 1911, when he left for its open support to the Italian occupation of Libya. Delegate to the peace conference in 1919, the following year he became a senator.

389 ASGOI, *Minute*, December 9, 1894.

390 *Ibidem.*

391 *La massoneria e Crispi*, in "L'Italia del Popolo", December 8–9, 1894.

republicans, and socialists). The latter counted 42 local notables belonging to Masonry (such as Pirro Aporti, Giorgio Sinigaglia, Antonio Maffi, Luigi Arienti, and the aforementioned De Cristoforis, Mussi, and Barbetta) and their debacle had wide echo.[392]

The electoral results proved the rapprochement with the Catholic Church had been a winning strategy and it would certainly have continued. During the following summit of the Council, in the second half of March, a new debate took place, but the result was—albeit several distinctions—an appeal for prudence.[393]

The final straw was the judgment delivered by the Supreme Council of the 33rd of the Ancient and Accepted Scottish Rite, which stated as «false and slanderous» the charges claiming the Grand Master—still Sovereign Grand Commander— had been condemned in Marseilles in 1844[394]. It was a shadowy affair that hit the headlines in 1880, when some newspapers published a verdict where a certain Adriano Lemmi, former shopkeeper, had been found guilty of theft. He had always warded himself by asserting this man was a namesake born in Florence and, at that time, he was in Constantinople. Despite his firm denials, the case had never been fully solved and had been cyclically brought back to light by his opponents.[395]

Many Brethren considered the paper produced by the Supreme Council, which also ratified it was not necessary to file a compliancy in the "profane" tribunals, as an act of overconfidence.[396]

On May 19, the Milanese lodge "Cisalpina-Carlo Cattaneo" sent a document to the press asking Lemmi to defend himself in court, to definitively dispel any doubt. Furthermore, it stated that Crispi should have been expelled

---

392 The complete list of the democratic electoral committee was published in "L'Italia del Popolo", February 4–5, 1895.

393 ASGOI, *Minute*, March 17, 1895.

394 *Un giudizio del Supremo Consiglio dei 33...*, in "Rivista della Massoneria Italiana", n. 9–11, 1895, p. 167. To confront the version, please refer also to *I 33∴ della massoneria scolpano Adriano Lemmi*, in "L'Italia del Popolo", May 22–23, 1895, and *Lemmi prosegue a negare*, in "Rivista Antimassonica", May 1895, pp. 236–237.

395 Fulvio Conti, item *Adriano Lemmi*, in *Dizionario biografico degli italiani*, vol. LXIV, Treccani, 2005, http://www.treccani.it/enciclopedia/adriano–lemmi_Dizionario–Biografico/ (September 20, 2018).

396 This was the opinion of Domenico Farini, president of the Senate. Domenico Farini, *Diario di fine secolo*, Bardi, Roma, 1961, p. 682.

"for his violent methods" and his collusion with the Vatican. At the end of this bursting note, the rebels claimed that, without response from the summits, they resolved to no longer recognize the authority of the G.O.I. [397]

The Grand Master had to take immediate action, since the revolt threatened to worsen—already a lodge, "La Ragione," expressed solidarity with the protesters—and therefore he decided to expel the dissidents: exactly 10 years after the last split, the Masonic unity was broken again.

When the Council of the Order met, some asked that, given all that was happening, the Grand Orient of Italy disclosed what political direction the Masonry had to follow. The aforementioned Fortis—a supporter of the Lemmi-Crispi axis—blatantly replied to the question by affirming that the G.O.I. wasn't supposed to deal with politics. This paradoxical answer showed how landmarks were brought up instrumentally only when defending the leadership. [398]

Beyond this debate, however, the main topic was the Milanese situation. The majority of the Council was in favor of mediation and therefore called for a lifting of the suspension. To this end, a commission was created to go to Milan and solve the issue.

Despite these attempts, the rupture was definitive. On September 2, an assembly was held in Milan, attended by about 80 Brethren from all over Italy, to discuss on how to create a new Masonic organization.

A working group was thus designated with the purpose of drafting the path to follow. [399]

Among the six members, four came from "La Ragione" and amid them emerged with particular emphasis the doctor—and fresh MP—De Cristoforis.

The group initially called itself Milanese Free-Masonry, then the name changed into Italian Grand Orient. This overhaul was largely the result of De Cristoforis's intense activity, trying to look beyond the narrow Lombard scenery and settle a national-level movement. Thanks to his commitment, the group obtained adhesions not only in Lombardy, but also in Liguria,

---

397   *La massoneria milanese ribelle a Lemmi e a Crispi*, in "L'Italia del Popolo", May 19–20, 1895; *Ribellione di massoni milanesi contro Crispi*, in "Il Secolo", May 19–20, 1895.

398   Marco Novarino, *Progresso e Tradizione Libero Muratoria*, op. cit., p. 122.

399   *Cronaca di Milano. Convegno massonico*, in "L'Italia del Popolo", September 1–2, 1895.

Tuscany, and Sicily. The peak was reached in 1898, when the Grand Orient of France decide to recognize it as the only Italian Obedience, lifting the support so far provided to the Grand Orient of Italy.

This dramatic tear had severe implications for the Italian Obedience. The criticism against Lemmi now came from the ranks of those who, till then, had always backed Crispi. The protest staged by Ernesto Nathan to express his dissent was significant: he refused to attend the Council work until light had been cast on the allegations against Crispi.[400]

In such a severe climate, the dissent from leading figures like Nathan and Bovio persuaded the Grand Master it was useless to persevere. Therefore, on October 28, Lemmi took the fateful decision to resign.

Immediately, there were attempts and pressures to get him back. Thus, almost two months were spent until, on December 23, 1895, Deputy Grand Master Achille Ballori publicly confirmed Lemmi had no intention of withdrawing his resignation. Therefore, according to the constitution, he would assume the full powers until the general assembly that would be held shortly thereafter. One of the most complex and contradictory periods of the Italian Masonic history was thus closed.

In June 1896, the plenary of the G.O.I. would identify Nathan, an Israelite born in the United Kingdom, the right man to lead the main Italian obedience in the twentieth century.

---

400 ASGOI, *Minute*, October 21, 1895.

4. The Grand Orient of Italy During Liberal Season, from Nathan to Ferrari

Emanuela Locci

4.1 Intro

On June 2, 1896, the Constituent of Grand Orient of Italy elects by an overwhelming majority Ernesto Nathan to the Great Mastery. Nathan was born in London on October 5, 1845 to Moses Meyer[401] and Sara Levi.[402] He lived the years of his childhood and training in a distinctly Mazzinian atmosphere, above all thanks to the engagement of his mother, a friend of Mazzini. In the English Nathan mansion, besides Mazzini, was attended by a number of renown personalities from Italian political and intellectual life: Aurelio Saffi, Maurizio Quadrio (who will give the young Ernesto lessons of Latin and French, always in touch with the family),[403] Federico Campanella, Ergisto Bezzi, Scipione Pistrucci; all exiles and in unsteady material conditions.[404]

Born in a Jewish family, he moved to Italy in 1859, after his father death; in Italy, he contributed with Unità Italiana headline. After a brief stay in Lon-

---

401 His father, Moses Meyer, born on April 22, 1799, in Rodelheim, near Frankfurt am Main, was a well-to-do merchant and stockbroker, who after long staying in Paris had settled in London, where on July 4, 1850, he had obtained his English citizenship. http://www.treccani.it/enciclopedia/ernesto-nathan_(Dizionario-Biografico)/ (November 18 2018)

402 Sara Levi, born in Pesaro on December 7, 1819, was a daughter of Angelo and Ricca Rosselli. After the premature death of the mother was hosted in Livorno by a relative, Emanuele Rosselli, a wealthy merchant with a representative office in London. It was probably he who combined the marriage with Moses Meyer, which was celebrated on May 29, 1836, according to the tradition of Jewish communities that favored unions among coreligionists. The couple settled in London and had, in addition to the five-year-old Ernesto, eleven other sons: David (1839), Henry (1840), Janet (1842), Adolf (1843), Harriet (1847), Joe (1848), Philip (1850), Walter (1852), Alfred (1854), Adah (1856), Beniamino (1859). http://www.treccani.it/enciclopedia/ernesto-nathan _(Dizionario-Biografico)/ (November, 18, 2018).

403 Anna Maria Isastia, *Scritti politici di Ernesto Nathan*, Bastogi, Foggia, 1998, p. 94.

404 Ivi, p. 7.

don from 1865 to 1870 (meanwhile, in 1867, he marry Virginia Mieli), he was recalled to the peninsula by Giuseppe Mazzini,[405] willing him in Rome as executive for Roma del popolo magazine. Settled in Rome, in 1888, he obtained Italian citizenship and gathered a broad group of intellectuals.[406] The year after he enters Italian political life by the Republican Party.[407]

4.2 Political Line

Beyond his masonic career, the political one is indeed relevant, as city councilor in Rome, from which he resigned in 1890 to protest against the track of Francesco Crispi.[408] He further was a provincial councilor in Pesaro and from 1895 re-elected to the Campidoglio, a post held until 1902. His political achievement led up to his election as mayor of the Eternal City. Nathan is an extraordinary example in the Italian political scenery for his very high moral rigor, grounded essentially on a convinced secular approach to the institution. Thus, from 1907 to 1914, Ernesto Nathan was mayor of Rome, leading a leftist coalition including radicals, republicans, socialists and constitutional democrats.[409] The Chamber of Labor also backed his candidacy.[410] Those were essential years for the close communal history, interested by the improvement of diverse ventures, as the innovation of building policy, the growth of education, citizen participation in the city govern, and the care of public hygiene. Nathan is accountable for the urban master plan, the institution of 16 primary schools, facilities made public, the recovery of the Agro Pontino swamp from malaria.[411] With the end of his term, the government entrusted him with assignments abroad, mostly in England and the United States.[412]

---

405 Nathan devoted much of his energy to the dissemination of the works of Giuseppe Mazzini, with whom his family, starting with his mother Sara, had a very close relationship. Mazzini and his supporters were always welcome in the homes of the Nathan family, both in Italy and abroad. Nathan's sister, Giannetta, welcomed Mazzini home in the last days of her life, and here the Italian patriot died, assisted in a loving and filial manner.

406 Vittorio Gnocchini, *L'Italia dei liberi muratori. Brevi biografie di massoni famosi*, Erasmo editore, Roma, 2005, p. 194.

407 Ernesto Nathan, *Noi massoni*, Bastogi, Foggia, 1993, p. 9.

408 See http://www.treccani.it/enciclopedia/francesco-crispi/ (November 18, 2018).

409 He was elected mayor with 60 votes in favor and 12 abstentions, no opposite.

410 Giuseppe Schiavone, *Scritti massonici di Ernesto Nathan*, Bastogi, Foggia, 1998, p. 21.

411 Ernesto Nathan, *Noi massoni*, op. cit., p. 11.

412 Anna Maria Isastia, *Scritti politici di Ernesto Nathan*, op. cit., p. 9.

4.3 Masonic Rise

R epublican, Mazzinian, mason:[413] these are the cornerstones of his
personal, intellectual, political, and corporative resume. Nathan's
Masonic career was very quick, he had been affiliated by Adriano Lemmi
to "Propaganda Massonica"[414] in Rome on June 24, 1887, and obtained
a Master's patent on February 3, 1893. In 1891, the Serenissimo Grande
Oriente Spagnolo entitled him as representative and Guarantor of Friendship at the G.O.I. The Italian Obedience corresponded recognizing Nathan
as Guarantor, Lemmi and Ballori—as endorsers—stressed the issue that
relations between the two Obediences would be ever more firm, to reach
the masonic brotherhood, pairing any gap amid men.[415] Same intentions
in the missive Nathan sent to the Spanish Obedience, as a gratitude for the
designation.[416]

In 1894, we find him I° Grand Watcher and only five years later leading the
prominent Italian masonic communion.

4.4 Nathan's First Grand Mastery

A s Grand Master, Deputy was Ettore Ferrari, another key player in the
Italian freemasonic environment. But he remitted his appointment,
since the republican belonging of both could have given a marked political bias, a danger for the institution itself.[417] In Nathan, the Grand Orient found the ideal profile, to accomplish the difficult target to lead Italian
Freemasonry in the new century, distancing it definitively from that heavy
legacy represented by Crispi. As first, merging the inner disagreements,
with a view to unity of the Communion. The issues counting masons and
still imperative were the fight against clericalism, and the commitment to
commemorate the Italian Risorgimento. Beyond that, Nathan was able to
indicate other marks: the struggle to dignify human existence and, last but
not least, the claim for accountability within the institution.[418] His view-

---

413 Please refer to Santi Fedele, *La massoneria italiana tra otto e novecento*, Bastogi, Foggia,
2011, pp. 47–50, for a deepening of the relationship between Masonry and Mazzini.

414 "Masonic Propaganda" [translator's note].

415 *Notizie massoniche*, in "Rivista della Massoneria Italiana", n. 7, year XXII, 1891, p. 108.

416 *Ibidem.*

417 Fulvio Conti, *Storia della massoneria italiana. Dal risorgimento al fascismo*, il Mulino,
Bologna, 2003, p. 149.

418 Marco Novarino, *Grande Oriente d'Italia. Due secoli di presenza libero muratoria*, Eras-

point on the relation between Freemasonry and civil society is right disclosed in his inaugural address: "è ora, o fratelli, di parlare chiaro ed alto, di ripetere ciò che noi siamo, dove andiamo; è ora che noi, puri di opera e di intendimenti, fughiamo dalla mente degli uomini di buona fede i fantasmi che la malignità cerca di evocare".[419]

To achieve these goals, Nathan from the very beginning of his office was very near to the various lodges in the Obedience; his travels[420] are often described on G.O.I.'s press, La Rivista della Massoneria Italiana, directed by Ulisse Bacci.

Returning to Nathan, it must be emphasized the approach Grand Master has toward political power is detachment. He repelled the acquiescence Obedience had shown toward institutional politics, and his mastery was also defined by the command of a departure from diplomacy. This issue was in sharp discontinuity with the past, represented by Crispi–Lemmi axis, while other features persisted. In particular, the anti-clericalism, Nathan considered one of the pivot of his mastery, is a benchmark of Freemasonry itself, as well as the revival of Risorgimento dimension of the masonic institution. This truly authentically patriotic dimension was a way to restore to Italian Freemasonry an image of full fairness. Its commitment both in the Institution and in the profane world, had to be carried out with two musts: integrity and square dealing.[421]

Back to the dualism masonry-statesmanship, it's remarkable in 1897 political elections Nathan, by a sheet sent to the Council of the Order of February 6, though leaving Brethen free to partake in political life according to their personal convictions, asked probity and properness in form. He also exhorted members to act in preventing reactions (pointing out clericals) from the key positions of Parliament. These general guidelines were then further extended in circular n. 36 of February 13, 1897, expounding the hurdle to overcome: ignorance, reaction, and corruption. Masonry, how-

---

mo, Roma, 2006, p. 48.

419 "it is now, Brothers, to speak clear and loud, to restate what we are, where we go; it is now we, pure in deed and intentions, let the ghosts malignity evoke throw off the minds of men of good faith." [translator's note]. Circular n. 29, June 12, 1896, in "Rivista della Massoneria Italiana", 1896, year XXVII, pp. 129–130.

420 Un'ultim'ora. Il Gran Maestro in viaggio, in "Rivista della Massoneria Italiana", n. 17–20, anno XXVII, 1896, p. 316.

421 Fulvio Conti, Storia della massoneria italiana, op. cit., p. 150.

ever, must care not to be dragged into political struggles cause if you let the "porta quello che si chiama indirizzo politico, vedrebbe uscire dalla finestra la concordia, la fratellanza, l'unità di intendimenti e di azione. La massoneria deve rimanere indipendente dagli uomini, dalle fazioni e dai governi".[422]

The Roman Catholic Church attacked masonry in those years; indeed, the struggle against the masons and their endeavors has been one of the great issues in Catholic propaganda throughout the nineteenth century in a methodical manner; the masonic question was intertwined with the loss of secular power. Therefore, Freemasonry was imputable for the Italian revolution, whose acme was the fall of Rome.[423]

Moreover, Freemasonry takes it upon oneself that amid its purposes, there was the contrast to clericalism and the Catholic Church. This struggle was only the prelude to reach the actual civil renewal of the country.[424] The Catholic Church could not remain defenseless before a pressing danger. Pope Leo XIII decided to eradicate this danger by gathering some cardinals, members of the Congregazione degli affari ecclesiastici straordinari,[425] to whom he asked for advice about a plot to combat Freemasonry.

The outcome then was the encyclical *Humanum genus* of 1884, as just the first in a series of pronouncements and condemnations of Freemasonry in Italy, whose reaction was fast and the strife against the Catholic Church stated as one of the institution's priorities in all areas of civil society. A struggle without quarter for both sides, aimed at the annihilation of the adversary. This was the scenery Nathan found at his very assignment, even worsened by his Jewish origins. At the base of anti-Semitic campaigns, Freemasonry and Judaism were often associated with all the possible duskiness. According to the Catholic press, Nathan was the embodiment of

---

422 "politics enter the door, you will see harmony, fraternity, agreement of intentions and action come out of the window. Masonry must remain autonomous from men, parties and governments" [translator's note]. Circular n. 36, febbraio 13, 1897, in "Rivista della Massoneria Italiana", 1897, year XXVIII, pp. 49–52.

423 The taking of Rome, also known as the breach of Porta Pia, was the episode of the Risorgimento, which sanctioned the annexation of Rome to the Kingdom of Italy. Happened on September 20, 1870, decreed the end of the Papal State as a historical–political entity and a moment of profound revolution in the management of temporal power by the popes.

424 Giovanni Miccoli, *Leone XIII e la massoneria*, in Gian Mario Cazzaniga (a cura), *Storia d'Italia, Annali 21, La massoneria*, Giulio Einaudi Editore, Torino, 2006, p. 195.

425 "Congregation of extraordinary ecclesiastical affairs" [translator's note].

a link affirmed for years. So, at the dawn of Nathan mastery, clericals enhanced their efforts. This situation forced personalities, as MP Giovanni Bovio, to take the defense of the Institution; indeed, Bovio went further, accusing the Society of Jesus[426] of being a sect, mighty and far more dangerous than Freemasonry. The dialectic clash is fair moreover in Italy the anti-masonic bias was also investing other areas, even secular, political, and media. At the June 1896 meeting, the Grand Master drew the attention of the leaders of the Grand Orient of Italy to the attacks the Institution was suffering from parliament. Thus, he proposes to write an open letter, to be published in major newspapers, to share the pillars on which Masonry is founded, which its aims. Meanwhile, Leo XIII, after careful attempts and propaganda, in 1896 promotes the international anti-masonic congress held in Trento, "posto sotto la protezione di Maria Vergine, di San Michele Arcangelo e di Sant'Agostino",[427] numbering 1,500 entrants.[428] The summits of the Catholic anti-masonic friary, led by Prince Guglielmo Alliata, president of the Unione Antimassonica Universale[429]—founded in 1893— were called upon the Congress. Beyond the specific presences, the location was not random; during 1545–1563 had been the beacon of Catholicism in the fight against Calvinism and Lutheranism. Thus, the city, in an ideal comparison in the fight against heresies—first represented by Calvinist and Lutheran doctrines, after by the secular-masonic ones—was chosen as a bulwark of confession. This concept is well expressed by the columns of "Osservatore Romano" in August 4, 1896: "Nessuna località, meglio di Trento poteva essere più adatta per un congresso anti-massonico. Tre secoli or sono, nella medesima città, un altro consesso di illustri personaggi si radunava a combattere la Massoneria d'allora ... d'allora in poi le idee sovversive contro le idee di Gesù Cristo, fecero strada e nella nuova manifes-

---

426 The Society of Jesus is a religious Order of regular clerics, founded in the fifteenth century by St. Ignatius of Loyola, whose members are commonly called "Jesuits" by the name of Jesus. The title of "company" comes from the order the military genius of founder himself imprinted on it. For more information, see http://www.treccani.it/enciclopedia/compagnia-di-gesu_%28Enciclopedia-Italiana%29/ (August 21, 2018).

427 "placed under the protection of the Virgin Mary, of St. Michael the Archangel and of St. Augustine" [translator's note]. Marco Novarino, *Progresso e tradizione libero muratoria. Storia del rito simbolico italiano (1859–1925)*, Angelo Pontecorboli Editore, Firenze, 2007, p. 129.

428 Rosario Francesco Esposito, *La massoneria e l'Italia. Dal 1800 ai giorni nostri*, Edizioni Paoline, Roma, 1979, p. 253.

429 "Universal Antimasonic Union" [translator's note].

tazione di sette massoniche si è perpetuata la guerra alla Chiesa, depositaria infallibile delle sacrosante verità della nostra fede".[430]

Trento had also been chosen since its belonging to Austria, where masonry had been banned. The Congress also aimed to strengthen the Church, overcoming internal friction that undermined its unity. The four points discussed during the conference: masonic doctrine, masonic drive, prayer, and anti-masonic action. The appointment was strongly backed by Catholic coteries all over the world, witnesses by allegiance from 568 localities, expressed by 1098 associations, 33 cardinals, and 209 bishops.[431] The media coverage of the event impressive thought the epoch. The Grand Master, in circular n. 32 of September 1896, explicit the position of Italian Freemasonry facing Trento meet. First of all, clear appears a disapproval to the Pope neglectful of the Gospel "ingiuria e predica lo sterminio, fino alla radice"[432] of men only willing common welfare. Nathan deplores the conduct of men who, under religious dress, do not shy away from a dishonest and unfair war. Masons are slandered, threatened, assaulted, because the enemies (the Church) see in the Institution a barrier, "un baluardo formidabile contro la vagheggiata restaurazione del suo dominio sui corpi e sulle menti".[433]

Even the not strictly clerical press was thrown at Freemasonry, the renown article by Romualdo Bonfaldini—former MP, State councilor, then senator, chairman of Press Guild and editor of "Corriere della Sera"—published at the beginning October 1896. Here, the author, besides referring to the Congress of Trento, addresses directly the Grand Master by words biased by the Freemasonry disrepute built on unproved facts, bearer of "influenze che apparvero ostili alla morale del paese".[434] Moreover, according to the

---

430 "No place, better than Trento could be more suitable for an anti-Masonic congress. Three centuries ago, in the same city, another group of illustrious personalities gathered to fight Freemasonry of the time ...from then onwards the subversive ideas against the ideas of Jesus Christ, made their way and, in the new embodiment of masonic sects, the war against the Church has been kept alive, an infallible depositary of the inviolable truth of our faith" [translator's note].

431 Rosario Francesco Esposito, *La massoneria e l'Italia*, op. cit., p. 254.

432 "to insult and preach the extermination, to the root" [translator's note].

433 "a formidable bulwark against the dreamed restoration of its dominion over bodies and minds" [translator's note]. Circular n. 32, September 15, 1896, in "Rivista della Massoneria Italiana", 1896, year XXVII, pp. 210–211.

434 "influences that appeared hostile to the morals of the country" [translator's note]. *Una opportuna risposta*, in "Rivista della Massoneria Italiana", n. 17–20, anno XXVII,

author "la massoneria odierna non può essere e non è popolare in Italia, perché il mistero personale di cui si circonda. ... Offre troppe occasioni di pensare come all'Istituzione degenerata premano più i vantaggi dei suoi adepti che le ragioni della giustizia".[435]

Nathan replied by pointing at issue: first of all, Freemasonry does not fight the criterions of Catholicism, except the dogma of faultlessness and of Popes' temporal power. The GM returns to the old accusations moved to the Institution on favoritism, greed, and immorality, firmly declaring it does everything in its power to dislodge those stakeholders in the structure.[436] Over and over again, Nathan was forced to return publicly to these topics, chiefly on the contrast between Freemasonry and the Church, each time trying to clarify its stance.[437]

A theme of mutual clash has been that of teaching Catholic religion in school. Masons willed an education prone to form free men, not tied to any dogma; Church indeed, stating Catholicism has always been a founding issue in Italian culture, claimed religion to be taught at school.[438]

At the end of 1896, Nathan, in continuity with Lmmi's plot, posed the need for the Institution to amply its presence in the government and bureaucracy, to keep its finger on the pulse on some main matters concerning State and its executive.[439] Moreover, the need to seal against clericalism and prevent Catholics meddling in local administrations, encouraged masons to engage more decisively in elections. Beyond this commitment, G.O.I. was at the forefront on people's liberty and self-determination,[440] especially in 1897, and through Ettore Ferrari, busily rooted the struggle for indepen-

---

1896, p. 280.

435 "today's Freemasonry can not be and is not popular in Italy, because of the personal gloom surrounding it [...] It offers too many opportunities to think as to a degenerate Institution more rewarding the advantages of its followers than the reasons of justice" [translator's note]. *Ibidem*.

436 Ivi, p. 282.

437 *Intendiamoci*, in "Rivista della Massoneria Italiana", n. 16–18, year XXVIII, 1897, pp. 241–244.

438 Marco Novarino, *Progresso e tradizione libero muratoria. Storia del rito simbolico italiano (1859–1925)*, Angelo Pontecorboli Editore, Firenze, 2007, p. 128.

439 Fulvio Conti, *Storia della massoneria italiana*, op. cit., p. 152.

440 Emanuela Locci, *La solidarietà tra popoli e garibaldini. Le spedizioni in terra ottomana*, in Pierpaolo Merlin (edited), *Solidarietà antiche e moderne. Un percorso storico*, Carocci editore, Roma, 2017, p. 106.

dence of Heraklion from the Ottoman domination. The masonic channels
were very active on this cause; the Grand Orient of Greece sent a circular
to the Obediences worldwide,[441] Italians responded with heartfelt words,
which recalled the brotherhood among mankind and allegiance to the ten-
et of solidarity amid people, especially those oppressed.

Ernesto Nathan further face another problem: dissident groups raising in
the G.O.I.

At the Orient of Naples some lodges, "La Vittoria,"[442] and "I figli di Garibaldi,"[443] decided to rebel against the government of the Order and—according to the Constitutions—the Grand Orient, to protect the masonic
togetherness, decided to demolish these[444] and expelling the Brethen who
had awakening the turmoil within.[445]

Beyond Naples, the Obedience had to deal with another internal issues
on unity: some lodges of Milan were further in disagreement with Rome
offices because of Lemmi conduction, specifically his intimacy with Crispi—reputed one of the greatest doers of the Banca Romana disgrace.[446] The
dissidents led by Malachia de Cristoforis,[447] after a short time, established
in Obbedienza with the name of the Italian Grand Orient[448] gaining inter-

---

441 *Notizie massoniche dalla comunione*, in "Rivista della Massoneria Italiana", n. 4, year
    XXVIII, 1897, p. 60.

442 "Victory" [translator's note].

443 "Garibaldi's sons" [translator's note].

444 ASGOI, *Decreto* n. 97, August 25, 1897.

445 ASGOI, *Decreto* n. 98, August 25, 1897.

446 The scandal of the Banca Romana was a political–financial case of national impor-
    tance at the center of the chronicles in 1892–1894 having as its central issue the dis-
    covery of the illicit activity of its governor in the previous decade. Council presidents,
    ministers, parliamentarians, and journalists were involved. Despite the gravity of the
    charge, the trials led to the acquittal of the accused. Even for Francesco Crispi, special-
    ly involved, the political consequences were minimal.

447 Malachia de Cristoforis was born in Milan in 1832, by Giovan Battista and Giovanna
    Adelaide Rota. An Italian patriot, doctor, and politician. He was a deputy and then a
    senator in the Senate of the Kingdom of Italy. It was initiated to Freemasonry on Au-
    gust 12, 1875, in "La Ragione" [Reason] of Milan, at the Obedience of G.O.I. For fur-
    ther information, see:http://www.treccani.it/enciclopedia/malachia-de-cristoforis
    _(Dizionario-Biografico)/ (August 22, 2018).

448 For further information, see: Marco Novarino, *Progresso e tradizione libero muratoria.
    Storia del rito simbolico italiano (1859–1925)*, Angelo Pontecorboli Editore, Firenze,
    2007, pp. 122–126.

national recognition by the Grand Orient of France, earning an unprecedented success. Nathan tried to recover relations with the Milanese lodges,
but the scenery worsened further and soon to the original protester joined
ateliers from Liguria, Tuscany, and Sicily. After the French confirmation,
Nathan had only to shut with the French of the Grand Orient[449] and to
expel the dissenting lodges.[450]

As seen, many of the hurdles Nathan was overwhelmed by came from Lemmi mastery, namely the bond G.O.I. had with Crispi. On April 24, 1898,
the Council of the Order was called to express on the request for Crispi
expulsion submitted by a bund of lodges. Here, Nathan considered a mediation and proposed to regard Crispi as mason in "sleep"; it was approved an
agenda that indeed proposed to quit with a discharge.

Problems didn't end anyway: brand new were to come. 1898 was an extremely difficult year for Italy, both from a social and financial side. This
out-came in popular riots bloodily repressed. The Grand Orient of Italy
kept away from political and street clashes, but did support the many destitute by meal dispensation and basic supplies. After May 8, 1898—the state
of siege proclaimed in the most tumultuous areas—the works of the lodges
dangerously located were suspended and freemasons asked to "ricondu-
rre la calma negli animi".[451] Nathan also asked Brethen to intervene where
possible, arranging popular kitchens or bread distribution to the neediest,
before hunger reaped the first victims, even considering institutional measures would have been obviously dilatory.[452] More, lodges were urged to
form a committee to check foodstuffs so as to survey the price trends of
basic supplies to prevent speculation.[453]

Despite the factual arbitration, the headmen of G.O.I. decidedly rejected
to support the protest, in an anti-government key. Fairly, in the late nine-
teenth- and twentieth-century Italy, Nathan's conduct imprinted by political separation actually unfolded with substantial prop to the government
and its actions. No surprise, appraising the first Pelloux ministry numbered
five initiated ministers (Camillo Finocchiaro-Aprile, Guido Bacelli, Pietro

449 Missive, Ernesto Nathan, May 14, 1898.
450 ASGOI, *Decreto* n. 107, May 6, 1898.
451 "bring calm in the minds" [translator's note].
452 Circular January 19 1898, in "Rivista della Massoneria Italiana", year 1898, XXIX, p. 4.
453 *Atti ufficiali della comunione italiana*, in "Rivista della Massoneria Italiana", n. 17–20, year XXIX, 1898, p. 258.

Lacava,[454] Alessandro Fortis and Nunzio Nasi), and an undersecretary of
state (Gaspare Colosimo).

In 1899, the constituent assembly of Rome approved the new Constitutions, endorsing Nathan again. The year after the Junta was renewed:
Ettore Ferrari (Deputy Grand Master), Antonio Cefaly[455] (Grand Secretary), Alessandro Aleggiani (Treasurer), Federico Fabbri (Orator), Silvano Lemmi (First Superintendent), Umberto Dalmedico (Second Superintendent).

In 1900, on the ballot appointment, after a general assessment, Nathan
had the lodges sent an invitation to "costituire al proprio interno una com-
missione per la organizzazione delle forze liberali in guisa da assicurare
loro il predominio nelle amministrazioni delle valli".[456]

The unprecedented results obtained in the term of 1902 by liberal and
democratic political groups and the retirement—by the Chamber of
Deputies—of the proposed law on divorce, a topic close to Freemasonry—the involvement in a judicial affair of Tullio Murri,[457] where he later
achieved in proving the absolute noninvolvement of him and the Institution, induced Ernesto Nathan and his junta to resign, also to prompt a
new mode.

So, the first Grand Mastery of Nathan ended due to his resignation in

---

454 Pietro Lacava was born in Corleto Perticara, Basilicata, on October 21, 1835, by Giuseppe Domenico and Brigida Francolino. His father was a lawyer of liberal ideas,
who played an important part in the revolutionary movement in 1848 and then in
the Lucan insurrection of 1860. He was a patriot and a leading politician, holding
numerous government posts. For more information, see: http://www.treccani.it/
enciclopedia/pietro-lacava_%28Dizionario-Biografico%29/ (August 20, 2018).

455 Antonio Cefaly was born in Cortale in 1850 and was for a long time an illustrious political exponent of his city. In 1882, he was elected deputy; in 1898, he was appointed
senator, playing important roles. There is no certain fact about his Masonic initiation,
but he was a member of the "Tommaso Campanella" lodge in 1894. He held many
posts in G.O.I. In 1900, he denied the Masonic membership of King Umberto I. He
died in Rome in 1928.

456 "set up a committee to organize the liberal forces to guarantee them premiership in
the guidance of the valleys" [translator's note]. Fulvio Conti, *Storia della massoneria
italiana*, op. cit., p. 167.

457 The Murri affair was a fact of chronicle of 1902, at the beginning of the Giolittian age,
with a wide resonance on public audience, ending with the condemnation for complicity of Linda Murri with his brother Tullio for the murder of the husband Count
Francesco Bonmartini.

1903,[458] the Deputy GM Ettore Ferrari replaces him till the ballot,[459] though the masonic career of Nathan is not over: we will find him again at the helm of the preeminent Italian Masonic communion from 1917 to 1919.

In early assessment, during his Grand Mastery, Nathan endowed G.O.I. with new headquarters, Palazzo Giustiniani,[460] a place with a torn history.[461] Already three years before, in 1898, the Grand Orient of Italy had rented the building belonging to Grazioli family and made its base on April 21, 1901, taking the name "Masoneria di Palazzo Giustiniani." During the installment, he delivered a speech aimed to depict what Masonry embodied, its profile, its issues. Particular emphasis was on the bond of brotherhood that unites Masons worldwide, despite the gaps distinguishing national Obediences.[462]

As for the mass of Obedience, Nathan asserted G.O.I. numbered 182 lodges (actually operative were 150).

The geographical allotment was as follows: 38 lodges in northern Italy, 54 in the center, 26 in the south, 22 in the islands, and 36 ateliers abroad. Many lodges in this period were straitened, so a comedown of fees and taxes was approved. This way, and remedying the insolvency, conditions could have been created even commoners could access the Institution. Indeed, during this period, there was a substantial increase in initiations. Unfortunately, the complete minutes of all the lodges have not yet survived (there are few kept in the archives, some incomplete), thus isn't easy to determine sharply the actual numerical consistency of the Italian communion. Approaching a quantitative analysis of the numerical thickness during Nathan's leadership,

458 Circular n. 45, November 15, 1903, in "Rivista della Massoneria Italiana", 1903, year XXXIV, pp. 260–261.

459 Circular n. 46, December 23, 1903, in "Rivista della Massoneria Italiana", 1903, year XXXIV, pp. 291–292.

460 Ernesto Nathan, *Noi massoni*, op. cit., p. 12.

461 At the beginning of 1926, Mussolini regime, after outlawing Freemasonry, acquired the building to the public domain and granted its use to the Senate, after the war followed a litigation quitted in amicable settlement for half a century, thus the branch of building overlooking Piazza della Rotonda remained in the availability of Freemasonry. Only in 1985, the Senate was able to dispose of almost the entire building, thanks to an agreement following which Freemasonry moved its headquarters to the Vascello manor on the Janiculum hill.

462 Ernesto Nathan, *La massoneria, sua azione, suoi fini*, Stabilimento tipografico Civelli, Roma, 1901, p. 6.

at first it might seem the Obedience has not grown. The situation is actually a bit more tangled: even if the full number is almost equal to the Lemmi period, we have to count 12 lodges merged together in Orients such as Livorno, Turin, Catania, and Siracusa. On the number of affiliates, there are no whole references to investigate; indeed, there are pleas for affiliations from priests, nobles, commoners, professionals, landowners, scientists, and other figures.

Shortly before the end of his work, the asset of the Order was a matter of confront. The Grand Master emphasized the time had come for Masonry to provide for the shielding of its patrimony, by a mandatory juridical capacity to be able to defend itself more effectively from defamation and slanders of its detractors. After a certain debate, the Junta was commissioned by the Grand Orient to compose a commission with the task of studying its juridical profile, without incurring, for the Institution, to the loss of its tradition and its rules.[463]

Probing Nathan's mastery, we often come across his speeches where usually from a definition of Masonry, he repute it a lifelong transforming institution. "Essa si muove e cammina con lo spirito dei tempi, non si fossilizza neppure nelle regole e nelle manifestazioni esterne che circoscrivono e distinguono il suo incedere".[464] More, what Nathan was interested in transmitting in and out from the Order were:

- Universal Masonry means the moral, intellectual, and material improvement of mankind. Freemasonry is one, but stands out in national, allied and supportive Communions across the globe.

- A national Masonic Authority leads the Italian Communion. It has the motto: freedom, equality, brotherhood, and is gathered under the traditional cosmopolitan formula A.G.D.G.A.D.U..

- The number of freemasons is unlimited. They mutually call Brethen: they do not mind gaps in their origins, classes, beliefs, and social conditions, and they distinguish one another only by degrees and offices in the Order. Training and assistance are mandatory engagements one to

---

463 Adunanza del consiglio dell'Ordine, in "Rivista della Massoneria Italiana", n. 9–12. Year XXXIV, 1903, pp. 130–132.

464 "moves and walks with the spirit of the times, it does not even become settled in the plots and outer signs that confine and distinguish its progress" [translator's note]. Giuseppe Schiavone, *Gli scritti massonici*, op. cit., p. 41.

another, within the limits of right and honest. They contract any commitment in the partnership with the promise on their honor and on their conscience.

- The lodges are governed by a unitary power called the Grand Orient of Italy and is chaired by a Grand Master.[465]

Fundamental to Nathan, the concept of patriotism, issue he defined in a speech of April 21, 1900 "il patriottismo è vissuto come dimensione sacrale, come fede nella religione civile dell'italianità".[466] Here, he further confirmed patriotism should be the core of the commitment Freemasonry lavished on civil society. Patriotism therefore had to be above politics, but at the same time transversally present. The action of Freemasonry is thus prime: doing everything in its power to return to Italy, to its undeceive or unconcerned citizens, the conscience and faith of the worth of debate. Here, Freemasonry has a dual function, patriotic and educational. Hence, also the heartfelt appeal of the Grand Master to avoid internal schisms, to uplift Freemasonry from politics and to unite all the fair and liberal men of any party, focusing them on a program with a pillar, the fight against clericalism and corruption.[467] Anyway, both the national and the internal unity were called to the Institution, though a scissure that raged on the board of officers rending in two: a radical-republican minority forwarding a line of anti-ministerial, mentioning Antonio Maffi, Salvatore Barzilai, Ettore Ferrari, etc.; the other, larger and moderate faction, instead advocated the idea of an absolute closeness to politics, to keep of the internal unity. Beyond Nathan, part of this was Alessandro Fortis, Camillo Finocchiaro-Aprile, Achille Ballori, and Antonio Cefaly. In spite of this divergence, however, ideological and historical items kept G.O.I. together and were rooted in being masons and Masonry. One was the ideal link between Freemasonry and the unitary state descending from the Risorgimento struggles. No one ever questioned this tie, nor the institutional set-up or the policy expressed by the government. Nor did anyone question the monarchy, not even when, on July 29, 1900, King Umberto I was assassinated by the anarchist Gaetano Bresci.[468] The Grand Orient of Italy promptly condemned the crime,

---

465 Ivi, p. 135.

466 "patriotism is lived as a sacral dimension, as faith in the civilized religion of Italian attitude" [translator's note].

467 Fulvio Conti, *Storia della massoneria italiana*, op. cit., p. 162.

468 Gaetano Bresci (Coiano, Prato, 1869—Penitentiary of Santo Stefano 1901). Weaver,

by Nathan is described as "un delitto che con la sua selvaggia impotenza, calunnia e deturpa di fango il nome della patria al cospetto del mondo".[469] Beyond the message of mere reproach of the criminal act itself, the facts gave Nathan the chance to state more strongly two basic concepts for masonry: patriotism and loyalty to the monarchy. Looking at foreign diplomacy, Nathan was always very active towards other Obediences, especially those subdued to overwhelming empires. Even during Ferrari mastery, he was always engaged in keeping relations with troubled Obediences since subjected to repression by the Hapsburg Empire or other crowns. When WWI broke out in 1914, Nathan strongly wanted Italy to go to war alongside the Allies; the annihilation of the Austro-Hungarian Empire was the crowning of the Italian Risorgimento affair. Undisputedly, Ernesto Nathan left a decisive mark in Italian Freemasonry during his leadership, especially in the first term.

4.5 From Ernesto Nathan to Ettore Ferrari

With decree n. 151, Nathan convened for Sunday, February 14, the General Assembly, for the election of his next[470] lasting from February 14 to 17, 1904, gathering 132 lodges and 11 upper bodies of the Scottish Rite which unanimously elected (139 votes) the successor of Nathan: Ettore Ferrari.[471] The proclamation, made by the former Grand Master, is covered by the applause of the Assembly. On the proposal of Ferrari, Nathan is proclaimed Honorary Past Grand Master.[472]

With this election "Dalla mano ferrea di Adriano Lemmi e di Ernesto Nathan il maglietto passava in quella vellutata di Ettore Ferrari".[473] He will

---

migrated to Americas, where he linked with groups of anarchists, returned home in June 1900 in order to kill King Umberto I. The monarch had already escaped two attacks, carried out by the anarchists Giovanni Passannante and Pietro Acciarito, but with Bresci had no escape. Sentenced to life imprisonment, the official version wants him to take his life a year later in his cell. http://www.treccani.it/enciclopedia/gaetano-bresci/ (July 18, 2018).

469 "a crime that with its savage impotence, slanders and spoils mud on homeland reputation in the world" [translator's note]. Fulvio Conti, *Storia della massoneria italiana*, op. cit., p. 163.

470 Decreto n. 151, in "Rivista della Massoneria Italiana", n.17–18, 1903, p. 262.

471 Ettore Passalalpi Ferrari, *Le muse e la politica*, Edimond, Città di Castello, p. 254.

472 Ivi, p. 255.

473 "From the iron hand of Adriano Lemmi and Ernesto Nathan the mallet went into

lead the Grand Orient of Italy from 1904 until 1917, fundamental years for the history of Italian obedience. Ferrari was born in Rome on March 25, 1845, and trained as sculptor and to art in general by his father, Filippo. In 1867, he took part in the failed insurrection attempt that was to break out in Rome against the papal government. In June 1877, he was elected city councilor of Rome, brought by the Circle of Fine Arts and the newspaper "Il Popolo Romano".[474] He kept the office, except for a brief interruption, until 1907. Among his first initiatives, there was a proposal for the building of Palazzo delle Esposizioni in Via Nazionale. MP by the electoral college of Perugia from 1882 to 1892, Ferrari sat in Parliament on the banks of the extreme democratic left and—straight Republican—always refused to meet the King and, coherently, in 1919, he rejected the nomination as life senator by minister Francesco Saverio Nitti. The artistic fame of Ettore Ferrari is due to two monuments, both in Rome: Giordano Bruno installed in Campo de' Fiori on 9 June 1889 with a massive public rally, and Giuseppe Mazzini of 1902–1911 on the Aventine,[475] but only placed in 1949.[476]

Returning to his Masonic career, it began in summer of 1881 on a proposal by Ulisse Bacci[477] in "Rienzi" lodge of Rome where he was Worshipful in 1892. Four years later. he became Grand Secretary with Adriano Lemmi and then Ernesto Nathan to whom he always remained amicably bound. GM Ettore Ferrari had a quite different idea, compared to that of Nathan on the role of Freemasonry in the civil society. He advocated the idea, and since its entry into Freemasonry had fought to achieve it, the Institution had to play a more active role in both homeland and foreign politics. Moreover, his inaugural address, pronounced on February 14, 1904, left no doubt about his will. He affirmed: "la massoneria non deve tenersi costantemente isolata e nell'ombra, ma scendere a contatto della

---

that velvety one of Ettore Ferrari" [translator's note]. Rosario Francesco Esposito, *La massoneria e l'Italia*, op. cit., p. 309.

474 "Roman's Folk" [translator's note].

475 https://tinyurl.com/yccmb35x (August 7, 2018).

476 Vittorio Gnocchini, *L'Italia dei liberi muratori*, op. cit., p. 120.

477 Ulisse Bacci was born near Florence in 1846, joined the Masonry in 1867 to become also General Secretary of the Grand Orient of Italy. In 1872, he became head of the magazine "Rivista della Masoneria Italiana." Of Republican orientation, in the pages of his paper he directed, stated for a non-confessional school and for the introduction of divorce in the Italian legal system. He wrote some texts of patriotic and anticlerical orientation and the book *Il libro del massone italiano* [*Handbook of Italian mason*]. He died in Rome in 1935.

vita, combattere alla luce del sole le sante battaglie dell'alta sua missione per la tutela della giustizia e per la grande educazione. Nuovi bisogni presentano nuovi problemi; nuovi problemi esigono nuove soluzioni; da nuovi doveri scaturiscono nuovi diritti: la massoneria non può, non deve chiudere gli occhi alla nuova luce, ma fissarla, scrutarla e dirigerla. Non deve cullarsi in teorie astratte, per quanto nobili ed elevate: ma affrontare i problemi dell'attualità in cui siamo concordi, rinvigorirsi nella soluzione degli interessi che alimentano la vita dei popoli".[478] In short, Masonry, to the new Grand Master, had to "get his hands dirty" in forming the society it was in.

Therefore, beyond the traditional matter of anti-clericalism and secularity of education, never adrift, the Grand Master called the Institution to a greater sensitivity and commitment to issues such as: social and labor lawmaking,[479] the institution of a body as peacemaker in the disputes between states; another subject dear to Ferrari was solidarity amid people, compelling in the case of countries fighting for independence and self-determination, as in the aforementioned Greek case of the island of Heraklion. In 1905, the Grand Orient of Italy fiercely objected against the repression of liberal movements in Russia, calling masons to unity against despotism.[480] The disastrous situation in Russia began with the war against Japan for Manchuria settlement. The continuous defeats put a strain on Russia and the Tsar's power was questioned by the masses pressing for the end of the war and the spread of civil liberties. In January 1905, a rally led by an Orthodox priest was going peacefully to the Tsar's palace to request a meeting and petition. The tsarist army opened fire, reaping several victims. The massacre brought down the liability of the monarch and dissent spread to many areas of Russia.

---

478 "Masonry should not keep itself constantly isolated and in the shadows, but to come into contact with life, to fight openly the holy battles of its high mission for the protection of justice and for great education. New needs present new problems; new problems demand new solutions; new duties arise from new duties: Freemasonry cannot, must not shut its eyes to the new light, but fix it, scrutinize it and direct it. He must not lull itself into abstract theories, however noble and elevated: but to front the issues of current affairs we agree, to invigorate oneself in the solution of the interests which nourish the life of people" [translator's note]. *Marco Novarino, Grande Oriente d'Italia,* op. cit., p. 50.

479 This issues are deepened in circular n. 49, *La parola del Gran Maestro,* in "Rivista della Massoneria Italiana", n. 3–6, 1904, p. 34.

480 *Informazioni, Per la Russia,* in "Rivista Massonica" n. 5–6, 1906, pp. 275–276.

These waves of protests had wide echoes both in the lodges indeed also in the ranks of the left[481] discarding awhile-internal disagreements to focus on the fight for human rights. Freemasonry led by Ferrari did not remain deaf to Russian facts and at the end of January, the Grand Master and his Junta responded to the Russian massacre by approving a statement: "la massoneria italiana, che con l'ideale e con il sangue edificò la libertà della patria e combatté in ogni tempo le battaglie della giustizia e della redenzione umana, alza un grido di degno per la cieca barbarie e le stragi orrende, con cui il despotismo teocratico in Russia risponde al popolo, che inerme chiede il suo diritto; ed invita tutti i centri massonici ed i fratelli di ogni terra a dar voti e a fare opere, perché quel diritto sia riconosciuto, e sulle rovine del privilegio, si affermi ancora una conquista del progresso civile".[482]

The mobilization of G.O.I. lodges had no precedents in the history of Freemasonry, the acts backing rebels are not limited to messages of solidarity, but they carried out initiative concerning the "profane" world in which the lodges had however a significant role. Under Ferrari mastery, then, the democratic turn of masonry was accomplished, flaunted by the new junta numbering outstanding members by the radical party as: Adolfo Engel (Deputy Grand Master), Gustavo Canti (Secretary), Rosario Bentivegna (Second Superintendent); a progressive liberal like Alessandro Aleggiani (Treasurer) and a Giolitti rooter as Giovanni Camera (Orator), MP and future undersecretary for finance in the Giolitti executive. Achille de Giovanni (First Superintendent), defeated in the electoral contest with Ferrari for the Grand Mastery, was also part of it. The democratic turning point was highlighted by the introduction, in the Constitutions of Obedience, of a note in article 1: the democratic principle of the political and social order.[483]

---

481 Fulvio Conti, *Storia della massoneria*, op. cit., p. 173.

482 "Italian masonry—which with the ideal and with blood built freedom of the country and fought every time the battles of justice and human redemption—raises a cry of disdain for the blind barbarity and the horrendous massacres, whom the theocratic despotism in Russia responds to the people, helpless asking for their right; and invites all the masonic centers and the Brethen of every land to vote and to act, so that right is recognized, and on the ruins of the privilege, a conquest of civil progress could still be affirmed" [translator's note]. *La solidarietà di Ettore Ferrari per i rivoluzionari russi del 1905*, in Anna Maria Isastia (a cura), *Il progetto liberal-democratico di Ettore Ferrari*, Angeli, Milano, 1997, pp. 217–232.

483 Fulvio Conti, *Massoneria e sfera pubblica nell'Italia liberale, 1859–1914*, in Gian Mario Cazzaniga (edited), *Storia d'Italia, la massoneria*, op. cit., p. 606.

This change had almost immediately positive outcome in the masonic field. First of all, Ferrari collected the rapprochement of the Milan team leading the split during Nathan office. Distancing features had vanished, so the idea of the uselessness of two separate Obediences began to be conceived. After some ineffective notices, in November 1904 an agreement decreeing the merge in G.O.I. of the Italian Grand Orient of Malachia De Cristoforis was signed, leading to the original obedience 36 lodges, 27 in Italy and 9 abroad. After this return, relations with the French freemasons of the Grand Orient were resumed; two definitely positive events for Ferrari mastery: *in primis*, the democratic inspiration of the Italian Masonic communion was stressed by the work of the Milanese lodges and *in secundis*, abroad, relations with one of the most illustrious. Obediences worldwide were resumed: the Grand Orient of France. In the same period, a narrow Sicilian protester group, the Sicilian Grand Orient of Palermo, entered the ranks of G.O.I., bringing some lodges founded on the island. Then, almost all the Italian masonry was united under the aegis of the Grand Orient of Italy.

While it seemed to run towards growth in terms of numbers and widespread acceptance, fronted unexpected problems. The first was the scandal involving the deputy Nunzio Nasi,[484] charged of embezzling for having seized large sums of state money during his political offices for personal use and to benefit his constituency. Not to undergo the trial, he took refuge first in Paris and then in London. When back in Italy, he was sentenced and his election deleted. From the Institution viewpoint yet again public opinion could associate its reputation to the corruption of one of its members, thus Nasi was subjected to a Masonic trial, judging him guilty and decreeing his expulsion. The political; parable of Nasi, however, did not stop with this "accident on the way" since by the protests of his faithful electorate was exculpated and readmitted to the Chamber of Deputies in 1913, elected both in Trapani and in Palermo, and re-elected in 1919 and in 1921, when he joined the Social Democracy. In the session of the House of November 16, 1922, during the debate on the confidence to the Mussolini government after the march on Rome, he held an acute speech, foreshadowing the anti-democratic and totalitarian nature of Fascism. In 1924 he applied against the fascist plank and was re-elected on the "Labor Democracy" list.

---

484 Nunzio Nasi was born in Trapani in 1850; professor of political economy was an academic at the University of Palermo. He was a Masonic Master from 1893. From 1900 until 1902, he was head of the Grand Lodge of Symbolic Rite. A prominent national politician, he was minister of public education in 1901 in Zanardelli executive.

He joined the Aventine, and in 1926 was declared decayed by the regime, with other dissident deputies.

He died in Erice in 1939.

Another serious problem was related to the tie amid Freemasonry and the Socialist Party.[485] Within this, in 1904, the voices against the masonic membership grounded and the instance to state the mismatch between the party and the affiliation to Freemasonry began to develop. A bunch in the party, the most conservative one, called for an internal referendum in 1905 raising the issue and providing the expulsion in case of masonic belonging. The Grand Master, aware of this, installed a commission with the task of verifying, within the single lodges, the effects that a positive response in the referendum could have had.[486] After verifying the actual presence of socialists among the columns of his temples, he informed the summits of Obedience they were but a few, and almost all questioned stated they wouldn't leave masonry. Anyway, the issue of socialism / Freemasonry did not resolve, was repeated indeed in all the socialist boards up to 1914.[487] Actually, the results of the socialist referendum did not wrong Grand Master's predictions: the small number of voters (11.776 out of 37.921) meant the base did not perceive the issue. The very outcome was the socialist hostility, bringing out the voters—even numerically narrow—disclosed they considered unsuitable socialism and masonry.

Also in the Republican Party, where Ettore Ferrari and other important members of Freemasonry belonged, a debate broke out on the plot of the socialist one. After lively discussions, we came to the conclusion that "crediamo che l'appartenere alla massoneria non costituisca un atto di incompatibilità o di indegnità per un repubblicano per la semplicissima ragione che siamo convinti che i principi fondamentali e animatori di questa associazione mondiale sono in armonia coi principi democratici e repubblicani".[488]

---

485 For further information on socialism and Freemasonry, see Marco Novarino, *Compagni e liberi muratori. Socialismo e massoneria dalla nascita del Psi alla grande guerra*, Rubbettino, Soveria Mannelli, 2015.

486 Marco Novarino, *Compagni e liberi muratori*, op. cit., p. 69.

487 Marco Novarino, *Massoneria e movimento operaio e socialista*, in Santi Fedele, Giovanni Greco (edited), *Massoneria ed Europa*, op. cit., p. 98.

488 "we believe that belonging to Freemasonry does not constitute an act of incompatibility or unworthiness for a republican for the very simple reason we are convinced the fundamental principles and animators of this world association are in harmony with

Besides these debates, triggering entourage close to masonry answering the "political-secular" attack and also to place the masonic issues toward the Catholic Church—about to play an increasing role within the civil society by an alliance with conservatives, an alliance troubling Italian masonic chairmen seeing the positions of the enduring "enemy" toughened by new detractors—Masonry did not remain restful. Ettore Ferrari prompted a Commission gathering Ernesto Nathan, Salvatore Barziali,[489] Emanuele Paternò di Sessa,[490] Agostino Berenini,[491] and Dario Cassuto[492] to draft a document that would give to all Masons firm guidelines. The results summed up in a circular by the Grand Master pointing out the peremptory refusal of any agreement with the Catholics and the prohibition for masons to deal with them under elections, penalty the expulsion from Obedience. Freemasonry leaders, while recognizing the freedom of feat in the political parties, censored this to be acted with clerical enemies.[493]

This stance, although firm, was almost immediately disregarded in 1906 elections, when some masons of Turin, in the civic term, allied with the Catholics. These—even if "in sleep"—were expelled since the Grand Master's dispositions made no exceptions. The choice, reputed by many parties too rigid, had immediate effect the resignation from the Board of Antonio Cefaly, in protest. The serious decision, however, was also warn within the Obedience, there was a certain turmoil and dissent to the track followed by Ferrari. In fact, the debate on the political line into the Grand Orient

---

democratic and republican principles" [translator's note]. Fulvio Conti, *Storia della massoneria italiana*, op. cit., p. 176.

489 Salvatore Barzilai was born in Trieste in 1860, was a lawyer, politician, activist in the Republican Party, and Minister. His Masonic career began in 1886 in "Universo" [*Universe*] loggia in the Orient of Rome.

490 Emanuele Paternò di Sessa was born in Palermo in 1847, of noble origins, became a famous chemist and taught first in Palermo and later in Rome. The exact date of his Masonic initiation is unknown, he was ordered Master in a lodge of Palermo in 1889.

491 Agostino Berenini was born in Milan in 1812, surgeon, politician and patriot, friend of Cattaneo, was amid the heads of the Five Days of Milan. In 1860, it was among the men who backed Garibaldi to the expedition of the Thousand. It was initiated in Freemasonry in 1866 toward "Progresso Sociale" [*Social Progress*] in Florence. Deputy in the VII legislature headed the extreme left and the radical party. He died in 1886.

492 Dario Cassuto, born in Livorno in 1846, was a lawyer and politician and became a senator. It was initiated to Freemasonry in the lodge of his hometown named after Giordano Bruno, on an uncertain date. In 1899, he was elected councilor of the Order. He died in 1920.

493 *La parola del governo dell'Ordine*, in "Rivista Massonica" n. 9, novembre 1905, p. 387.

was about to come and a proposal by three politicized lodges ("Popolo Sovrano" [*Sovereign People*] of Turin, "Avvenire Sociale" [*Social Advent*] in Reggio Calabria e Cisalpina-Carlo Cattaneo in Milan) was supported. It consisted of a partial adjustment in the first article of the Constitutions, the new text told: Italian communion advocates the democratic principle of the political and social order.

From this, the Obedience shown how preeminent the democratic frond was, defining the will of most of the Italian masons of the Grand Orient, and by this, it felt entitled to give even more firmness to its purposes. Following this mandate in 1906, Ferrari invited the lodges to comment on two central issues: universal suffrage and the burden of primary school teachings to the state. On both fronts, Ferrari intended to mobilize the country and the political camps. During this period, there was also a rapprochement with the socialist party, hoping to mend the relations between. Freemasonry decided to take a closer look at the issue of cooperative associations and of social housing, dear both to democrats and socialists.

So Freemasonry was engaged on several fronts, even new, but hadn't drop its anti-clerical vocation; proving the endurance on this issue, voted a harsh censure against one of its leading exponent, Alessandro Fortis who—in an electoral speech—declared that there was no longer a clerical danger in Italy, opposite to what was stated by G.O.I. more annoyed by the coalitions of clerical and moderate working side by side. This position of Ferrari, so rigid and unwilling to welcome colliding voices, gave rise to a current invoking the return to "initiatory tradition and statutes." This minority remained unheard; lodges were called to act in the front line and masons in first person to built "popular blocs"—electoral alliances between the progressive parties—which had as a direct effect the birth of many leftist administrations.[494] One of the most striking results of the "blockade policy" was the election of Nathan as Mayor of Rome in 1907.

Freemasonry and left-wing parties had common programmatic points that acted as binders in the chance of political agreements, one of these was the topic of secular teaching in schools, so that growing illiteracy would be overcome. Obviously, the convergence on such these issue was considered bearing issues in the strengthening of the secular state.

The battle for a lay school, however, did not see all the Italian freemasons

---

494 Fulvio Conti, *Storia della massoneria italiana*, op. cit., p. 179.

agree with the line from the summits of Obedience; the most conservative fringe of the Grand Orient of Italy, already shown its vision in 1906, began to organize a wider movement of internal dissent, carrying to the great masonic crisis of 1908.

4.6 The Schism, the Birth of the Great Lodge of Italy

C utting back the dynamics of the split in the G.O.I., the spark started precisely from the secularization of schools. Leonida Bissolati, a socialist deputy, filed a motion in the Chamber of Deputies against religious education in primary schools. Presented in 1907, was however discussed in 1908. Shortly before the parliamentary debate, Ferrari decided to write to all Masonic MPs to suggest a positive vote on the motion.[495] The motion was though rejected even thanks to the vote of some masonic deputies—not once but twice: another deputy, Vittorio Moschini, presented in turn a motion, with the same substantial content but with a less sharp architecture. Giovanni Giolitti had publicly impeded this; well aware, it would have negative consequences in bonds with Catholics. From a political viewpoint, the rejection was attributed to the scarce political plot of Bissolati, not testing the very chance of victory.

The disapproval determined a strong disdain among the columns of Italian communion. Ettore Ferrari, who had spent so much about, decided to take disciplinary measures against those who had not voted the motion, actually ditching it. "Guilty" deputies were thus expelled from the communion on Article 129 of the Constitutions.[496] According to the results of an internal investigation in Parliament, there were 38 Masonic deputies, whose 17 backed Moschini, 11 voted against, and 10 were absent. This internal problem overlaid another one, the unification of Rites, here the Great Lodge of the Symbolic Rite was favorable, while the Supreme Council of the 33 was against. Saverio Fera, at that time Sovereign Grand Commander of the S.R.A.A., opposed the Order's decision to take action against unwilling members. This was actually a war declaration against Ettore Ferrari, his junta, and his management. Fera replaced the resigning members of the Council with others of his own trust and assumed the defense of the deputies. This dramatic situation was consummated on the eve of an important masonic meeting: the General Assembly for the year 1908. Here, was the as-

---

495 *Penosi doveri*, in "Rivista Massonica" n. 3–6, 1908, pp. 50–52.

496 Marco Novarino, *Progresso e tradizione*, op. cit., p. 175.

sessment of Obedience, an absolutely positive one with a growth of G.O.I. that passed from 195 lodges of 1904–301 in 1907, whose 251 belonged to the Scottish Rite and 50 to the Symbolic one. Two hundred and sixty-six lodges were on Italian territory while 35 abroad. In addition, 71 triangles were established, including 65 of Scottish rite and 6 of Italian Symbolic Rite.[497] Scanning the numbers, the Grand Orient was going through an unprecedented phase of development, with a fairly homogeneous geographical spread, with the foundation of lodges in territories until then outside the Masonic circuit. During the General Assembly, frequent references were made to the Fera affair and the MEPs under investigation. Rosario Bentiveglia declared in resolute terms, it was mandatory to continue on the line proposed by Ferrari, aiming higher: forming an anti-clerical political block, to direct the parliament toward the ends shared by Freemasonry, deleting all political, social, and religious opportunism. The reference to Fera and the dissident masonic deputies was evident. Fera reacted to these criticisms with disciplinary measures on masons and entire lodges, within the framework of S.R.A.A. The situation became even more severe when in June 1908, Ferrari supported by Ernesto Nathan managed to resume the leadership of the Supreme Council and give Achille Ballori (previously resigned) back its leadership. Fera's reaction was fast and fierce: at the beginning of July 1908 spread a decree declaring G.O.I. irregular and asked all lodges belonging to the Scottish Rite to rely upon the Supreme Council.[498] As an immediate response, Ferrari reunited the Grand Orient Committee in an extraordinary and urgent session and decreed the expulsion of Fera and all upholding Brethen .

From that moment began the dispute between the new Obedience founded by Fera, the Grand Lodge of Italy and the Grand Orient of Italy for the recognition as the only legitimate masonic Communion in Italy by foreign Obediences. Moreover, the decision to G.O.I. and found another masonic communion was the result of years of veiled internal dissensions, always alive, between a strongly progressive anti-clerical faction—, seeing in Ferrari, more than in Nathan, its champion—and a minority faction, liberal though conservative.

This split, however harsh for inbound matters and international recognitions, was not that messy on a quantitative level. In August 1908, Ferrari

---

497 *Una circolare del Gran Maestro*, in "Rivista Massonica" n. 7–8, 1908, p. 146.

498 *Informazioni*, in "Rivista Massonica" n. 11–12, 1908, p. 285.

published a circular describing the situation regarding the split: nine lodges had left the Grand Orient of Italy, the "XX Settembre" [*XX September*] in Florence (Fera was the Worshipful), the "Anglia" of Naples, the "XX Settembre" of Formia, the "Charitas" from Misilmeri, and the Palermo lodges "Giorgio Washington," "Risveglio" [*Awakening*], "Sicilia Risorta" [*Risen Sicily*], "Palermo" and "Sondesmos." Two upper bodies of the Rite, the Chapter of Palermo and the Areopagus of Reggio Calabria,[499] also left the Supreme Council. The new Obedience settled in Piazza del Gesù; amid its personalities, we mention—beyond Saverio Fera himself—, John Chamber, John Miranda, Leonardo Ricciardi, Francesco Pellicano, Cesare Pastore, Enrico Pegna, Carlo Ferretti, Theofilo Gay, Costantino Gregorio Carelli , Leonardo Bianchi, Giovanni Francica Nava, Giovanni Ameglio, Enrico Presutti.[500] After a few months, Dario Cassuto, Raoul Vittorio Palermi,[501] Arturo Vecchini, Temistocle Zona, Alessandro Delli Paoli, and Giovanni Lavanga were also expelled.

The Grand Master of G.O.I., with some satisfaction, said: the attempt of the secessionists is completely and miserably failed,[502] but many years to come, the two Obediences continuously revived the digits.

In 1909, the Grand Orient of Italy with its 15,000 members was one of the mightiest communions in the European masonic scenery. More, almost as a proof of the excellent state of health enjoyed by Obedience, also thanks to the income of more modest social classes, Palazzo Giustiniani was acquired.

4.7 Freemasonry and Political Life

This new democratic vocation had produced an exponential development of forces and human resources, but few realized that an overly "civil–political" bias could have distorted the Obedience for what concerned its masonic tradition. The political line held by Ferrari allowed in-

---

499 Rosario Francesco Esposito, *La massoneria e l'Italia*, op. cit., p. 323.

500 Some of these masons, Francica Nava, Ameglio, and Bianchi, returned to their decisions and moved back to the ranks of G.O.I.

501 Raoul Vittorio Palermi was born in Florence on May 20, 1864, in a wealthy family. There is little information about his youth, but in the second part of his life, he played an important role in some domestic political events. He began in Freemasonry and was one of the key-players of the birth of the Gran Loggia d'Italia (GLI), Obedience he led from 1919 to 1925. http://www.treccani.it/enciclopedia/raoul-vittorio-palermi_(Dizionario-Biografico)/ (August 7, 2018).

502 Fulvio Conti, *Storia della massoneria*, op. cit., p. 187.

deed Freemasonry to have a primary role in political decisions, or a strong influence in governmental life, but at the same time, this media overexposure was a source of conflict that eventually weakened Italian Communion, as the attacks the Institution suffered from the socialists, who had not downsized their idea of Freemasonry, indeed far from it. Socialists began to think Masonry with its proper vocation to overcome social classes mischanced the proletariat issues; it was therefore mandatory to separate Masonry and socialism. This vision had been carried on for years, since the beginning of the century, but in the Socialist Congress of 1910, the incompatibility topic was re-proposed, through two agendas, one by Gaetano Salvemini.[503] This motion—inviting all not Freemasons socialists not to embrace the Obedience and those already belonging to egress—, had 6,606 votes.

The situation re-emerged two years later with the Congress of the party in Reggio Emilia, where the issue was at the center of the debate. Benito Mussolini supported the agenda declaring the Masonic institution had to be defied cause it "portatrice di quella politica bloccarda che deforma i caratteri specifici dei partiti politici".[504]

In both the dates, the legal number of consents necessary to validate the statement was failed, thus the question was postponed to the Congress of 1914.

But the winds opposed to Freemasonry were not just mounting within the Socialist Party, even within the Republican Party, they distanced from the Institution, explicitly in 1912 during its meeting in Ancona. According to the most unrelenting wing, Freemasonry was responsible—with its stuck

---

503 Gaetano Salvemini, historian and politician (Molfetta 1873—Sorrento 1957). Joined the PSI, he deepened his reflections on the link between socialism and the southern question, criticizing the tendency towards northern worker protectionism. The attention to nation issues led him to argue with the government of Giovanni Giolitti. He directed, with Antonio De Viti De Marco, the weekly "L'Unità," through which he acted a profound influence on the political debate. Interventionist in 1915, he was a deputy in 1919. In 1925 he founded the anti-Fascist clandestine daily "Non mollare!" [*Do not give up!*]. Arrested, expatriated in France, where he was amid the founders of Giustizia e Libertà [*Justice and Freedom*], and then in the United States. From 1933, he taught Italian history at Harvard University, then assumed the U.S. citizenship. Back home, in 1948 was reinstated in Florence. http://www.treccani.it/enciclopedia/gaetano-salvemini/ (August 7, 2018).

504 "was the bearer of that blockade policy that deforms the specific characteristics of political parties" [translator's note]. Marco Novarino, *Grande Oriente d'Italia*, op. cit., p. 55.

plot by the trend to compromise amid similar political entities—of the loss of republican identity. The removal was there, but not the statement of discordance; so much so that in 1913 Eugenio Chiesa,[505] a Republican MP, was initiated in a lodge of G.O.I. The Catholic Church itself would have played a fundamental role in the excited exile years of the Grand Orient of Italy.

From now on Freemasonry had to officially shield from socialists, albeit not them only. From many parts, G.O.I. was appointed of scarce patriotism. These charge, the masonic summits rejected as defamatory, referred to the matter of the war in Tripolitania in 1911. Then, masons who in the Italian lodges of the Ottoman Empire had asked the leaders of G.O.I. to intervene with the Italian government to avoid a humiliation of the Empire. Italian Freemasonry declared the Tripoli enterprise was essential for Italy. If something could be done, it would have to before: it was late, the weapons had already been taken; otherwise, it would have sounded as an attack against the interests and dignity of Italy. The patriotic position of Italian Freemasonry was fair, first the interests of the Fatherland, and for it the principle of brotherhood solidarity was sacrificed. The Grand Orient of Italy, moreover, had been openly in favor of Italian intervention in Libya, for a range of reasons, from the economic to the social and descending from the "civilization" Italy could bring into this territory. To Masonry, the Italian presence was remarkable, diverse lodges were founded, both at the Obedience of G.O.I. and the fresh Grande Loggia d'Italia.

Although the Grand Orient of Italy was variously engaged, its leaders managed to organize an important event, the 1911 International Congress.[506] Welcoming 2000 Masons from all the Italian districts and delegates of 21 foreign Obediences, was organized for September 20 at the National Theater of Rome. During the afternoon, a procession with 300 Masonic vessels passed through the streets from Palazzo Giustiniani. The central topics were: the anti-clergy action of Freemasonry; public charity; essence and boundaries of solidarity among Brethen of universal Freemasonry; the

---

505 Eugenio Chiesa, was a prominent politician before the advent of fascism; he was born in Milan on November 18, 1863, militated since youth in the Republican party. He was a deputy from 1903 to 1926, the year when he had to flee from Italy since the fascist persecution of Freemasonry.

506 *Informazioni. Congresso massonico universale*, in "Rivista Massonica" n. 1–4, 1911, pp. 72–77.

merger of ceremonies, gestures, signs, words concerning the first three degrees of Masonry worldwide.[507]

In May 1912, Ferrari was reconfirmed at the head of the Italian Communion; there—two Piedmontese lodges, the "Dante Alighieri," and the "Cavour"—reissued the theme of female Masonic belonging. Even in this case, it did not go beyond pledge, the question wasn't addressed properly and no progress was made.[508] At the Constituent, the Grand Master presented a balance sheet on the asset of the Communion. Again the budget was more than flattering; there were 431 lodges and 131 Triangles. The discussion heated on the unification of the Rites, the S.R.A.A., and the Italian Symbolic, but no final determining was reached. More to the confirmation of Ettore Ferrari as Grand Master, the new Junta was elected, with Gustavo Canti Deputy Grand Master and Alberto Beneduce, Alberto La Pegna, Gino Bandini, Carlo Berlenda, Pellegrino Ascarelli. Beneduce was assigned the trust to hold relations with the Political Commission within the Council of the Order numbering Malachia de Cristoforis, Adolfo Engel,[509] Giovanni Ciraolo, Giovanni Antonio Vanni, Salvatore Barzilai, Agostino Berenini, Mario Chiaraviglio, and Teodoro Mayer.[510]

The new Junta gave a renewed impulse to the path always supported by Ferrari, and looked with interest at the new scenario from the broadening of male suffrage. The Grand Orient did not minimize the impact the new electorate—essentially of laborers and peasants—could have on the ballots. By Masonry, these were under the influence by the Catholic Church. Thus, Beneduce drew up a list of measures necessary to counter clerical forces. First, the dissemination of popular education; the reform of taxes, the local ones mostly. The vocation of initiatives was popular: to approach the "base." Furthermore, the agricultural problem had to be solved, especially in southern Italy, and to think of workers' pensions. In October 1912, Gino Bandini promoted the institution of a defined structure to coordinate the Masonic activities during the terms: a central masonic committee was

---

507 Rosario Francesco Esposito, *La massoneria e l'Italia*, op. cit., p. 326.

508 See Emanuela Locci, *Storia della massoneria femminile. Dalle corporazioni alle obbedienze*, BastogiLibri, Roma, 2017, pp. 105–138.

509 Adolfo Engel was born in 1851, was an engineer and politician in the ranks of the Radicals. Initiated at the Freemasonry in 1884 in Milanese "La Ragione," over the course of his Masonic career, he played roles of primary importance, both in the Grand Orient and in the Scottish Rite. He died in Rome in 1913.

510 Fulvio Conti, *Storia della massoneria italiana*, op. cit., p. 225.

established, that would gather the numerous committees at local level. A real war machine, although Ferrari, worried this overexposure could damage the Institution, didn't agree. In case of victory, there would be a risk of weakening the parties close to the Institution, in case of defeat, the Masonry could have become the main scapegoat. The works began, thanks also to Barzilai, who hastened to reassure Ferrari of the absolute confidentiality that would protect the work of the Grand Orient. In this span, so rich in initiatives—see the contribution of G.O.I. in the birth of the Banca Nazionale delle Casse Rurali—the Institution had to cope with the controversy due to the resignation of Gustavo Fara, war hero who had distinguished himself in Eritrea and in Libya.

Not that much his resignation, as his past masonic membership raised the question, in some newspapers, of the influence Institution had in the army and in the magistracy. The words to describe Masonry were textually: Masonic Octopus.[511] Paolo Spingardi,[512] minister of war, pronounced very harsh words toward Freemasonry but did not support the discordance between political offices and Masonic affiliation.

G.O.I. reacted immediately to these attacks and rejected as absurd and ridiculous the hypothesis the Masonic belonging could create duties opposite to the discipline of the military hierarchy.[513]

As if the situation was not already deranged, the Italian Masonic Communion handled also the hostility by nationalists; actually not new, though worsened.[514] Luigi Federzoni,[515] leader of the nationalists, declared it was

---

511 Fulvio Conti, *Storia della massoneria italiana*, op. cit., p. 228.

512 Count Paolo Spingardi (Felizzano 1845–Acqui 1918) was a General, professor at the School of War (1886–1887), was also undersecretary (1903) and then (1909–1914) four times Minister of War. Called back into service in 1915, he was chaired by the central commission of prisoners. He was also a deputy (1904), and a senator (1909). http://www.treccani.it/enciclopedia/spingardi-paolo-conte/ (August 8, 2018).

513 *Informazioni. Adunanza del Grande Oriente*, in "Rivista Massonica", n. 9–10, 1913, pp. 219–223.

514 *La parola del Gran Maestro*, in "Rivista Massonica" n. 15–16, 1913, p. 347.

515 Luigi Federzoni (Bologna 1878–Rome 1967). Political man and writer, leader of the Italian nationalist movement and founder of its organ, L'idea nazionale [The national idea] (1911), deputy in 1913, interventionist and highly decorated, in the first postwar period. He supported the fusion of the nationalists in the Fascist Party, was later Minister of the colonies (until June 16, 1925), of the inner affairs and again of the colonies (6 November 1926–18 December 1928). Senator since 1928, he held the presidency of the Senate from 1929 to 1939 and the Accademia d'Italia from 1938 to

mandatory to erase definitively the leverage Masonry exercised on Italian civil society. Patriots saw in the Institution all the evil according to their ideology: bourgeois reformism, cosmopolitan humanitarianism; the last in particular thought preventing the raise of national hegemony. For its part, G.O.I. believed nationalism was paroxysmal patriotism and it would only harm the nation. The situation appeared to fall in 1913 when G.O.I. refused to participate in a confront with nationalists, whose reaction was to indict an investigation into Freemasonry. Many public figures were called to express an opinion on the Institution and many—from Benedetto Croce,[516] to Pasquale Villari,[517] and Giovanni Amendola[518]—were not positive. The only voice that arose in defense of Freemasonry was that of Ivanoe Bonomi,[519] who openly declared the attitude on Freemasonry was absolutely persecutory. Beyond the single statements, the inquiry itself had quite other meanings, the summit of the Grand Orient realized such an

1943. In 1943, he pronounced against Mussolini in the session of the Grand Council on July 25. http://www.interno.gov.it/it/luigi-federzoni (August 8, 2018).

516 Benedetto Croce (Pescasseroli, February 25, 1866–Naples, November 20, 1952) was a philosopher and historian and although he did not lack critics and adversaries, he appears to be the essential figure in Italian cultural life in the first half of the twentieth century. http://www.treccani.it/enciclopedia/benedetto-croce/ (August 10, 2018).

517 Pasquale Villari was a historian and a politician (Naples 1826–Florence 1917). Exile in Florence after having partaken in the Neapolitan movement of 1848, he taught history at the University of Pisa (1859). National member of the Lincei (1878), deputy (1870–1876; 1880–1882), senator (from 1884), was Minister of Public Education (1891–1892). http://www.treccani.it/enciclopedia/pasquale-villari/(August 10, 2018).

518 Giovanni Amendola (Naples, 15 April 1882–Cannes, 7 April 1926) was an Italian politician, journalist, and academic. He was elected for three legislatures as a deputy, later in the fascist period, he was strongly critical of the regime, becoming one of the most renowned anti-fascists in Italy. He was one of the promoters of the Aventine, he conceived it as the seat of legality, opposed to the government and the House, considered illegal; and opposed both the various attempts, advocated by Republicans and Garibaldians of the "Italia Libera" [Free Italy], of armed insurrection, and to ally the opposition from Aventin to the Communist one. After the murder of Giacomo Matteotti, Amendola was also threatened and twice beaten, the last beating of 1925 proved fatal, in fact Amendola died after two years because of the injuries reported. http://www.treccani.it/enciclopedia/giovanni-amendola_(Dittà-Biografico)(August 10, 2018).

519 Ivanoe Bonomi (Mantova 1873–Rome 1952). Italian politician, amid the founders of the Socialist Reformist Party (1912), he held diverse government posts, but with the advent of fascism, he withdrew from political life. He returned there after the liberation of Rome, becoming one of the key figures of the early republican age. http://www.treccani.it/enciclopedia/ivanoe-bonomi/ (August 10, 2018).

important part of the political, economic, and intellectual class had this sensing: a conventicle of intrigue, ill reputation, cronyism, completely ignoring the contribution the Institution had given to the national identity: its aims, programs, its battles in view of equality amid men. In this sad moment for the Italian communion, it appeared the struggle for the divorce, the enlargement of the right to vote, the abolition of the death penalty, had no meaning.

One of the few who in this chaos, even emotional, of strong disappointment, the right detachment and right mind on the real reasons for the attack on Freemasonry was Achille Ballori.[520] He declared: "senza dubbio si combatte la massoneria perché si sa che essa si occupa di elezioni politiche e quindi la guerra e lo spirito antimassonico che si diffonde e si organizza nell'esercito, nell'armata, nella magistratura, nelle amministrazioni pubbliche per combattere e neutralizzare l'azione politica dell'Ordine. Se è così la lotta non cesserà che ad elezioni avvenute".[521]

Ferrari strengthened this concept and stated: "la campagna non ci giunge inattesa alla vigilia dei comizi politici ed amministrativi era prevedibile ed inevitabile".[522]

The speeches of Ferrari and dignitaries of Grand Orient, or magazines such as "Acacia" and "Rivista Massonica" were no longer enough to reach a wide audience and to obtain consent, for this the settling to fund some progressive headlines that were already published was taken.

---

520 Achille Ballori was born in the province of Pisa in 1850, becoming a doctor, he was head of the hospital in Mantua and the united health center in Rome. Here, under Ernesto Nathan, he was councilor for hygiene. In 1874, he was given the rank of Master in "Umanità e Progresso" [Humanity and Progress] of Pisa, while in 1891, he was Worshipful of "Rienzi" lodge in Rome. In 1890, he was elected first Grand Superintendent, and in 1893, Deputy Grand Master. Six years later, he became Sovereign Grand Commander of S.R.A.A.. In 1917, he was the only candidate for the Grand Mastery, as Ferrari's next, but on October 31—same year—he was shot dead in Palazzo Giustiniani in Rome, by Lorenzo d'Ambrosio.

521 "No doubt Freemasonry is fought because it deals with political elections and therefore the war and the anti-masonic spirit that spreads and organizes itself in the army, in the courts, in public administrations to fight and neutralize the political action of the Order. If this is the case, the struggle will only cease after the elections" [translator's note]. Fulvio Conti, Storia della massoneria italiana, op. cit., p. 233.

522 "the campaign does not reach us unexpected on the eve of the political and administrative rallies, was predictable and sure" [translator's note]. Ibidem.

But the most important move was to found in November 1913 a new week-ly "L'Idea democratica"[523] under the direction of Gino Bandini, a member of the Executive Committee and of Italian Radical Party, for about six years was the most important channel between masonic and profane world.

The years before WWI weren't laidback: against socialists, nationalists, clericals, all this while the politics of the Blocks,[524] Masonry warmly sup-ported was in crisis.[525]

With the clericals, the struggle was timeworn, in the early twentieth cen-tury, they were not the most disruptive, but they returned with leagues with the sole purpose to fight Freemasonry. Even if short-lived, it's worth mentioning the foundation, in 1913, of the National League against Se-cret Associations by deputy Romeo Gallenga Stuart and Count Demetrio Baldelli-Mombelli, whose aim was: to fight freemasonry and all secret bod-ies since they keep undercover on their constitution and statutes.

Nothing could be more untruthful, as both documents were public.[526]

The 1913 terms saw the Catholic electorate in the front row, thanks to the "Gentiloni agreement," between liberals of Giovanni Giolitti and the Ital-ian Catholic Electoral Union (UECI), presided over by Vincenzo Ottorino Gentiloni in view of the elections policies of 1913. It marked the official entry of Catholics into Italian political life. At the beginning of the twen-tieth century, the declarations of Pope Pio IX on the "non-profitability" of believers' partaking in political activity were still in force in the Catholic world. But the environment of lay associations was constantly moving. In-side the Opera dei Congressi—the main Italian Catholic fellowship—the group of Fry Romolo Murri[527] ruled, supporting the need to prefer a tacti-

---

523 "Democratic Idea" [translator's note]. See Anna Maria Isastia, *La Massoneria al con-trattacco: "L'Idea democratica" di Gino Bandini (1913–1919)* in "Dimensioni E Prob-lemi Della Ricerca Storica"1/1997, pp. 259–287.

524 See also Demetrio Xoccato, *La massoneria di fronte alla crisi dei blocchi popolari: la guerra di Libia (1911–1912)*, in "Tetide. Rivista di Studi Mediterranei", n. 1, year 1, 2015, pp. 1–18.

525 Marco Novarino, *Progresso e tradizione*, op. cit., p. 206.

526 Ivi, p. 210.

527 Romolo Murri (Monte S. Pietrangeli 1870–Rome 1944). Priest since 1893, advocate of a greater political commitment of Catholics, he acted as a critical voice toward the conservatism of the ecclesiastical hierarchy, seeking a reconciliation between social-ism and the social doctrine of the Church. For more information, see http://www.

cal agreement with socialists rather than supporting liberals, but in 1904, Pope Pio X intruded dissolving the body.

Vincenzo Gentiloni, and the convenient Catholics, instead lined up with the monarchy and liberals to arrest socialists, Marxists, and anarchists. Pio X, who in the decree *Lamentabili sane exitu* of 1907 had condemned 65 modernist propositions and soon afterwards imposed the "excommunication" of modernism in the encyclical *Pascendi dominici gregis*, also shared this attitude, aimed at preserving the traditional values. The outcome of political polls of 1913 decreed the success of the agreement: liberals scored 51% of the votes, with 260 elected. The Socialist elected representatives were 58, reformists (Italian Socialist Reformist Party) 21, while radicals achieved a good success with 73 elected (including Murri), 34 Catholics (nonmembers of the Liberal Party), and 5 nationalists. Gentiloni compact led to the merge between the Risorgimento strand and the catholic tradition; the two, united, formed a large majority in the country.

Here, Freemasons sought among their ranks the deputies who, not to lose the seat, had recourse to the vote of Catholics, and a list of these politicians was published on the "Idea Democratica." The quarrel raged within the Masonic Communion, from many sides measures to punish those failing the lines of Grand Orient were called. Beyond that, there was a fair majority of radicals in the rows of Freemasonry. In the 1913 voting, Freemasonry was often not able to concretely support the radical candidates; an example is the refusal to fund the campaigns of Alberto la Pegna, Filippo Virgili, and Romolo Murri.[528] However, compared to 1908, the presence of masons in Parliament had empowered: 90, thus one on five was a freemason. Returning to the linkage between Freemasonry and socialism, in the congress of Ancona of 1914, two distinct motions were presented, one by Giovanni Zibordi, who asked for incongruity and the other for opposing orientation, therefore favorable to the double belonging, presented by Alfredo Poggi.[529] Benito Mussolini, who at that time was director of the socialist newspaper "Avanti" supported Zibordi. After a long debate, an overwhelming majority, decree not just the incompatibility, but also the immediate expulsion of socialists joined

---

treccani.it/enciclopedia/romolo-murri/ and https://tinyurl.com/y9lt9fqk (August 28, 2018).

528 Fulvio Conti, *Storia della massoneria italiana*, op. cit., p. 236.

529 Marco Novarino, *Grande Oriente d'Italia*, op. cit., p. 55.

to Masonry approved his motion.[530] Ferrari's reaction was explained in a circular of May 3, 1914: "dopo il voto del congresso di Ancona non vi può essere dubbio sulla condotta che debbono tenere i massoni iscritti al Partito Socialista ufficiale. Se vi è tra essi qualcuno che è disposto a piegarsi al novissimo dogma del partito, esca senz'altro dalle nostre file, dove noi vogliamo uomini di fede sicura, coscienza salda e dignitosa, volontà libere e forti. Attendo da voi, non oltre i quindici giorni da oggi, l'assicurazione che il pensiero del Governo dell'Ordine è stato da tutti sentito".[531]

In the General Assembly of May 1914, the Grand Orient of Italy had the chance to evaluate the last years of activity, and also to appraise the situation concerning the internal management of the Order, it was decided—for example—to set improvements in the Constitutions making viable to lodges to increase influence and decision-making power in the running of Obedience. Another issue to be addressed Ferrari faced was the groundless rumors, which concerning the acquisition of Palazzo Giustiniani. He sent an open letter to "Corriere della Sera" to detail the steps of the sale, disentangling there had been any cheating by the contractors.[532]

After a few weeks by the General Assembly, Italy was on the abyss of the First World War. On July 31, 1914, Ettore Ferrari delivered a circular to all the lodges: "Un'ora tragica volge sull'Europa e minaccia di travolgerla tutta nel più spaventoso conflitto che la storia ricordi. Il governo dell'Ordine, conscio dei propri doveri, va adoprandosi con ogni possibile sforzo perché l'azione di tutti i grandi orienti si svolga concorde e conforme ai principii universalmente riconosciuti dalla massoneria, per salvare la civiltà umana dal flagello che le incombe o almeno temperarne le conseguenze. La pace è senza dubbio, nostro costante ideale, perché è condizione prima d'ogni

---

530 Marco Novarino, *Massoneria e movimento operaio e socialista*, in Santi Fedele, Giovanni Greco (edited), *Massoneria ed Europa*, op. cit., p. 105.

531 "after the vote of the congress of Ancona there can be no doubt about the conduct that must be held by the Masons enrolled in the official Socialist Party. If there is someone among them who is willing to bow to the very last dogma of the party, he will surely come out of our ranks, where we want men of sure faith, firm and dignified conscience, free will and strong will. I await from you, no later than fifteen days from today, the assurance that the thought of the Government of the Order has been felt by everyone" [translator's note]. Rosario Francesco Esposito, *La massoneria e l'Italia*, op. cit., p. 334.

532 Ettore Passalalpi Ferrari, *Le muse e la politica*, op. cit., p. 347.

progresso; ma se la fatalità degli eventi potesse compromettere l'integrità della patria, trovi essa, per la difesa dei suoi supremi interessi, concorde in un solo volere il popolo italiano. Rifuggano le logge dall'associarsi a moti incomposti e tumultuosi; cerchino anzi d'impedirli. Essi gioverebbero solo a spingere i governi sulle vie della reazione. Se mai suoni l'ora delle dure prove, non mancherà la nostra voce per confortarvi ad affrontarla con lo spirito di sacrificio e con la fede dei padri".[533]

Clear the stance of Freemasonry in the question; besides the obvious plea to masonic ideals, we see the first marks of patriotism. It's favorable to the intervention of Italy alongside the forces of the Entente. After the first doubt, more by prudence than by the lack of conviction for the feat itself, Ferrari spoke straightly for the intervention of Italy. Italian Freemasonry, represented by G.O.I., as previously during the war in Tripolitania, would have respected and supported the choices made by the government. Then Italian Obedience went further; in fact, since August 1914, it arranged a body of mason volunteers, disposable to the government, underlining their belonging to Freemasonry and the loyalty toward the state. In October, a committee raised with the main task to organize the propaganda pro armed intercession. At the end of the same month, Gustavo Canti in a meeting in Turin openly slandered Germany, forced to take power and not to regard the statements.[534] In Italy, to Canti, the enemies to be defeated were: the clericals and the socialists, not new, but well known by the Institution. From autumn 1914 on Masonic channels, ideals such as patriotism and national belonging were repeatedly claimed. Certainly, in G.O.I., there were dissonant positions on the conduct: one was that of Senator Antonio Cefaly, playing in years leading roles in the communion.

---

533 "A tragic hour turns on Europe and threatens to overwhelm her in the most frightful conflict that history remembers. The government of the Order, conscious of its duties, must be used with every possible effort to ensure the action of all the great orientations is conducted in accordance with the principles universally recognized by Freemasonry, to save human civilization from the scourge that looms or at least temper the consequences. Peace is undoubtedly our constant ideal; because it is a condition before any progress; but if the fatality of events could compromise the integrity of the country, find it, in defense of its supreme interests, the Italian people in one will agree. Refuge the lodges from joining unaccompanied and tumultuous movements; rather try to prevent them. They would only be good for pushing governments on the path of reaction. If you ever hear the hour of the hard trials, our voice will not fail to comfort you to face it with the spirit of sacrifice and with the faith of the fathers" [translator's note]. *In difesa dell'Ordine*, in "Rivista Massonica" n. 2, 1914, pp. 85–87.

534 Fulvio Conti, *Storia della massoneria italiana*, op. cit., p. 240.

The question is defined when Italy enters the war, Masonry as interventionist, will always work during the war.[535] Even before the decision, Freemasonry on its own initiative essentially funded the enterprise of Garibaldi volunteers, many Masons amid, who led by Peppino Garibaldi[536] left for the front in France as part of the foreign legion and fought more than once in the Argonne zone.[537] In the weeks before Italy's entry into the war, Ettore Ferrari and Ernesto Nathan went to the United States; as soon as they received the official news that Italy had declared war they immediately returned to their homeland.[538]

Here, the exposition of the history of G.O.I. is due to the skilful pen of Nicoletta Casano; to comment on the masonic history of Ettore Ferrari, I quit by saying in June 1917, Ettore Ferrari joined the Paris Congress where The Entente Masonries, without British ones, met to establish a project of the League of Nations. Fearing the Italian delegation would vote in favor of the principle of self-determination, such a hostile campaign took place in the press that prompted Ferrari to put the Grand Master's mandate back on November 25 of the same year. In April 1918, he was elected Sovereign Grand Commander of the Supreme Council of S.R.A.A., a post he held until his death. In 1919, he was appointed Honorary Past Grand Master. From the end of 1922, he devoted every effort to reinforcing the Scottish rite. The following year he traveled throughout Italy and it is clear the Insti-

---

535 *Informazioni. All'inizio della guerra europea*, in "Rivista Massonica" n. 7, 1914, pp. 315–316.

536 Giuseppe–Peppino–Garibaldi (1879–1950) was an Italian general firstborn of Ricciotti Garibaldi and then nephew of Giuseppe Garibaldi. At the age of 18, he joined his father to fight in Domokos, Greece, alongside people who had rebelled against the Ottoman Empire. In 1903, he went in South Africa under the British Empire (his mother, Constance Hopcraft, was English) against the Boers. Later, he partook in Venezuelan revolution against dictator Julián Castro and he waged in Guyana and Mexico. After a few labor experiences in Romania and Panama, he returned to Mexico to struggle against dictator Porfirio Díaz during the Mexican Revolution. In 1912, he was again in Greece with his father and brothers. From 1913 to 1915, he lived in the United States. Back in Europe, he battled in WWI. At the end, he left his military career to undertake trades between United States and London, however not that successful. In 1922, he entered politics, opposing Benito Mussolini and the National Fascist Party, he became promoter of antifascist actions, with the support of Domizio Torriggiani. In 1926, he left for United States, to home come in 1940. With the armistice, the Germans halted him. War over, he retired to private life and died in Rome in 1950.

537 In Argonne clash, two nephews of him—sons of Ricciotti—died, the very young Bruno and Costante.

538 *Informazioni. Il ritorno in patria*, in "Rivista Massonica" n. 6, 1915, p. 280.

tution was shrinking to defend against fascist attacks, even with the entry
of representatives of the Symbolic Rite among the Scots. In May 1923, Ferrari rearranged the Superior Chambers and decided to publish "Lux," the
monthly bulletin of the Rite, to carry on a free thought that fused socio-cul-
tural issues with esoteric problems. Still at the end of 1924, he committed
freemasons to defend the secular values of the Risorgimento. Opponent
of fascism, he rejected all public offices.[539] The fascist violence struck him
several times; his studio of sculptor was turned over many occasions. Ferrari did not dissolve his Rite even after the approval of the law, November
1925, against the secret societies, commissioned by Mussolini. Guarded
by the police, he was denounced on May 25, 1929, on charges of attempt
to reorganize the Masonry, and warned. He was in fact in correspondence
with Giuseppe Leti, a lawyer and known anti-fascist moved to France, his
lieutenant, who in May 1929 passed on full powers. He died in Rome on
August 19, 1929.

His Masonic thought can be briefed as follows: "La Massoneria non è un
partito o una corrente. politica, nel significato che comunemente si dà alla
parola; ma una scuola e quasi vorremmo dire una grande Chiesa cattoli-
calaica che aduna e accorda uomini di diverso credo politico in un ordine
più elevato di eterni principi umani. E ben possiamo affermare, come af-
fermiamo che essa è apolitica, intendendo ch'essa è non già fuori della vita
nazionale, bensì fuori dagli angusti cancelli dei partiti, al di sopra delle
piccole e grandi competizioni di fazione. Ma essa si muove ugualmente
e profondamente nell'orbita della vita pubblica creando le vaste correnti,
disciplinando e organizzando le agguerrite falangi che agiscono in difesa
della libertà e per la conquista di sempre maggiori progressi nel campo
morale e civile".

---

539 https://tinyurl.com/yccmb35x (August 7, 2018).

5. Luster and Misery of Italian Freemasonry Between the Great War and Fascism

Nicoletta Casano

The history of Italian Freemasonry at the beginning of the 20th century arose from two different accounts including a patriotic narrative, the legacy of Risorgimento, and from an internationalist one. This duplicity clearly shows how in just over 20 years, this establishment moved from playing a progressive political national role to being a scapegoat for the state.

This chapter will display the historical reasons for this dichotomy and show how this affected the Italian civil frame and its profound changes.

5.1 The Homely Political Commitment of Italian Freemasonry at the Beginning of the 20th Century

Unlike the Anglo-Saxon world, the Freemasonic institution in Western Europe became deeply rooted and engaged in the political and social scenario of the countries it existed in at the end of the 19th century.

At the start of the 20th century in Italy, much of the liberal and democratic political grade was involved in Freemasonry. To understand this phenomenon, note the number of Masonic affiliations quadrupled from 4,000 to 5,000 at the end of the 19th century to 20,000 in the early 20th century. Moreover, at the time no other fellowship, which covered political parties too, was so rooted in Italian territory.[541]

One of the main causes for this breakthrough came from the crisis that the Catholic Church experienced in the legacy left by the *siècle des Lumières* and the French Revolution. In some European countries, this birthed anti-clerical movements and drove notable lay reforms in others.[542]

---

541 Fulvio Conti, *Massoneria e identità nazionale nell'Italia unita* in José Antonio Ferrer Benimeli (edited), *La Masoneria Española y la crisis colonial del 98*, vol.II, VII Simposium Internacional de Histoire de la Masoneria Española, Barcelona, diciembre 3–6, 1997, Zaragoza, 1999, pp. 966–968.

542 Hervé Hasquin, *I fondamenti dello spirito laico nell'Europa contemporanea*, in Aldo

Italy experienced the birth of an anti-clerical movement which gathered all progressive forces against the advance of a union appointed by Pope Pio X to partially overcome the forbiddance for Catholics to partake in the political life of the country, called *non expedit*.

This combined with political tensions led the Italian Freemasonry to define its position in the Constitutional Convention convened in 1906. The Constituent of 1906 voided the first article of the Italian Masonic Constitution pointing the lodges of the Italian Communion to deal with all the issues affecting the political life of the country.[543] This was due to a certain "historical casualty" which committed Italian Freemasonry to the social development of the nation. It provoked reactions in both Masonic and political contexts.

To Masons, the political commitment of Freemasonry was one of the causes generating the split within the Supreme Council of Italy from which, a new Masonic Obedience called the Grand Lodge of Italy was born a few years later.[544]

Politically, however, the Freemasonry of the Grand Orient of Italy openly became the ideological promoter of the progressive anti-clerical movement known as the "Popular Blocks"[545] which quickly imposed itself on the Italian political scene.

Alessandro Mola (edited), *Stato, Chiesa e Società in Italia, Francia, Belgio e Spagna nei secoli XIX–XX*, Bastogi, Foggia, 1993, pp. 33–45.

543 "Rivista Massonica", maggio 31, 1907, pp. 217–219.

544 Fernando Cordova, *Massoneria e politica, 1892–1908*, Laterza, Roma, 1985, p. 288, On this topic about the conflict born in the Supreme Council of Italy, see also: Fulvio Conti, *Storia della Massoneria Italiana dal Risorgimento al Fascismo*, Il Mulino, Bologna, 2003, pp. 180–186; Aldo Alessandro Mola, *Storia della Massoneria Italiana dalle origini ai nostri giorni*, Bompiani, Milano, 2006, pp. 327–331; Luigi Pruneti, *Quel che accadde nel 1908*, in "Officinae", a. VII, n°4, December 1995; Anna Maria Isastia, Alessandro Visani, *L'idea laica tra Chiesa e Massoneria. La questione della scuola*, Atanòr, Roma, 2008, pp. 26–64.

545 "Popular Blocks" [translator's note]. For an argument on the "Popular Blocks," see: Fulvio Conti, *Massoneria e identità nazionale*, op. cit., 2003, pp. 207–215; Ferdinando Cordova, *Agli ordini del serpente verde*, Bulzoni editore, Roma, 1990, pp. 10–16; Enrico Decleva, *Anticlericalismo e lotta politica nell'Italia giolittiana. II: L'estrema sinistra e la formazione dei blocchi popolari (1905–1909)*, in "Nuova rivista storica", vol. LIII, year 1969, Società Editrice Dante Alighieri, fascicolo V–VI, pp. 541–617.

5.2 The Political Commitment of Italian Freemasonry at the Beginning of the 20th Century in the World

The empowerment of the role of Italian Freemasonry in home politics is equally reflected in foreign policy.

For a brief overview: Italy faced the late century as a new national political body boldly walking on the stage of international alliances starting with the Franco-Prussian conflict in 1870. This clash between two key nations of the old continent sets the international community a new reality in Europe: the survival of States is granted by peace, a precarious balance that must be shielded through agreements and blocs.

Here, the pacifist movements prevailed and amid them, the Masonic one. From the Franco-Prussian conflict to the outbreak of WWI, the pacifist appeal expanded and gained traction within a shared platform variously developed in international masonic congresses, the Bureau International des Relations Maçonniques (B.I.R.M.).[546]

This participation of masons and lodges in the debates on international pacifism corresponds to the reawakening of the "coscienza della necessità di un dialogo tra le obbedienze europee al di là delle frontiere nazionali".[547] At the birth of the working men's "Internationals"[548]—plus socialist and anarchist—masons, which pursued "uno scopo identico, per mezzo di metodi differenti"[549] also willed to create an international federation. Their urge was strengthened by a charitable imprint which is the basis of modern Masonry.

---

546 Nadine Lubelski-Bernard, *Freemasonry and Peace in Europe, 1867–1914*, in Charles Chatfield, Peter Van De Dungen (edited), *Peace Mouvements and Political Cultures*, The University of Tennessee Press/Knoxville, 1988, pp. 84–87.

547 "awareness of the need for a dialogue between European obediences beyond national borders" [translator's note]. Pierre-Yves. Beaurepaire, *L'Europe des francs-maçons, XVIIIe–XXIe siècles*, Belin, Paris, 2002, pp. 246–247.

548 At the Paris Congress of 1889, the *Second International* or *Socialist International* whose permanent seat is in Brussels in 1900 and the secretariat entrusted to the Belgian Camille Huysmans. For further information, see: Georges Haupt, *La Deuxième Internationale, 1889–1914: étude critique des sources, essai bibliographique*, Matériaux pour l'histoire du socialisme international. 2. Série, Essais bibliographiques, Mouton, 1964, Volume 1.

549 "an identical purpose, by means of different methods" [translator's note]. Edouard Quartier-La-Tente, *Le Bureau International de Relations Maçonniques pendant les 18 premières années de son existence. Son histoire, son but, ses difficultés, son activité, son avenir, 1902–1920*, Imprimerie Büchler & Cie, Berne, 1920, p. 1.

The representatives of the Obediences in France, Belgium, Switzerland, Hungary, Italy, Spain, Greece, Portugal, Brazil, Australia, and the State of Massachusetts (United States) engaged in the Universal Masonic Congress convened in Paris in 1889. From this meeting came the idea of founding the B.I.R.M. that would be established in 1902. Other national Obediences joined the *Bureau* during its 18 years.

At the international masonic congress called by the B.I.R.M. at the end of August 1904, masonic issues that were previously unappraoched are discussed to give an initial structure to the International Bureau. Among these debates, some were intended to develop a program of effective standards that would eventually be the foundation of international Freemasonry. This appointment stated that masonry must contribute to uplifting people, peace, and propaganda of the International Arbitration, following the assets of the diverse firms for peace.[550]

However, this stunning project had limits on both a basic and a pragmatic level. From a substrate approach, a "universal" congress yearning had been more of an ideal than a fact. Despite the enthusiasm at the time, the worldwide activity of Freemasonry had always been narrowed because of the "purely masonic" parting among different groups of Obediences. The goal of the B.I.R.M. was to gather "irregular" Obediences of continental Europe and Latin America. They were the opposite are those following the Anglo-Saxon ritual and doctrine, the "regular" Freemasonry. This gap between the two main masonic parties compromised the force and influence of bodies like the B.I.R.M., though exceptions, as regular Obedience (the Great Alpine Lodge) joined this association and also holding the presidency throughout its existence.

Despite this eternal controversy in irregular and regular masonries, the breaking point of the B.I.R.M. was effectively the alignment of national Obediences with the position taken by the respective countries during WWI.[551] The case of the Grand Orient of Italy was exemplary in this sense.

---

550 Centre d'Etudes Maçonniques a Bruxelles (ormai CEDOM), *Archives de Moscou*, 114-1-79. Congrès International Maçonnique de Bruxelles 1904. Note et Projet présentés par le Frère François Nicol.

551 José Gotovitch, *Franc-maçonnerie, guerre et paix*, in "Les Internationales et le problème de la guerre au XX siècle", Ecole française de Rome, 1987.

5.3 WWI: Patriotism and Pacifism Compared

During his fourth term, in September 1911, Giovanni Giolitti committed Italy to war in Libya against the Ottoman Empire while holding a certain sovereignty over Libyan territories. Freemasonry was living the apogee of its hold on Italian politics thanks to the success—mostly in Rome—of the progressive coalition known as the Blocchi Popolari[552] who is the patron.

The council of the G.O.I. stated it was essential the Grand Master send a handbill to all the lodges to share the following:

> "Italian Freemasonry wants the greatness of the country and therefore must await the events, rooting for the victory of arms; every brother must work to people keeping harmony and devotion; the Grand Orient will have to act for the unity of democratics, preventing the effort from being exploited by the conservatives and clericals."[553]

Thus showing steadiness, on July 31, 1914, the Grand Master Ettore Ferrari sends to the Venerable and Brethen of the G.O.I. a circular alleging peace was the abiding ideal of his Obedience by far, as a condition of any progress. Nevertheless, the fatality of events can compromise the integrity of the country. Therefore, to the interest of the latter and in the name of the institution he headed, Ferrari urged the country to act in agreement with the will of Italians.[554] The fatality of the events above refers to the outbreak of the WWI. During this time, the Italian Freemasonry goes against its peaceful beliefs once more, though, in order to accomplish a precise task.

Rather than an announcement on the same evening of July 31, the general assembly of the Grand Orient of Italy concluded to support the country going to war next to the Entente rather than joining the Triple Alliance—which it was part of—with the drafting of a very tough public statement against Austria. However, it would have been wise not to outface before the political parties to avoid the pontifical hostility aimed at

---

552 For further information, see Marco Cuzzi, *Dal Risorgimento al Mondo nuovo. La massoneria nella Prima guerra mondiale*, Mondadori education, Firenze, 2017, pp. 33–47.

553 Archivio Storico del Grande Oriente d'Italia (ASGOI), *Processi verbali del Comitato Esecutivo*, 253° session, September 28, 1911.

554 "Rivista Massonica", n°7, 1914, pp. 315–316.

both war and Freemasonry. In response, the text of the discussed notice was then changed.[555]

A few months later, most of the European states entered the war. Italy, as avowed, kept itself out from the intervention alongside its allies of the Triple Entente.

The masonry of the Grand Orient of Italy reacted with a note draft on September 6, 1914, and solemnly read during the feast—yet celebrated in a more discreet tone—of September 20, 1914.

Here, the G.O.I. expresses its regrettable displeasure the decision of Italy's allied empires to throw Europe into the war. Instead, it pulls Italy not to stand aside of this tragic conflict sentencing the future of Europe.

His argument mainly concerns homeland crucial threat: the completion of national unity. The G.O.I. even forecasts change not made effectual soon risks being always postponed. From its stand, the State has the right to adjust to the will of the Italians to resolve. Masonry, its part, guarantees the commitment to the nurturing of national principles.[556]

After this communiqué, the Grand Orient of Italy has truly accomplished the goal it claimed: becoming the main propelling force bulk a public opinion in favor of the intervention of Italy in the war next to the Entente.[557]

Concretely, beyond to the notorious prompted initiatives[558]—as the Central Committee of interventionist parties and the expedition, in Argonne, directed by Giuseppe (called Peppino) Garibaldi—masonry has sponsored and inspired a whole series of steps able to empower and ignite the audience and to convince it of entering into war as an imperative.[559] For instance, events organized to welcome French and Belgians sent to Italy to exhort the country to flank the Entente. The G.O.I. hopes this way to set freedom both

---

555 Gerardo Padulo, *Contributo alla storia della massoneria da Giolitti a Mussolini*, in "Annali dell'Istituto per gli studi storici", VIII, 1983–1984, Il Mulino, Bologna, 1984, pp. 269–270.

556 "Rivista Massonica", n. 7, 1914, pp. 319–322.

557 Giuseppe Leti, *Il Supremo Consiglio dei 33 per l'Italia e le sue colonie*, NY Publishers, Brooklyn, 1930, p. 145; Gino Bandini, *La massoneria per la guerra nazionale (1914–1915)*, *Discorso detto a Palazzo Giustiniani il XXIV maggio 1924*, Roma, edited by Roman Masonry, 1924, p. 5.

558 Marco Cuzzi, *Dal Risorgimento al Mondo nuovo*, op. cit., pp. 65–124.

559 Gino Bandini, *La massoneria per la guerra nazionale*, op. cit., pp. 82–98.

to the oppressed Brethen in the "seized" Italian territories and to Belgium, where the invaders "avevano brutalmente offeso la giustizia e l'umanità".[560]

Using conventions as war propaganda was at the time a new agent figured by French to promptly reach the heart of a neutralist nation like Italy. The French orators André Weiss and Charles Richet arrive in Rome on September 12, 1914, and hold a conference on civil right violation in Belgium and France.[561]

In these forums, the speakers avoid to show sharp positions not to prescribe their will to the audience. They only try to move them, to be outraged by the tragedy happening in the occupied countries.[562]

In Italy, as the lecturer and Belgian politician Georges Lorand states in his report, the lectures were promoted by interventionist parties, republicans, reformist socialists, and the democrats, but above all by the masonic lodges where these factions were ascendant.[563] Many are the evidences of this crucial role played by the Grand Orient of Italy, either kept in coeval papers or in retrospect documents both by masons, such as Giuseppe Leti and Gino Badini, and other beholders.[564]

War ended, in a letter sent on September 28, 1919, to the Grand Orient of Italy, the Grand Master of the Grand Orient of Belgium, Charles Magnette, credits Italian freemasonry a pivotal role in the politics that brought the nation on the battlefield next to the Allies.[565]

---

560 "They had brutally offended morals and mankind" [translator's note]. *Ivi*, p. 62.

561 Michel Dumoulin, *La propagande belge en Italie au début de la première guerre mondiale*, in "Bulletin de l'Institut historique belge de Rome", 1976–1977, n. XLVI–XVLII, pp. 343–344.

562 C. Saldari, *La propagande belge en Italie pendant la Ière guerre mondiale*, mémoire ULB, 1974–1975, pp. 32–33.

563 Archives du Ministère des Affaires Etrangères-Bruxelles (désormais A.M.A.E.B.), Film n°85, Dossier n°93, Propagande, Guerre 1914–1918 et après-guerre, Propagande en Italie, Dossier n°11, II, Rapport de M. Lorand adressé à M. Carton de Wiart, sur son activité en Italie, September 16, 1916.

Archives Générales du Royaume de Belgique (désormais A.G.R.), *Archives de la famille d'Alviella*, dossier 74, *Informations belges*, N°810 bis, 13/09/1918, *Un solennel hommage rendu à la mémoire du député belge Georges Lorand*, discours de Goblet d'Alviella à l'occasion des funérailles de G. Lorand.

564 On this topic, see the synthesis by Gerardo Padulo, *Contributo alla storia della massoneria*, op. cit., pp. 279–294.

565 "Rivista Massonica", 1919, n°8, p. 178. A copy of this missive can be found in CE-

The statements by nonmasons on the effectiveness of Italian ateliers in interventionism come mainly from the Prime Minister (1919–1920), further journalist and party man, Francesco Saverio Nitti who, in his memoirs, asserted masonry had representatives and agents in all main centers and sometimes even in the more peripheral ones.

As Nitti stated, simultaneously no political party could stage public meetings and rally as Masonry did. On these appointments, it also succeeded in inducing nation-concerned movements that, actually, did not consist.[566]

At last, the memoir by Prime Minister Antonio Salandra—before the war—can't be even ignored: none can refrain from recognizing the constant work done by freemasonry until the establishment, in November 1914, of a central committee of the interventionist parties.[567]

However, it should be remarked this position belongs only to the Grand Orient of Italy. The masonry of Piazza del Gesù—or the Great Lodge of Italy and the relative Supreme Council of the Ancient and Accepted Scottish Rite—are instead neutralists. The motif evoked in backing this view is the oath the Scottish rite masons make as loyal observers of the laws: they are given the duty to support the nation and not to object it. This unfolds the neutrality of this Obedience has been as the Italian State and, at Italy's entry into the war, its granting the cause of the Entente.[568]

Briefly, as with the war in Libya, at the outbreak of WWI, the Grand Orient of Italy keeps coherent with its patriotic principle declared in the first paper released in the constituent assembly of 1906. However, in the span Libya conflict–WWI, a fundamental shift happened. The Grand Orient favors Italy's intervention in the war before its homeland and maintains its line despite the neutrality proclaimed by the state. What concerns the Grand Orient now is the integrity of principles and land: Italy as a nation, and this goes beyond mere patriotism.

A symptom of nationalist feelings sprouted during the war. A phenomenon

---

DOM, *Archives de Moscou*, 114-2-201, doc.106.

566 Giampiero Carocci (edited), *Francesco Saverio Nitti, Scritti politici, vol. VI, Rivelazioni, meditazioni e ricordi*, Editori Laterza, Bari, 1963, p. 452.

567 Antonio Salandra, *La neutralità italiana (1914), Ricordi e pensieri*, Mondadori, Milano,1928, pp. 219–220 quoted by Fulvio Conti, *Massoneria e identità nazionale*, op. cit., 2003, pp. 242–243.

568 "Rassegna Massonica", year VIII, 1918, n°1, p. 16.

that strongly clashes with the international pacifist movement, which the Italian Freemasonry of the G.O.I. partakes and therefore confirms what has been claimed previously: the B.I.R.M. as a platform to enact world peace-keeping was a projection rather than a real commitment.

5.4 Nationalisms Compared

The G.O.I. therefore had cunning and ideological reasons to urge the Italian State to engage in the First World War and its drives about are widely reported in Italian and international history.

However, there have not been just bright comments on Italian Freemasonry commitment in favor of intervention. The neutralists—on one side—including the Catholics who tried to belittle the interventionism by branding it was backed worldwide by masonry since its hatred of Catholicism.[569] New political enemies lay on the other: nationalists formerly interventionists, but rooting the Triple Alliance. The detractors of the Grand Orient therefore defamed Freemasonry position by accusing it of willing Italy alongside the Entente because of its Francophile disposition and certain sentimentality.[570]

The traditionally opponent voice of the Catholics, in the second decade of the twentieth century, then joins that of a new political movement, the Italian nationalist association.

The Italian nationalist association as a movement was born in 1910 and, two years later, on the time of its congress held in Rome, it votes an anti-masonic agenda.[571] The first reason is a summary approach to the internationalism of Freemasonry overlooking the patriotism of the mentioned institution. The second reason is the harmful opinion on Italian Freemasonry backing the popular Blocs. The breaking point is reached when in 1913, the G.O.I. does not accept a public debate with the nationalists and when "Idea nazionale" [*National Thought*], weekly magazine by nationalists, begins an inquiry amid coeval party men and intellectuals about the thought, the action and the objectives of the masonic institution.[572]

---

569 Gino Bandini, *La massoneria*, op. cit., p. 93; C. Saldari, *La propagande*, op. cit., pp. 163–164.

570 Gino Bandini, *La massoneria*, op. cit., p. 59.

571 *La scissione al Congresso nazionalista*, in Archivio Centrale dello Stato (ormai ACS), MI, DGPS, DIV. Aa. Gg. Riservati "Atti sequestrati alla Massoneria" b. 1; "Rivista Massonica", n°4, 1914, pp. 164–166.

572 ASGOI, *Processo verbale del Comitato Esecutivo*, 65° session, July 23, 1913 "[...] L'opin-

This inquiry, commissioned and directed by Luigi Federzoni—who would become Home Secretary in 1924–1926—is displayed as a short questionnaire whose first inquiry is about the suitability in modern times of such a "secret society," the second refers to the humanitarian and cosmopolite though of Freemasonry and the third to its visible and hidden action in Italian community.[573]

The result of this inquest discloses the actuality of a diffuse adverse feeling toward Freemasonry. The institution defends itself by asserting the defamatory campaign is only prone to gather votes and creates a headline for the "profane" world, the "Idea democratica" [*Democratic Idea*], a masonic weekly journal for all.

With the rise of fascism, the nationalists—at the time of the march on Rome pretty wary of the new political corps[574]—join the new party between February and March 1923[575] fetching, as presented later, their anti-masonic propaganda apparatus.

5.5 Benito Mussolini and Masonry

The Italian dictatorship was the first to persecute Freemasonry in Western Europe in the *entre-deux-guerres*.[576]

In Italy, anyhow, official positions against masonry came more than a decade earlier, very popular in some political milieu, the same even Benito Mussolini began.

---

ione dominante è che non bisogna rispondere, ma bisogna invece farne partecipi i giornali amici affinché loro possano parlare di questo referendum ridicolizzandolo, in quanto in fondo non è altro che un'arma per la lotta elettorale". ["[...] *The prevailing opinion is that we must not respond, instead take part in the amicable newspapers so that they can talk about this referendum ridiculing it, since it's basically nothing but a weapon for the electoral struggle"]* [translator's note].

573 *Inchiesta sulla Massoneria*, forewords by Emilio Brodero, Arnaldo Forni Editore, 1979, (Milan Prints anastatic reproduction), p. 1.

574 Renzo De Felice, *Mussolini il fascista. L'organizzazione dello Stato fascista, 1925–1929*, Giulio Einaudi Editore, Torino, 1995, pp. 366–369.

575 Ivi, pp. 501–506.

576 Nevertheless, Masonry was first persecuted in Hungary in 1919 by Bela Kun, during the brief span of the Soviet republic, and the following year by the regent Miklós Horthy. In 1921, the affiliation to Freemasonry is also interdicted by the Communist International. Santi Fedele, *La massoneria italiana nell'esilio e nella clandestinità, 1927–1939*, Franco Angeli, Milano, 2006, p. 165 ; Grand Orient de France, Suprême Conseil pour la France et les possessions françaises, *Compte-rendu des travaux du Grand Orient*, du 1er octobre au décembre 13, 1920, pp. 67; 78–79; 93.

If we want to backtrack the impulse of the oppression by the dictator to come, we must point out Mussolini expressed a particular hostility toward the masonic institution already at the origins of his political line amid socialists.

A certain historiographical tradition would trace this enmity to his exile in Switzerland (1902–1904), when Mussolini would have been twice rejected for initiation to the Swiss lodges. Then his political activity was already considered subversive and therefore not tuned with the affiliation to Freemasonry. Once back in Italy, he would have made one more attempt, but to no avail.[577]

However, there is no file or proof in favor of this statement. After all, this story had already spread during Fascism. The Grand Master of the Grand Lodge of Italy, Vittorio Raoul Palermi, would have been actually the responsible to release and disseminate the dispatch, first in America through his followers.[578]

What's fair, however, is that Benito Mussolini as a party man made his debut as a socialist. His imprint was part of the legacy of his father Alessandro, a socialist activist, together with republicanism and anti-clericalism.[579]

Began at the end of 1909 with an appointment as cabinet officer in the socialist federation in Forlì (Romagna) and as head of the section newspaper, entitled "La lotta di classe" [*The class struggle*]. In this first phase, he is clearly inspired by the young magazine "La Voce" [*The Belief*]. Without being a disciple, he experiences the influence of Gaetano Salvemini, set in the polemic against socialist reformism and against the politics of Popular Blocks, represented by Masonry. To Mussolini, beyond secrecy, ateliers constitute a real danger for socialism, as an obstacle to its renewal. Freemasonry exerts "bourgeois" pressures within the socialist party.

By his words: "Il socialismo è movimento, la massoneria immobilità; il primo è un operaio, la seconda una borghese".[580] Even in the anti-clerical

---

577 Alberto Cesare Ambesi, *Storia della massoneria*, Giovanni de Vecchi Editore, Milano, 1971, pp. 204–205; "Rivista Massonica", N.3, marzo 1971, p. 148.

578 "La Fenice", n°. 8–9, marzo 2–9, 1924, p. 3.

579 Renzo De Felice, 1995, *Mussolini il rivoluzionario 1883–1920*, Giulio Einaudi Editore, Torino, pp. 3–8.

580 "Socialism is movement, masonry lull; the first is a handyman, the second a bourgeois" [translator's note].

struggle, Mussolini doesn't admit compromises with Freemasonry—forerunner of the anti-churchly strive within the Blocchi Popolari—claiming this radicalism within socialism, both as anti-clerical that of republican.

Hence, at the XIV congress of the socialist party in Ancona during 1914, Mussolini is author, with Giovanni Zibordi, of a charter condemning masonry against socialism. Approved.[581] Benito Mussolini joins the assembly as delegate of Milan section, already nationally renown within the party, but—above all—as head of the socialist daily paper "L' Avanti" [*Onward*].

In the end, the general assembly of the G.O.I. of May 1914 approved the ousting of Brethen intervened in Ancona and granting the Mussolini-Zibordi agenda.[582]

Despite the anti-masonic campaign by socialists and patriots plus the adverse outcome from the quest by "Idea Nazionale," after the general elections of November 1913, the entity of masons in the Italian Parliament largely grew.[583] The politician and intellectual Antonio Gramsci stated in his notebooks masonry under the great effort of Ettore Ferrari (1904–1917) was one of the most efficient forces in the anti-clerical labor, a real attempt to oppose a weir to consequences of clericalism.[584]

After the war, the time of the vote in Ancona seems very far, further the oncoming dictator and masonry seem to have found an agreement during the campaign rooting Italy's intervention in the WWI. Masonry, however, was quite far from the picture of Mussolini and the revolutionary socialists besides him. To those indeed the ultimate goal was the social revolution, not even people deliverance from the invaders, as for masonry.[585]

War ended, the Italian political scenario revised with the birth of the popular (Catholic) party and Fasci di combattimento [*Fighting Leagues*] in 1919. Popular Blocks steadily lost their weight.[586]

---

581 Ivi, p. 112–127.

582 Fulvio Conti, *Massoneria e identità*, op. cit., p. 223.

583 Ivi, p. 237.

584 Ferdinando Cordova, *Massoneria e politica*, op. cit., p. 296.

585 Gino Bandini, *La massoneria*, op. cit., pp. 107–108.

586 Fulvio Conti, *Massoneria e identità*, op. cit., p. 265.

5.6 Freemasonry and Fascism

The Great War has caused such a gap in contemporary history up to change balances appearing to be everlasting. As far as we are concerned, contradictory, relations between Mussolini and masonry seem to improve. Therefore, it's not surprising to see the Grand Orient of Italy and the Grand Lodge of Italy quite favorable to the original fascism.[587]

To consider Italian Freemasonry position about, just note a few passages of dispatches by the head of the Grand Orient, a few days before the march on Rome—the Sovereign Grand Commander Ettore Ferrari—and a brother of the Great National Lodge of Italy in March 1923.

The Grand Master of G.O.I., Domizio Torrigiani publishes—on October 19, 1922—a long missive where he endorses what already declared December 1921: it was not interdicted to masons to remain in the *Fascio*—rather, they had free will. The Grand Master fosters this by stating fascism is such a fresh phenomenon not to pursue an outside observer to front clashing tendencies. The purpose of Brethen hanging on the *Fascio* must be to preserve the best issue direction not to turn hostile to the principles professed by Freemasonry.

Torrigiani keeps on by noting Italian Freemasonry admits none if not swearing devotion to his country till the last strew of bleeding. This keeps "antinational" parties away from the masonic institution. According to Torrigiani, fascism then held within touching popular moods, the very substance of the nation. Fascism must therefore be taken in continuity to the masonic ideals of freedom, fraternity, and equality.[588]

Over the other Obedience, the Grand National Lodge of Italy, the scenario is far more mingled because of a deeper involvement with Mussolini of his Grand Master—and Sovereign Great Commander in the Supreme Council of *Piazza del Gesù*—Vittorio Raoul Palermi; the issue will be unfolded below. The General Assembly of *Piazza del Gesù*, held in Rome on March 21, 1923, sow a high masonic dignitary from Bologna praising the deed of the Great Master, with a special regard to his support to the advent of fascism. The hint is to the accusation against Palermi of masonic treason, after his speech of February 1923. According the prominent orator, Palermi instead

---

587 Renzo De Felice, *Mussolini il rivoluzionario,* op. cit., p. 287.
588 *Circolare 28,* ottobre 19, 1922, in "Rivista Massonica", 1922, n° 7–8, pp. 146–150.

helped to free Italy from the nightmare of demagogues and of subversive follies. More, he backed fascism to assert itself in the name of the homeland—sick and eager to resume its range—and finally urged the revolution of the Black Shirts and the march on Rome. For all these, Palermi is rather a source of pride for his masonic order.[589]

This situation stands roughly the same, depending on the specific cases of the two Obediences, up to the first shock given by the regime to Freemasonry with the statement of incompatibility to the double membership of the Fascist party and Freemasonry, voted by the Great Fascist Council on February 14, 1923. Anyway, the masonic attitude towards Fascism is a sensitive matter, to handle with care not to miscarry—as by Aldo Allessandro Mola—both an "excess of merit" and a certain "indignity" referred to the role played by Obediences in the rise of Mussolini.[590]

The Italian scholar recalls this way those who judge masonry as the spark of fascism at a certain political and ideological level. Mola simply argues there were masons in the Fascist ranks as in the other camps.

However:

> At no time the Grand Mastery did express briefly, if not abridge, the specter of the diverse ideal items, as well as ideological and political, expressed in the Family. Nor was his task.[591]

With regard to masons embracing the original fascism, if it's correct the two representatives of national Freemasonry Obediences gave their *placet* to Mussolini at the time of the march on Rome, we must detect between Domizio Torrigiani and Vittorio Raoul Palermi. Torrigiani, and therefore, the official position of the Grand Orient of Italy, does not differ from the majority of political corps and free-democratic audience urged same way and judging fascism mandatory to pull the country out of the quagmire.[592] Palermi instead helps Mussolini in order to turn to his favor the conflict with Palazzo Giustiniani. A material, not just political, support.

---

589 "Rassegna Massonica", 1923, n°1–2–3, p. 7.

590 Aldo Alessandro Mola, *Storia della massoneria,* op. cit. pp. 486–493.

591 *Ivi*, p. 492. The same issue in developed in Marco Novarino, *Grande Oriente d'Italia. Due secoli di presenza liberomuratoria,* Erasmo Edizioni, Roma, 2006, pp. 64–65.

592 Renzo De Felice, *Mussolini il fascista. La conquista del potere, 1921–1925*, Giulio Einaudi Editore, Torino, 1995, pp. 348–353 e Angelo Tasca, *Naissance du fascisme*, Editions Gallimard, Paris, 2003, pp. 289–296.

Just to disclose: Palermi meets Mussolini a few days before the march on Rome and later, holding to his international network, he proposes a trip to America to reassure the Anglo-Saxon confreres about the character of the new Italian government.[593]

Mussolini advantages of masonry backing—mainly that of *Piazza del Gesù*[594]—but a few months just after the rally, the Duce induces the fascist masons to choose between the two.

> [...] il Grande Consiglio fascista, presieduto dal Signor Mussolini, ha adottato l'ordine del giorno seguente : Considerando che gli ultimi eventi politici, l'attitudine e gli auspici della massoneria offrono motivi fondati di pensare che la massoneria perseguiti un programma e adotti metodi che sono in opposizione con quelli che ispirano tutta l'attività fascista, il Grande Consiglio fascista invita i fascisti che appartengono alla massoneria a scegliere tra il partito fascista e la massoneria perché, per i fascisti, esiste una sola disciplina: la disciplina fascista; una sola gerarchia: la gerarchia fascista; una sola obbedienza: l'obbedienza assoluta, devota e quotidiana del capo del fascismo.[595]

This agenda was voted unanimously by the Grand Council, with the exception of four abstentions, those of Giacomo Acerbo, Alessandro Dundan, Cesare Rossi, and Italo Balbo.[596] Thus, Freemasonry in the main shows shocked a little by this statement. A fair case is the handbill no. 25 of the

---

593   On the abetment of Vittorio Raoul Palermi and Mussolini, there are direct evidences by two fascists and masons of *Piazza del Gesù*, ovvero Michele Terzaghi, *Fascismo e Massoneria*, Milano, 1950, pp. 59–60 and Cesare Rossi, *Trentatré vicende mussoliniane*, Casa Editrice Ceschina, Milano, 1958, pp. 142–144.

594   Renzo De Felice, *Mussolini il fascista*, op. cit., pp. 348–353.

595   "[...] the Grand Fascist Council, presided over by Mr. Mussolini, adopted the following agenda: Considering the latest political events, the attitude and the hopes of Freemasonry offer reasons to mind masonry pursues a program and adopts methods in opposition to those inspiring all fascist activity, the Grand Fascist Council invites fascists who belong to Freemasonry to choose between the party and Freemasonry since, to comrades, there is only a discipline: the fascist one; only a hierarchy: the fascist one; an Obedience: the absolute, devoted and daily Obedience of the head of fascism." [translator's note]. "Bulletin de l'Association Maçonnique Internationale", n. 5, 1923, p. 100.

596   Italo Balbo was one of the quadrumviris of the "March on Rome." For more details, see Marie Rygier, *La Franc-Maçonnerie italienne devant la guerre e le fascisme*, 1930, pp. 180–183.

Supreme Council of Palazzo Giustiniani where, two days later, the Sovereign Grand Commander Ettore Ferrari, after heralding his order prop to fascism, writes serenely "Crediamo, e vogliamo augurare, che quel partito s'inganni",[597] considering the young party, for its rawness, is not yet capable of quiet meditations. The Council of the Order of the Grand Orient, by its Grand Master Domizio Torrigiani, at the gravely summoned meeting on February 18 to discuss this topic, rather disclosed its good proneness to assent to those Brethen tendering for *Fascio*. The Council is indeed sure these people will cultivate anyway the patriotic feeling cultured in the lodges.[598]

This risky scenario in a short time would have turned into a source of hurdles to masons. The first person to be hit was ramblingly the avowed pro-fascist Vittorio Raoul Palermi. The day following the fascist resolution, Palermi pretended the ruling concerned only Palazzo Giustiniani[599] and afterward made staunch declarations of loyalty to fascism.[600]

This behavior is scarcely welcomed by a part of the Brothers who, for some years now, have been wary of Palermi regarding a possible accord with G.O.I.[601] Consequently, during March 1923, these officially revolted against Palermi founding the "Movimento di redenzione massonica"[602] with a magazine called "La Fenice" [*Phoenix*]. The movement decides Palermi must resign as Grand Master and be freed from Freemasonry. Palermi didn't, but in December 1923, the separatist lodges merge with the G.O.I. considerably weakening the Great Lodge of Italy.[603]

---

597 "We trust and wish that party gets wrong." [translator's note]. ACS, MI, DGPS, DIV. AA. GG. RISERVATI "Atti sequestrati alla Massoneria", b. 2.

598 "Rivista Massonica", 1923, n° 2–3, pp. 36–39.

599 "La Fenice", giugno 30, 1924, p. 2.

600 Palermi processes the "new declaration of principles" and has it approved by its Supreme Council on December 17, 1922, to please the dictator. Then, Mussolini himself endorses it as establishes like a Masonic principle "we must first of all be Italians and then masons [...]". Since 1923, this rule has been introduced in printed rituals. U. Triaca, op. cit., p. 58. We found several models of oaths allowing access to the different degrees of obedience in Piazza del Gesù in ACS, MI, DGPS, DIV. AA. GG. Riservati, "Atti sequestrati alla Massoneria", bb. 2, where the next formula is always present: "It is forbidden for affiliates to do anti-religious propaganda, while they must consecrate all their acts, all their struggles to the homeland. Italy above all. First Italians, then masons".

601 "La Fenice", n°15, July 29, 1923, p. 4.

602 "Movement for masonic redention" [translator's note].

603 Fulvio Conti, *Massoneria e identità nazionale*, op. cit., pp. 307–308.

On the side of the Grand Orient, there was the will to avoid the genesis of a public opinion opposite to fascism, though the fracture amid this and Freemasonry already occurred in May 1923, and the first fascist attacks against the lodges' venues.[604] Ending the year, in Rome, the deputy Giovanni Amendola, a mason of the G.O.I.,[605] theosophist and future animator of the anti-fascist schism in the Italian parliament known as "Aventino," is onset by fascists.[606]

The murder of the Socialist deputy Giacomo Matteotti in June 1924[607] highlights the abyss of violence fascism has plunged the country: that's the outset of a gross crisis, thus known as "crisi Matteotti".

This plight was itemized by Aventino—which was the protest of congressmen opposing fascism on the assassination of Matteotti—followed by the birth of "antifascismo unitario",[608] to which the Grand Orient of Italy too adheres.[609] More, by acquainting the breakup in the Fascist party between "moderates and normalizers" and squads and die-hards. They pled Mussolini in their respective opposed directions. Despite significant difficulties, he seems to find a way to restore consensus within the party, heading rather toward resoluteness and, to face its opponents, promulgates the first restrictive measures on press. At the Grand Fascist Council held on July 22, 1924, he claims there are no longer any different inner tendencies: the motto is "to live dangerously." Here, Mussolini once again takes a personal position

---

604 Ivi, pp. 309–310.

605 Ivi, p. 438.

606 Anna Maria Isastia, *Massoneria e Fascismo*, op. cit., p. 52.

607 The Socialist MP Giacomo Matteotti was kidnapped in Rome on the afternoon of June 10, 1924 after leaving his home and was later assassinated. On August 16, morning, his body was found outside an abandoned farmhouse in the countryside which was 150 mt far from Via Flaminia in Rome. Even if there is no file proving Mussolini's direct charge for the murder, the clues carrying within the Fascist party have been pretty obvious from the beginning. For more information on this, see Mauro Canali, *Il delitto Matteotti*, Il Mulino, Bologna, 2004.

608 "Constituent antifascism" [translator's note]. The diverse anti-fascist tendencies of this moment are recognized as participating in a single struggle. Leonardo Rapone, *L'Italia antifascista*, in Giovanni Sabbatucci, Vittorio Vidotto (edited), *Storia d'Italia vol. IV, Guerre e fascismo 1914–1943*, Laterza, Roma-Bari, 1997, p. 502.

609 On the sentence of fascism for the murder of Matteotti by the Supreme Council of Palazzo Giustiniani, see circular n°47, June 17, 1924. ACS, MI, DGPS, DIV. AA. GG. Riservati "Atti sequestrati alla Massoneria", b. 2. It must however be specified Giacomo Matteotti was not a mason.

against masonry—definitively, after the crime Matteotti, behind the enemy lines—both G.O.I. and the Great Lodge of Italy; another agenda, by the nationalist Emilio Brodero, confirms the simultaneous belonging to Freemasonry and the fascism conflicting. The Council points out as a main task the struggle against Freemasonry with an absolute, mandatory, and eternal priority to the accomplishment of "nation" against any humanist and universal ideology.[610]

After the "case," the violence of fascist sections against their detractors became unruly for Mussolini himself. The masonic venues are the priority target throughout 1924.[611] From now on, every hap is a chance to Ettore Ferrari to condemn Fascism, as shown by official papers.[612] Domizio Torrigiani—ever closer to Aventino—responds harshly to the fascist violence in a letter of complaint addressed to the Prime Minister.[613]

With his speech of January 3, 1925, to the Chamber of Deputies, the Duce establishes his dictatorship. After the Executive proposes a bunch of draft laws to the Senate, including that of January 12 to narrow the labor of secret societies—masonry, subtly onset.[614]

This project was discussed in the Chamber in May.

It's the time of Antonio Gramsci's[615] notable speech on Freemasonry, in his only address to the Chamber. The farsighted Communist deputy states he assumed this ban on masonry—or rather, secret venues, since freemasonry is not fairly mentioned in the text—is just a step toward the total interdiction of fellowship, mostly labor unions. The first persecutions of the communists have begun yet. Gramsci also reports during his oration Mussolini declared Italian inner unity is finally accomplished at the expense of

---

610 Renzo De Felice, *Mussolini il fascista*, op. cit., pp. 660–670.

611 Ivi, pp. 673–767.

612 Supremo Consiglio di Palazzo Giustiniani, Circolare n. 49, Roma settembre 20, 1920; ACS, MI, DGPS, DIV. AA. GG. RR. "Atti sequestrati alla Massoneria" 1870–1925, b. 1, Supremo Consilio dei 33.·. d'Italia e sue colonie. Convegno dei presidenti degli aeropaghi della giurisdizione italiana, December 21–22, 1924.

613 CEDOM, Correspondenza Grande Oriente del Belgio-Italia, *Protesta del Gran Maestro della Massoneria contro le devastazioni fasciste delle logge*, Roma, September 18, 1924.

614 Renzo De Felice, *Mussolini il fascista*, op. cit., pp. 120–121.

615 See *sub verbo* Antonio Gramsci in Franco Andreucci, Tommaso Detti (edited), *Il movimento operaio italiano: dizionario biografico, 1853–1943*, Editori Riuniti, Roma, 1975.

Freemasonry. Though this organism, to Gramsci, then embodied in Italy the spirit and the very system of the capitalist bourgeois class. Thus, who fights Freemasonry oppose to liberalism and bourgeoisie tradition. Once, Vatican was against masonry: his class enemy. The deputy stressed fascism would replace Vatican on this field and its social effects.[616]

An analogy to reflect on; shortly after—in 1929—the Patti Lateranensi amid State and Church were signed.[617] In fact, the persecution of Freemasonry would have served Mussolini strategically to approach not just patriots, as seen, but even Vatican. To nationalists, it's meaningful the spokesperson for the draft law sanctioning masonry in January 1925 was that same Emilio Brodero who released the query on freemasons made more than a decade before. At the time of the first vote on incompatibility in 1923, this decision aimed, certainly to support the nationalists, but also to please the Vatican.[618] Father Giovanni Caprile states that, however, there is no file consisting the hypothesis the persecution of Freemasonry by the establishment would have the purpose of facilitating dealings with the Vatican.

The Grand Orient of Italy shield by convening a constituent assembly in September where Torrigiani is confirmed as Grand Master and, ongoing trend, is given extraordinary powers.[619] On September 20, the Manifesto of the Grand Orient strongly criticizes fascism, which does nothing but enhance the strength of attacks on masons. The climax was reached on the night between October 5 and 6, 1925, night known as "San Bartolomeo di Firenze" referring to the murder harshness some Florentine masons were subdued.[620] The seriousness of this matter compels Mussolini to abolish the "leagues"[621] by moving partakers into the voluntary militia. During the incidents in Florence, masons of this city were victims of violence of such

---

616 Antonio Gramsci, *Ultimo discorso alla camera, maggio 16, 1925*, R. Guerrini, Padova, 1951.

617 See the paper by Ubaldo Triaca in "Bulletin de l'Association Maçonnique Internationale", n. 29, 1929.

618 Renzo De Felice, *Mussolini il fascista*, op. cit., p. 505.

619 Fulvio Conti, *Massoneria e identità nazionale*, op. cit., p. 317.

620 The massacre of Florence begins with the homicide of the fascist militant Gambaccini partaking, with his comrades, in one of the expeditions of the "leagues" to obtain information on masons by an old Venerable. Ricciotti Garibaldi, *La Franc-Maçonnerie italienne et le Fascisme*, L'Eglantine, Bruxelles, 1926, pp. 23–26.

621 Aldo Alessandro Mola, *Storia della massoneria*, op. cit., pp. 567–569 ; Fulvio Conti, *Massoneria e identità nazionale*, op. cit., pp. 316–317.

ferocity the government thought convenient to censure headlines' reports to release an official version. For the first time since fascism arose, measures were taken against order bailees and turmoil-makers. Until then, the excesses kept unsanctioned as the authorities silenced the deal and/or aldermen pronouncing a sentence and risking, as happened, the reprisals of guilt's comrades.

5.7 The End of the Allowed Endurance of Freemasonry in Italy

Exactly one month after the massacre in Florence, Mussolini exploited another fact drawing attention on masonry.

On November 4, 1925, the socialist deputy Tito Zaniboni[622] tries to call a halt of Duce's life without achieving. The general of WWI, mason and favorable to early fascism, Luigi Capello, is forthwith jailed as a partner in crime.[623]

The failure of Zaniboni was ultimately the righteous chance for Mussolini to reawaken the picture of the political and masonic conspiracy; even if stays more as a myth than reality. The dictator thus did nothing but awakening a customary cliché anytime a certain public hostility toward Freemasonry is craved. The masonic conspiracy prosaism will later be typical of the other despotisms of the twentieth century. These have actually often resorted to the "anti" elements of the system: anti-masonism, anti-Judaism. Mussolini will recur on the occasion of Jewish persecution.

The plot would then have been hatched by Zaniboni with the help of anti-fascist politicians, masons and refugees to France;[624] instead, he acted alone

622 Tito Zaniboni was a member of the Unitary Socialist Party. A tenacious opponent of fascism since the beginning. After the murder of Matteotti and the failure of the opposition and the Aventine, he argued as mandatory to change strategy and to get, at the limit, to tyrannicide. Aldo Chiarle, *1927: Processo alla massoneria*, Bastogi Editrice Italiana, Foggia, 2002, p. 10.

623 Aldo Alessandro Mola, *Storia della massoneria*, op. cit., pp. 570–573. For a more detailed reading, see Laura Capello, *n°. 3264 (Generale Capello)*, Garzanti, Milano, 1946. Probably, Capello loaned money to Zaniboni, but was not part of the planning of the attack. Nevertheless, in April 1927, the special court sentenced him to 30 years imprisonment and was thus robbed by the army. He died in Rome on April 25, 1941. "Rivista Massonica Italiana", febbraio-marzo 1923 e ASGOI, Processo verbale del Comitato Esecutivo, March 3, 1923; Vittorio Gnocchini, *L'Italia dei Liberi Muratori. Piccole biografie di massoni famosi*, Erasmo Editore, Roma, 2005.

624 Renzo De Felice, *Mussolini il fascista*, op. cit., pp. 139–149; 503–511.

with the complicity of Carlo Quaglia, the catalyst of the whole affair.[625]

Once discovered the conspiracy, Mussolini receives inbound a wide public proof of sympathy, cause of the outrage happened. Outside the country, the general impression was the "plot" as result of a beautiful machination.

With no hesitation, the Duce dissolves the unitary socialist party—enlisting Zaniboni as Matteotti—and raises a real attack against the Grand Orient of Italy, whose headquarter, Palazzo Giustiniani, will be seized without ever being returned.[626] All the lodges are unavailable[627] and the bill—called "against the secret societies"—on the "Regolarizzazione dell'attività delle associazioni, enti ed istituti e dell'appartenenza ai medesimi del personale dipendente dallo Stato, dalle province, dai comuni e da istituti sottoposti per legge alla tutela dello Stato, delle province e dei comuni" (legge del 26 novembre 1925, n°. 2029, in Gazzetta Ufficiale, 28 novembre, n°. 277)[628]— is quickly discussed to the Chamber and Senate and made law on November 20, 1926. The promptness this law was approved after the failure of Zaniboni is not a case. What happened to Mussolini disparaged anti-fascists, provoking politically a real race for fascism. In other words, the failed attack had very favorable political–parliamentary consequences toward the Duce: all the plans by the government are approved.[629] Perhaps, it was not just a chance the attempt took place timely, just before the opening of the judicial debates on the Matteotti affair.

Thus, on November 22, by the extra powers attributed to him, the Grand Master Domizio Torrigiani notified a decree (n. 434) which he suspended

---

625 Michele Terzaghi, *Fascismo e massoneria*, op. cit., pp. 116–117.

626 In 1926, the State declares Palazzo Giustiniani's purchase by G.O.I. in 1901 as invalid. The motive was at that time the State didn't apply its preemptive right on an asset of historical interest. In 1926, it did, but paying the purchase price of 1901, far from the value of 25 years later, above all considering the monetary devaluation occurred with the war. Santi Fedele, *La Massoneria italiana*, op. cit., p. 16.

627 Aldo Chiarle, *1927: Processo alla massoneria*, op. cit., p. 11.

628 "Allocation of the activity by associations, institutions and their enlisting of civil servant and employees of bodies subject by law to the appointment of the State, the provinces and municipalities" [translator's note]. Cfr. law November 26, 1925, n. 2029, in *Gazzetta Ufficiale*, November 28, n. 277. Lelio Barbiera, Gaetano Contento, Paolo Giocoli Nacci, *La associazioni segrete. Libertà associativa e diritti dell'associato tra legge Rocco (1925) e legge sulla P2 (1982)*, Jovene Editore, Napoli, 1984.

See Ruffini, Corradini and Rocco speech in CEDOM, Correspondance G.O.B.-Italie ; Ricciotti Garibaldi, *La Franc-Maçonnerie italienne*, op. cit., pp. 26–34.

629 Renzo De Felice, *Mussolini il fascista*, op. cit., pp. 150–163.

all the masonic lodges and societies of any nature, related to the Obedience of the G.O.I. which—from this very moment—cease to exist in Italy. In the second item of the same document, Torrigiani resolves the Grand Orient of Italy embodies the heart of the masonic order and accepts the provisions of the law. To this, he established a "Comitato ordinatore" formed by Giuseppe Meoni, Deputy Grand Master Ettore Ferrari, Attorneys Ugo Lenzi and Solitine Ernari, Sir Costanzo Novero, and Grand Commander Cerasola. This committee has the task to provide support to troubled Brethen; care the interests of the Grand Orient and examine whether—when— would be restored masonry in Italy.[630] Even if Freemasonry willed to legitimate, fascism would not have allowed it since in the transition to the solo party system,[631] with the Royal Judgment of November 6, 1926, the "Testo unico delle leggi di pubblica sicurezza"[632] n. 1848 in *Gazzetta Ufficiale*, November 8, n. 257) even harder rules were ratified on the ordnance of institutions outside the party.

The violence waged against the masons since 1924 has pulled to plunge the liberal state. The ban on lodges instead represented the first legal persecution of an ideological group, running ahead those of the parties and the trade unions. Freemasonry was therefore the first victim of the dictatorship.

On November 23, 1925, the Grand Master of the Grand Lodge of Italy Giovanni Maria Metelli, lacking Palermi, decrees the same the denouement of all the ateliers in the Obedience. Palermi, on his return, tries to keep alive a certain nonoffensive form of Freemasonry against fascism, defeating in the early autumn of 1926.[633]

In April 1927, Torrigiani, in the meantime gone to France, was arrested after his homecoming due to the Zaniboni trial and the Grand mason Luigi Capello summoning to testify. He is recalled actually for being implied in the affair. The trial ended on April 23 with a sentence of 30 years of im-

---

630 "À S.E. Il Capo Della Polizia, Roma il 27 novembre 1934, l'Ispettore generale di PS" ACS, MI, DGPS, DIV. AA. GG. RR. "Atti sequestrati alla Massoneria" 1870–1925, bb. 1.

631 Renzo De Felice, *Mussolini il fascista*, op. cit., pp. 210–221.

632 "Consolidation law on public security" [translator's note].

633 Between the end of 1927 and the beginning of the following year, some fascists who were masons from Piazza del Gesù thought to give life to a national Freemasonry of Scottish Rite to support the Regime in the same precincts of the same rite. Italo Balbo would have been the leader, while the Grand Master would have been Arturo Reghini, since Palermi was no longer feasible. Santi Fedele, *La massoneria italiana*, op. cit., pp. 24–25.

prisonment for both Zaniboni and Capello. The Grand Master instead is sentenced to five years of confinement in Lipari, not because of the attempt against Mussolini he had not clearly taken part, yet for igniting unrest against the Regime and the State.[634] A warning was also inflicted on Meoni, Deputy Grand Master: exile and secrecy are the only option to surrender.[635]

This enactment is tenable with the believers of the masonic order indeed: loyalty and Obedience to the institutions and laws of the state.

Nevertheless, when Homeland becomes liberticidal, tyrannical, totalitarian—as with fascism—every mason can make his free will prevail in actions.[636]

What happened with the inward statement to dissolve lodges and Obediences was the righteous measure to shield the masons. The real difficulties came actually soon after freemasons found themselves at the crossroads between submission and exile abroad.

5.8 Conclusion

During the Fascist dictatorship, some courageous masons will continue to "work" in their homeland in hiding, while it was precisely abroad Italian Freemasonry in the Grand Orient of Italy tried to survive as "in exile" Obedience.

After WWI, the international masonic network to survive changes in tune, not in core. Then, the blatant failure of the *Bureau International des Relations Maçonniques* follows the breakdown of the *Association Maçonnique Internationale* (A.M.I.) to oppose the totalitarianism.

In the *entre-deux-guerres*, masonic internationalism has shown its further limit by not allowing the pursued lodges—above all, the Italians—to officially re-establish abroad, due to a regulatory issue concerning the criterion of territoriality defining an Obedience. Principle not to disregard to avoid a custom. The disappearance of national masonries due to persecutions is perforce followed by the end of the A.M.I.[637]

---

634 Santi Fedele, *La massoneria italiana*, op. cit., p. 14.

635 Aldo Alessandro Mola, *Il Grande Oriente d'Italia dell'esilio (1930–1930)*, Erasmo, Roma, 1983, p. 18.

636 Eugenio Bonvicini, *Massoneria moderna. Storia, ordinamenti, esoterimo, simbologia*, Bastogi Editrice Italiana, Foggia, 1994, p. 16.

637 For an in-depth analysis, see Nicoletta Casano, *Libres et persécutés. Francs-maçons et laïques italiens en exil pendant le fascisme*, Garnier, Paris, 2016.

Italian Freemasonry has therefore succumbed in the twofold hope of homeland rise from the post-war crisis—then from fascism—and of retreat in the arms of international brotherhood. Insanely, it was therefore the sole victim of its workhorses: that patriotism and cosmopolitism enduring 50 years of glory, from the Risorgimento to the late liberal era.

6. THE GRAND ORIENT
OF ITALY IN EXILE

Emanuela Locci

The 1925 is evoked in the Italian Masonic entourage as the black year: that year the executive under Benito Mussolini promulgated the law on "Allocation of the activity by associations, institutions and their enlisting of civil servant and employees of bodies subject by law to the appointment of the State, the provinces and municipalities",[638] known as "the rule against Masonry." Scanning carefully the text the name of Freemasonry is never mentioned, instead when the Chamber of Deputies discussed its articles, it appeared almost obvious it was conceived right against that institution.[639] Not a few addresses are heartfelt against masonry to prompt catholicity, seen as a founding feature of Italian community. One of the few dissenting opinions was that of Antonio Gramsci who, on May 16, struck with sharp words the Chamber not to allow the law to get voted.[640]

With the approval on November 1925, Mussolini government plot was indeed accomplished: deleting Masonry from political and civil scene. It had been several years the Institution had being targeted by determinedt and heady attacks,[641] since its maturing a openly contrary winding against fascism, thought often yielding, if not in an fair agreement with the policies pursued by Fasci.

The situation collapsed after the failed attack on Mussolini's life by the MP Tito Zaniboni and the alleged accomplice General Luigi Capello, both masons. On November 22, 1925, a few before the law that would have ban Masonry for roughly 20 years, the Grand Master of G.O.I. Domizio Torrigiani issued the decree to state as dissolved Obediences ateliers.[642] Afterwards,

---

638 *Parliamentary Acts*, session of Saturday May 16, 1925.

639 Anna Maria Isastia, *Massoneria e fascismo*, Libreria Chiari, Firenze, 2003, p. 13.

640 *Discorso di Gramsci alla Camera*, May 16, 1925, p. 48.

641 Anna Maria Isastia, *Massoneria e fascismo*, op. cit., p.

642 "Rivista Massonica". Year LVI. April 1926. NN. 1–2, pp. 18–19. It wasn't viable to detect the number, just the press release sent by G.O.I. to the Stefani agency, announcing the dissolution of Obedience.

a committee was set up within the Grand Orient of Italy in charge to aid Brethen —then an amount of 20,000—who had found themselves in strain. Since 1925, Italy wouldn't number any established masonic Obedience.[643]

Struggles are yet to come for Italian masons. GM Torrigiani is detained and sentenced to restriction in Lipari island for five years, since he is recognized guilty for "riots against the regime and the state." The same doom of many initiates to Freemasonry.

Between 1926 and 1928, the state of Italian Masons is pretty severe, many are arrested due to their belonging, thought it hasn't been officially active since 1925 and Brethen are forced to meet in a nonritual manner. Already since 1926, countless members moved to an exile abroad, along with representatives of disbanded political parties and/or editors whose newspapers had suffered the same measure. Several found themselves working side by side in LIDU, an anti-fascist organization born in France acting from abroad to get rid of fascist regime. France was—together with Switzerland—one of the countries of election of Italian masonic and dissident exile. French authorities stand Italian exiles devised politically to continue their struggle; this hospitality was effective also on the Masonic level, many thus found hospitality in both ateliers of Grand Orient of France and Grand Lodge of France. The situation in France became actually entangled when some members of G.O.I. laying in French territory stated the need of a Scottish rite chapter; for this purpose, Ettore Ferrari—then expiring—sent a letter to Giuseppe Leti, with a decree attached to re-institute the Supreme Council, capable then to allow again the rise of Grand Orient in due course. Ferrari departs a few months later,[644] marking with his death an era in the history of Italian Freemasonry and ushering a hard new one finding Freemasonry defeated by fascism while engaged in its erection outside Italy. An issue forthwith posing a legitimacy matter of a Grand Orient not drawing its lawfulness from a regularly convened Grand Lodge, or deriving powers from the GM in charge, who is its holder. Another flaw arose: could a Grand Orient of Italy be established in a territory—like France—where masonic organs already lived?

The territorial restriction topic came into play, whose nonobservance would have denied any recognition by the whole regular Masonic system.

---

643 Fulvio Conti, *Storia della massoneria italiana*, Il Mulino, Milano, 2003, p. 320.

644 Santi Fedele, *La massoneria italiana nell'esilio e nella clandestinità (1927–1939)*, FrancoAngeli, Milano, 2005, p. 43.

The condition, though peculiar in exile, was not a due reason to derogate. Despite the obstacles, in 1929, Giuseppe Leti resolved to rebuild G.O.I. in exile.

The decision was firm for several reasons: fascism was not expected to overturn in a short time and the awareness the long-lasting uncertainty would lead to the disintegration of the foreign lodges depended on the Institution, though not yet subdued to 1925 law outcomes, as this legislative provision could only be applied within national borders. Abroad ateliers lasted and got on acting autonomously, but underwent the merging pressures by other present Orients—Tunisia case is distinctive—where French and Italian had been for decades. A key role in backing the Grand Orient of Italy played the Argentine lodges, recognizing in Alessandro Tedeschi a champion of Italian Freemasonry. The lodges concerned were "Labor et Lux" of Thessaloniki, "Rienzi" in Rome, "Ettore Ferrari" of London, and "Giovanni Amendola" of Paris. The initiative to found an Italian Obedience in exile was taken by Leti, who on January 12, 1930, declared formally re-established it. The Grand Master was not appointed out of respect for Torrigiani, still in confinement. The office was also left vacant, covered only in 1926 by Meoni—no longer in restraint but still under strict surveillance. Eugenio Chiesa is named Second Deputy Grand Master. Obedience headquarters is set in the practitioner seat of Francesco Galasso, in London. The summits are getting ready to receive the mandatory acknowledgments for the life of Obedience itself, while the issue discloses: at the AMI congress, the Italian delegate, Arturo Labriola, is not admitted in September 1930. The reason for this denial is essentially in the unfeasibility for the international Masonic body to recognize as an heir of the former G.O.I. this new Obedience, entering into the conflict of legitimacy already outlined, in 1929. The situation is promptly reviewed in Grand Orient gathering of October 1930, where diverse attitudes from AMI shown off; suspending for a while the plead on international endorsement, the main task is to disseminate worldwide the update of G.O.I. rebirth in exile with a circular letter sent in 1931 to all the world's Obediences. Meanwhile, Labriola is appointed Second Deputy Grand Master, replacing Chiesa, departed a few months earlier. Same 1931, the first return to the statement missive came—mostly opposing, i.e. they didn't recognize the Obedience; the only exceptions were the Spanish, inviting Italian Brothers to their international forums, Uruguay, and some other Obediences from South and Central America—where Italians found the Cuban support—, while for Asia a positive response came from the Grand Lodge of Philippines.

At the end of 1931, after the resignation of Labriola, Alessandro Tedeschi was elected as Second Deputy Grand Master, but a few months after his election he was "promoted" to Grand Mastery, with the proper powers repletion.

In April 1932, Torrigiani, now elderly and ill, after serving his sentence of confinement, returns home, but under strict surveillance. He died a few later, on August 31, 1932.[645]

Meantime, Obedience is debated amid financial affairs, new charter devices—tied to the arrangement of the organs of the G.O.I.—and questions related to rituals, with a particular regard to the sharp observance of the Rite to grant the continuity of initiatory tradition. More, during the Tedeschi mastery, the thorny issue of international recognition, with Tedeschi and Leti on different minds, resolute the first in claiming the descent from G.O.I. by Palazzo Giustiniani, more attentive to the diplomacy the second, persuaded of the need of international endorsement to survive. At the end, Leti approach prevails and the first steps are toward resuming deals with the AMI. From the very beginning, delivering the record required isn't viable, such as the dissolution decree of 1925, which did not include the lodges abroad. The other big deal was the principle of territoriality. Even if the arrangements were carried out with commitment, it is almost fair they are doomed to failure; in February 1934, the official response comes. A denial.[646]

Set aside the international issues, delicate asset matters scourge the Obedience, and the diatribe sets around its patrimony. Quite substantial in 1925, due to unfavorable investments, it had progressively thinner. Meoni had assumed its care in 1926, and since then the situation had progressively worsened, the reason—as well as erroneous speculations—on the dozens of subsidies Meoni delivered to destitute Brethen because of Fascism. This controversies continued even after Meoni passing, who had died in such desperate conditions to clear any doubt about his good imprint.[647]

This miserable situation continued throughout the '30s, lodges did not pay any fee, though the deeper reason lied in the evidence members, often exiles, lived in serious hardship. In spite of this, the Obedience engagement didn't stop: Tedeschi was confirmed Grand Master for the years

---

645 Santi Fedele, *La massoneria italiana*, op. cit., p. 91.

646 Ivi, p. 107.

647 Ivi, p. 126.

1935–1941, years when the condemnation of fascism in Italy is steady and wide, in particular for crimes committed in Ethiopia. In 1936, Tedeschi denounced the infamy of the use of gas on the population, weapon called "the shame of our century."

Another compelling stance is that against the growing danger posed by Nazism for peace worldwide. For other nefarious historical events, G.O.I. is openly siding—at the outbreak of civil war in Spain, for instance, Italian Obedience condemns the coup leaders and declares its support for the legitimate republican government. In recent years, Freemasonry is indeed seriously endangered throughout Europe; not just in Italy is affected by the fascist attack, but the situation breeds elsewhere: Germany is affected by the Judeo-Masonic conspiracy bias, due to which the whole nine Grand Lodges in the wide German Masonic system are dissolved. In Portugal, Freemasonry was not officially forbidden, but the hatred was such as not to allow the regular activities of the Grand Lusitanian Orient. In Spain, the scenery was, if possible, even more dramatic after the military uprising of July 1936: Masonry was persecuted and systematically annihilated. From West to East, the frame keeps the same, even in Turkey, Masonry was not flourishing. In 1935, Atatürk government decreed the closure of all the bodies not under the governmental aegis. Freemasonry went into sleep until 1948, though the Supreme Council still operated, which even received state financial support. Notwithstanding, the idea of creating a supranational organization that served as a link amid all these persecutions was born among the exiled Italians. The accomplishment is hard, since the Masonic groups are scattered, as is the Italian community, and broadcasting is pretty arduous. Among thousands of tiring, Leti and Tedeschi succeeded in organizing, in June 1937, the Assembly of G.O.I.—the last organized in exile and extended to representatives of foreign Obediences. Really, the initiative did not have the deserved outcome, the attendance was of only 10 masons: a modest appointment. This upshot stresses the fragility of a small group of men who indeed tenaciously tried to keep alive the Masonic tradition throughout Europe. All is not lost, some ateliers located abroad, but under the auspices of G.O.I. persisted in their activities, in masonic traditions, and even in the struggle to fascism. While Italian Freemasonry efforts amid ado, winds of war blow off. In 1938, the Sudeten question was raises, setting a sudden matter of awareness to the Masons. What should have been their attitude in the case of an Italian call to arms? A refuse to war in an anti-fascist key is the response.

To the worrying scenery for the Italian communion is added the mournful news, June 1, 1939, of Giuseppe Leti passing. He, who had held the fortunes of Italian Freemasonry for over 10 years, was missing at a definitive moment. A few weeks later, the WWII broke out. The departure of Leti leaves all responsibility for the survival of G.O.I. on Tedeschi shoulders. Aware even his end was near, he calls new polls to give Obedience a new lease on life. Three days after convening the ballot the war began; given the unsteadiness, Tedeschi proposed David Augusto Albarin as Deputy Grand Master Added. Albarin was Worshipful of the "Cincinnato" lodge in Alexandria, Egypt. This location granted it safe at the time of 1925 law and again in that sad juncture.

Tedeschi dies on August 19, 1940, a few hours after his departure the German police showed up at his dwelling to arrest him. Notable was his widow behavior, who—in order to save any Masonic document from Nazi requisitions—decided to hide the files in her husband's grave. The archives were recovered 11 years later, even if not unscathed, and returned to G.O.I.

Albarin will labor till 1943 to provide the continuity of the Grand Orient of Italy in exile. After the end of WWII and the fall of fascism, the Institution is attempted to start again even to fulfill the huge sacrifices made not to succumb to the Fascist regime. To 1947 dates back the decree where Guido Lay, as new Grand Master, recognizes the struggle of the exiled masons within a wider recognition of the work done by the Italian Brethen who honored the Institution.

Thus closes the span of G.O.I. in exile, definitive players of this part of its history being Giuseppe Leti and Alessandro Tedeschi, who—by their own drive—managed G.O.I. not to be forever wrecked.

7. Italian Communities and Freemasonry Abroad

Emanuela Locci

7.1 Intro

Italian Masonry, notably the one represented by Grand Orient of Italy (G.O.I.) often overcame national boundaries to reach far lands. Thus, many are the ateliers founded by the appointment of G.O.I. outside Italy—from Africa to Asia and Americas. Here, we'll focus on Italian lodges established in Turkey, Egypt, Tunisia, Libya, and Eritrea. The time lapse goes from 1861 to 1955.

The lot considered has been wholly part of Italian communities based in diverse territories. Many are the reasons of Italian presence abroad, from economic and social to colonization purposes. The birth and development of masonic groups bond to nowadays-avowed Palazzo Giustiniani is tied to the growing migration in the Mediterranean shores and beyond.

The first case study is related to G.O.I.-bound cells in the Ottoman Empire by then.

In this dominion, since Middle age, many were the Italian groups. Traders were deeply involved in seashore traffics in Empire cities such as Constantinople, Salonika, and Smyrna. Their nature was assorted: swashbuckling, traders, sailors, and soldiers for hire, political refugees, and friars. Italian migration has always been lively and people were growing in number and influence.

In 1871, Ottoman Empire-based Italians were roughly 10.000 units.[648]

7.2 The Early Italian Ateliers in the Empire, L'Unione d'Oriente, and Italia

When G.O.I. defined the lodge institution, the Empire already numbered other Freemasons practices from France and Britain.

---

648 Marie Carmen Smyrnelis, *Une Ville Ottomane Plurielle, Smyrne aux XVIII et XIX siècle*, Isis Press, Istanbul, 2006, p. 80.

The first acknowledged Italian atelier is "L'Unione d'Oriente" [*Orient Union*], affiliated to Turin G.O.I.[649] No more items on: it's not listed in any official minute on 1861–1971 spans.[650] The second in order of birth, named "Italia," was built in Constantinople in 1862; recently, the record found allowed to drawn the identity of founders and members. Certified facts are scarce, but among the Brethen is counted for sure Marquise Camillo Caracciolo di Bella, Italian Realm ambassador to the High Port.

The effective Italia Brethen' list in 1864 shed some light on its story. This paper allows us to grant the identity and amount of active masons. Inspecting the items comes out the members were not just Italians: Hebrews, Greeks, and Armenians. In 1864, there weren't any Ottomans: their partaking is late. The comp shows immediately the adherence to the universality assumption in masonry and its openness to diversity of confession and ethnicity thus meeting in this institution.

Two years since its foundation, according to the document abovementioned, it consisted of 70 active members plus 9 to be.

Some names recur in "Italia Risorta" [*Resurged Italy*] records, a lodge risen from the ashes of Italia in 1869, two years after its quitting for inside conflicts frustrating the routine.

Among the charity activities by Italia, the key one was establishing a primary school addressing migrant children and concerned customers without nationality bias. The school was aimed to keep the Italian history, customs and idiom alive becoming one of the most outstanding education institute with an exquisite secular profile as willed by founders and Provost, freemasonry member Trinca. The atelier featured also by other philanthropic initiatives, such as the sanitary assistance during the cholera epidemic in 1866, rewarded by Ottoman government. Commendation came from Italy too: Grand Master Ludovico Frapolli appointed Worshipful Antonio Veneziani deputy of G.O.I. to European Turkey.[651]

---

649 October 8, 1859, *Ausonia* lodge was established in Turin. A few months before, *Grande Oriente Italiano*—better known as *Grande Oriente di Torino*—arouse with the aim to start a Great National Lodge. Cfr. P. Buscaglioni, *La Loggia Ausonia e il primo Grande Oriente Italiano,* Edizioni Brenner, Cosenza, 2001.

650 ASGLT, *Logge italiane in Turchia* (edited by Archivio Storico Grande Oriente d'italia, here from ASGOI), Roma, July 2005, p. 1.

651 ASGLT, op. cit., p. 2.

In 1865, Italia was embedded in the official list of G.O.I. appointed lodges, joined the Constituent Assembly of Genoa but couldn't be represented by any member.

Despite the gains, in 1867, Italia disrupted the activity, many Brethen questioning on the easiness in approving undignified members. A concurrent issue in ceasing was finances, due to the school high cost of keeping.[652]

Anyway, same year, Francesco Abbagnara represented the atelier during the Constituent and Executive Assembly in Naples. The other Italian ateliers partaking were "Stella Jonia" [*Ionian Star*] from Smyrna Orient, founded in 1864, "Anacleto Cricca" from Magnesia—born in 1867 by the founder of the same name (1824–?), and "Macedonia" from Salonika Orient, established in 1864 by Han Barouh Coen, a Hebrew hailing from Italy.[653]

Despite the ceasing of Italia, Italian freemasonry in Istanbul was still alive and a new lodge, named "Italia Risorta," arouses—whose title reminding the prior institution and recalling the aspiration of Risorgimento.

7.2.1 Italia Risorta

"Italia Risorta" was founded on March 10, 1869, as the very first under G.O.I. purview, based in Rome. At the end of 1869 Worshipful was Antonio Geraci and registrar Enrico Ottoni.[654]

In 1871, the mason, deputy, and then senator of Italian Realm, Mauro Macchi, was the spokesman in the Constituent Assembly in Florence at the end of May, while Giuseppe Mazzoni (1808–1880) did it the year after. In 1875, the lodge chooses Antonio Barbagallo as Worshipful, Stefano Tundra first proctor, Vincenzo Della Mea second proctor, Gennaro Marchesi orator, and Luigi Cattolinich as deputy. All distinguished members in the Italian community.

On March 20, 1875, the lodge appointed Giuseppe Garibaldi Worshipful for life since its members—as well as Italy based masons—had a profound esteem for Garibaldi and his acts as for Giuseppe Mazzini, so that Italian

---

652 Thierry Zarcone, *Mystiques, Philosophes et Franc- Maçons en Islam*, I.F.E.A., Maisonneuve, Paris, 1993, p. 213.

653 Sam Levy, *Salonique à la Fin du XIXe Siècle*, ISIS Press, Istanbul, 2000, p. 74.

654 ASGLT, op. cit., p. 3.

Brethen living in Istanbul supported the campaign by "Trionfo Ligure" [*Ligurian Triumph*] in Genoa to erect a monument to Mazzini.[655]

The year after, by order n. 10—effective in August 18—, G.O.I. suspended its works; notwithstanding, less than two years after it raised again under the direction of Antonio Geraci, leading up to 1889 when awarded for his masonic engagement with a honor gold medal by Orient appointed lodges of Constantinople.[656] In 1887, vice-Admiral Woods Paşa (Henry Felix Woods), Worshipful of Bulwer lodge, promoted Geraci British mason for his qualities.[657]

In the span 1890–1891, the atelier was mastered by Attorney Giorgio Furlani and in the forthcoming four years by Worshipful Raffaele Ricci. During his mastery activities held over,[658] but soon after Brethen Geraci, Guerraccino, Catalani, Reiser, Atlas and Luzzena were solicited to start it up again thus re-activating the lodge the following year.[659] From 1909 to 1911, Worshipful was dean Raffaele Ricci and in 1913, the lodge suspended its feat once again, resuming in 1919, with Ricci still mastering. In 1921, a new Worshipful was elected—Giulio de Medina—while in the ensuing round, Raffaele Ricci succeeded anew.

In 1925, Worshipful was Alberto Fano.

In the masonic scenario of Istanbul, the Brethen often worked in diverse cells even not in Italian Obedience and in leading roles. It's the case of Veneziani, Worshipful in "Italia" and co-founder of "L'Unione d'Oriente" were he was deputy. Giorgio Guarracino in 1868 was Worshipful in the Azize lodge and first proctor in "L'Unione d'Oriente."

Geraci, Worshipful in "Italia Risorta," was an active member in "Bulwer" lodge—British Obedience—while Woods Paşa, Worshipful in Bulwer, was also Brother in "Italia Risorta." This mutual insight eased the dissemination

---

655 *Trionfo Ligure no. 90* in Genoa has been founded in 1856 and yet lies under *Grande Oriente d'Italia*.

656 ASGLT, op. cit., p. 3.

657 Angelo Iacovella, *La massoneria in Turchia: la loggia Italia Risorta di Costantinopoli*, in "Studi emigrazione", no. 123, 1996, p. 402.

658 ASGOI, *Decreto Grande Oriente d'Italia n. 58 del 1895*, Roma.

659 ASGLT, op. cit., p. 3.

of revolutionary ideas from Risorgimento, producing effects on formerly initiated Ottomans.[660]

"Italia Risorta," despite some admin criticism due mainly to the shifting of G.O.I., cast itself in the masonic entourage of the Ottoman capital. It lavished in many charitable acts appointed by the sultanate and worked continuously for all the reign of Abdülhamid II, differently from French lodges, become sleeping. Officially didn't act for revolutionary purposes and this shielded them from interdiction hitting many other cells in the capital. No clue on direct involvement in the complot by Young Ottomans first and Young Turkish then, but easily balls and feasts weren't just for charity. During these meetings, masonic propaganda took place and arguably the Italian freemasonry in Salonika was the moonlight harbinger of Young Turkish movement.[661]

The lodge had a modest insight in Ottoman society according to the number of members.

Generally speaking, the membership had a constant ranking and initiatives were narrowed but not ceased only before 1908 Revolution, Libyan war, and WWI. The activities stopped definitively in 1923, when Atatürk republic began.[662]

7.2.2 *La Fenice, La Sincerità, and La Speranza and Bisanzio Risorta*

Other ateliers relying upon G.O.I. served in Istanbul, albeit not fundamental as "Italia Risorta."

"La Speranza" [*Hope*] was established in August 25, 1867, following the Scottish Rite Ancient and Accepted. After just two years, modestly running indeed, the outstanding attendants stated to merge with Brethen from "La Fenice" and "La Speranza" to build up "Azize."

"La Fenice" [*Phoenix*] was founded on March 15, 1868;[663] scarce are the documentary sources on, we can resume it didn't overcome the first year. The gathered masons soon decided to close the temple and join the Brethen from "La Sincerità" [*Honesty*] and "La Speranza," forming

---

660 Thierry Zarcone, op. cit., p. 214.

661 *Ibidem*, p. 215.

662 Angelo Iacovella, op. cit., p. 404.

663 ASGOI, *establishment Seal n. 2194.*

"Azize," whose infos are narrowed to the start—1869—and the name of the first Worshipful, Giorgio Guerracino, already known in other masonic entities.

"La Sincerità" was founded August 5, 1868, under the aegis of G.O.I.[664] We should wait the beginning of twentieth century to face the birth in Constantinople of a new Italian lodge; "Bisanzio Risorta" [*Resurged Byzantium*] was thus founded in 1908. Its first Worshipful, and institutor was Nicola Forte, teacher in the head male school. From 1909 to 1910, Edoardo Denari—engineer and wealthy businessman—was Worshipful. During his mastery, the lodge was engaged in the charter of the Great Ottoman Orient. In 1911, due to the conflict between Italy and Ottoman Empire to possess Libya, the lodge diminished its significance up to resolve in closing in 1913.[665] After 10 years, Worshipful Jouhami resumes it again: no more info we possess about its routine.[666]

7.3 Italian Freemasonry in the Region

Coming next Istanbul as the political and cultural center of the Empire, Smyrna (now Izmir) and Salonika were the main cities for business and heritage. Masonry had a remarkable outcome there—Salonika mainly—and leaded on Empire issues.[667] In just Smyrna, there were 13 ateliers founded during 1860–1870: 7 British, 5 Italian, 1 French, and 1 Greek.

The Italian settlement in Smyrna dates back to far times and the first documents come from 1700s, when Venetians and folks coming from Ionian isles were roughly 2,000 units.[668]

7.3.1 Orhaniye

Italian masonry came to Smyrna in the second half of 1800s; the first lodge—"Orhaniye"—was founded on March 28, 1868, by the appointment of Italian Grand Orient ratified by a masterly seal numbered 1993 and recognized by Scottish Rite Supreme Council on August 5 1898.

---

664 *Ibidem.*

665 ASGOI, *Decreto del Grande Oriente d'Italia n. 139*, November 24, 1913, Roma.

666 ASGLT, op. cit., p. 5.

667 Thierry Zarcone, op. cit., p. 274.

668 Marie Carmen Smyrnelis, op. cit., p. 75.

Its uniqueness consists in only Turkish idiom rituals;[669] more, unusually than ever, the Worshipful was often a Muslim.

"Orhaniye" gave the setting maul to Enverî Efendi, head of Health Department in Smyrna, who represented the lodge in the Constituent Assembly taking place in Rome during 1874.[670]

All its chief mates in 1870 were Muslims; it happened only in 1909 with the establishment of the Great Ottoman Orient.

In 1872, Worshipful was Giorgio Tamajo,[671] representing the Brethen in Florence Constituent Assembly same year on May. Afterward, it mysteriously ceased but re-opened the next year. "Orhaniye" shared the same domicile with other lodges: 3 Italian plus other 3 British, while in 1878 had legal residence to Doctor Anacleto Cricca's manor.[672]

7.3.2 Armenak and Stella Jonia

"Armenak" was a Scottish Rite atelier depending by G.O.I. and founded on February 18, 1870, by seal no. 3408. In 1873, Acop Sivagian was Worshipful and in 1977 joined Rome Constituent albeit sent no representative there. This lodge moved its legal residence to Doctor Anacleto Cricca's house, as the one abovementioned.

"Stella Jonia" was born in 1864 and in its minute Anacleto Cricca is logged; born in Bologna in 1824, son of Pietro, medical doctor, initiated in 1849 under patent no. 01447.[673]

Cricca played as delegate in the structure and was endorsed with the 33rd degree of Ancient and Accepted Scottish Rite.

Captain Anastasio Giulì, adhering to Palermo Supreme Council Obedience under patent no. 106,[674] founded "La Fenice" on February 1868.

---

669 ASGLT, Koray Özalp, Bület Çetiner, *Türk Masonluk Tarihi, vol III,* Istanbul, 1974, p. 17.

670 ASGLT, 2005, p. 9.

671 In 1871, Giorgio Tamajo was elected Sovereign Knight Commander by the High Council of Scottish Rite Ancient and Accepted.

672 ASGLT, 2005, p. 10.

673 ASGOI, *Registri Matricolari loggia Stella Jonia,* p. 3.

674 ASGLT, 2005, p 7.

Worshipful was Costantino Tritafillis, soon replaced after resignation by Temistocle Iatros. In 1868, the lodge passed to G.O.I. Obedience. Establishment seal no. 2304 stated its recognition and membership.

In 1872, Ludovico Frapolli became Worshipful and following year again Iatros.

In 1884, "La Fenice" was in G.O.I. yearbook as first range lodge, but its activity suspended due to financial issues related to Great Orient grants, then formally "dismantled" with act no.108bis. [675]

In 1911, during the political crisis between Italy and Ottoman Empire cause of the control over Libya, "I Mille" [*The Thousands*] came into be obeying to G.O.I. Followed The Scottish Rite and its first Worshipful—and founder—was Attorney Samuele Ventura. By reason of Italian–Turkish war, the lodge became effective only by the election of Enea Brunetti in 1913, with residence to the Italian Consulate since 1922 cause his being a staffer. After this year, no more record are available on.

7.4 Italian Freemasonry in Salonika, Macedonia Risorta, and Labor et Lux

A rich and gross Italian colony was in Salonika, the interest in creating a lodge there is dated back to the 70s of the nineteenth century.[676] In 1864, Macedonia was build up as a cell of Italia starter lodge in Istanbul. According to the 1867 Great Orient Dispatch,[677] "Macedonia" acted exemplary, but at the end of 1800s, events lacked so much so in September 1900 Ettore Ferrari coming for a visit hailed Brethen to liven up.

"Macedonia Risorta" was born by the ashes of Macedonia in 1902 under G.O.I. In 1904, Emanuele Carasso was elected as Worshipful keeping the office up to 1909 when he moved to Istanbul to take part to the Ottoman Parliament as member after 1908 revolution. This atelier gathered men aimed to change the face of the Ottoman Empire coming from diverse backgrounds and nationality. Among its members, there were İsmail Hakki Cambulat, Chief of Staff Captain, Zade Refik Bey, Secretary of Justice, Mehmet Talat, Midhat Sükrü, and Rahmi Ben Riza.

---

675 ASGLT, 2005, p. 8.

676 Orhan Koloğlu, *L'influsso della massoneria italiana sulla rivoluzione dei Giovani Turchi*, Quaderni della Casa Romena, I.C.R., Bucarest, 2006, p. 132.

677 ASGOI, *Le logge italiane in Oriente*, in *Bollettino del Grande Oriente* 1867, p. 185.

Between 1902 and 1908, 188 members joined, whose 23 where Officials from the II and III Corps of the Imperial Army. The massive military presence wreaked havoc thus some affiliates left to adhere to "Veritas" French lodge.

Besides "Macedonia Risorta," in the early 1800s, "Labor et Lux" was founded by masons formerly coming from it. In this new institution, the effective rite was the Scottish Ancient and Accepted. Into the minutes of 1907 and 1909, we read the lodge was active and leaded by Worshipful Giacomo Carasso, coming from "Macedonia Risorta" himself.

7.5 The Role Played by Italian Masonry in 1908 Revolution

Ettore Ferrari, G.O.I. Grand Master, openly supported the Turkish revolution of 1908. The raise of Abdülhamid II caused a stop in lodges affairs, but Italian freemasonry couldn't back this condition any longer. The status hindered masons to support Italian community, often in miserable conditions due to frequent epidemics or fires commonly occurring in the old district of Constantinople.

To face this impasse and wake the works up again the Grand Master Ernesto Nathan send sculptor Ettore Ferrari—then Deputy Grand Master—as person in charge in the Ottoman Empire.[678] The journey took place during September 1900 and urged inactive Freemasons of Constantinople, Salonika, Smyrna. The outcomes weren't late: the old "Macedonia" lodge in Salonika began again as Macedonia Risorta based in Rue Boulma Giani. Italian masonry on behalf of Emanuele Carasso heard the alarm call by Young Turkish. Revolutionaries gathered in a location aside to "Macedonia Risorta," taking advantage of the imperial discharge policy for abroad people and their asset. Other Italian idiom lodges welcomed demanding Young Turkish, the movement empowered and some activists became masons.

The Head of Young Turkish accepted new activists with a ceremony taken partly by masonic ritual: the candidate faced a deputation of movement executive Committee and examined on his political beliefs and attitudes. If the outcome was positive, he was sworn upright with the right hand upon a gun on an altar, stating: "I swear to tear my blood till the last drop for freedom,

---

678 ASGLT, *Selanik'te Kurulan Localar*, in *Mimar Sinan*, Istanbul, 2003, p. 21.

to give perfect accomplishment to the orders by agitation Committee and follow the purpose it sets".[679]

The purpose of this revolutionary wave was to set back the Constitution, suspended by the Sultan soon after became in law. Abdülhamid, thanks to his thick network of spies—due to avoid a violent death or to be over-threw—knew many military officers moved to liberal ideals and revolutionary principles. Salonika was almost besieged by the Empire troops, two generals were sent to dismantle the movement and put "Macedonia Risorta" under strict surveillance. On March 1908, police moved into the atelier location to catch the minute and other compromising documents: unluckily for them Worshipful Emanuele Carasso had been promptly informed and took away every detrimental paper.[680]

A second sortie by police was unfruitful again: nighttime during a plenary meeting, a member informed the assembly about plain-clothes policemen waiting outside the Brethen. Inside, key members of the Committee, as Rahmi bin Riza, Diamid and Talat were attending. In the end, the activists mingled with the crowd of Freemasons; in the leaving, mess agents were not able to pick any up.

Emanuele Carasso in 1908 went in Istanbul with Talat and same here Ottoman police tailed them night and day. Authorities thought they were about to pull some outstanding personalities to join the revolution. Carasso was blocked and questioned, but didn't betray his fellows. A probe, based on the clergymen Carasso spoke to, was open with no success.[681] This continuous hazard urged the Brethen to shot the time to batter the sultan despotism down. A share of them was involved in propaganda, while the officers from the II and III Corps of the Imperial Army arranged the guard. A third part straightly pressed the Sultan and Ministers to restore the Constitution. Revolution triumphed peacefully thanks to this plan. When the State adopted again the Constitution, Talat was elected House vice-President, Rahmi and Emanuele Carasso were congressmen in Salonika district. On December 31, 1908, "Macedonia Risorta" counted 177 members.

---

679 Thierry Zarcone, op. cit., p. 245.

680 Angelo Iacovella, *Gönye ve Hilal*, Tarih Vakfı, Istanbul, 2005, p. 41.

681 Evram Galante, *Histoire des juifs de Turquie*, Isis Press, Istanbul, 1985, vol. 8, p. 56.

7.6 The Italian Settlement and the Grand Orient of Italy in Egypt

The presence in Egypt of Italian traders, coming from seaside towns such as Naples, Amalfi, Genoa, Pisa, and Ancona, dates back at least to the Middle Ages, even if they were not proper communities, since their stay was seasonal. We will have to await the rising of Mehmet Ali (1769–1849) to record a noticeable increase in the Italian presence and assist in the strengthening of the colony, thanks to the sharp regeneration interesting Egypt during his term. He broadly encouraged the European emigration, French and Italian in particular, precisely to modernize the country, as European staff was pretty experienced and employing it mainly in the army and in the public running.

This large community resided almost exclusively in the main urban centers, Alexandria, Cairo, and Port Said.

The invasion by British troops in 1882 and the joint political supremacy of England did not downsized Italians in Egypt, which had been representing the natural outlet of our immigration in the Mediterranean, second only after Tunisia, which has always been the elected country of Italian resettlement, exerting an attraction that no other Mediterranean country has managed to match. Italian Freemasonry expands in the Mediterranean outskirts even before the Unification of Italy; during the first Constituent Assembly of G.O.I., held in Turin in 1861, Egyptian delegates from "Isis," "Pompeja," and "Eliopolis" entered. Two years later, deputies of two other lodges, "Caio Gracco" of Alexandria and "Alleanza dei Popoli" [*Alliance of Peoples*] from Cairo,[682] were added to the Masonic assembly of Florence. During span 1868–1870, the Italian Consul outlines the situation of his community, highlighting the weight of Freemasonry, thought as an organization of subversives and evildoers, and emphasizing the links between it and homeland active rebels. The presence of Italian masonry in Egypt thus was always substantial, but a noticeable decrease happens after WWI and the almost complete fade after 1925.[683]

---

682 Fulvio Conti, *Entre orient et occident. Les loges maçonnique du Grande oriente d'Italie en Méditerranée entre les XIX et XX siècle*, in Marta Petricioli (edited), *L'Europe méditerranéenne*, n. 8, Bruxelles, 2008, p. 113.

683 Jacob M. Landau, *Prolegomena to a Study of Secret Societies in Modern Egypt*, in "Middle Eastern Studies", vol. 1, n. 2, 1965, p. 163.

Between the mid-nineteenth century and WWI, 32 ateliers arose, including 19 in Alexandria, 9 in Cairo, and 4 in other minor locations. In the luster from 1920 to 1925, the lodges became 26, including 12 in Alexandria, 8 in Cairo, and 6 in close to the Suez Canal.

During the reign of Fuad I (1922–1936), many worked under the protection of the King, mason himself,[684] but with the advent of fascism, the Italian Consulate was commanded by Mussolini to close the eight Italian ateliers of Alexandria in Egypt, gathering together roughly 800 members. On November 7, 1937, "Giordano Bruno," "Cincinnato I," and "Cincinnato II" held a plenary meeting "in the shadow of Egyptian independence, following the end of the Capitulations", as written in the official invitation. There were about 300 masons of diverse nationalities and, in the days following, leaders of the Italian lodges met with to attempt a re-asset.[685]

7.6.1 Italian Lodges

Amid the early ateliers, we're aware in Egyptian territory, there are "Caio Gracco," "Fratelli Repetti" [*Repetti Brothers*], and "Alleanza dei Popoli" [*People Alliance*], already working just after the Unification of Italy.[686] There are scarce documentary records, but as far as the first is concerned, it is determined in1862–1863 Worshipful Master was Arturo Piazza.[687] In 1863, the "Alliance of Peoples" in Cairo succeeded, with its sole wherewithal, in funding and managing a small hospital garrison and its members also planned the opening of an international college. His Worshipful E. Rossi, personal doctor of the Prince of Egypt, was awarded the title of Bey. In a letter of April 1863, he outlined masonry scenery in Egypt, especially the proselytizing action Italian Freemasons were carrying out in the local society.

The opening to the outside of the lodges, toward the community that housed them, constituted a peculiar trait of Italian Freemasonry here. At first lodges kept only Italian citizens, but soon they opened the temple to the local population. It was part of its cosmopolitan hint—much felt at

---

684 *Appunti sulla massoneria italiana in Egitto*, in "Rivista Massonica", n. 8, 1978, p. 510.

685 Virginia Vacca, *Curiosa conseguenza dell'abolizione delle Capitolazioni: ricostituzione di logge massoniche italiane*, in "Oriente Moderno", XVII, n. 11, November 1937, pp. 584–585.

686 ASGOI, *Minute, Grande Oriente d'Italia n. 349, July 5, 1862.*

687 ASGOI, *Minute, Riunione tenuta dal Grande Oriente d'Italia, May 19, 1863.*

the dawn of the institution's development—but which had been fading, when not dispersing, in the following centuries. On May 22, 1875, a lodge numbering exclusively Egyptians "Luce d'Oriente" [*Light of the East*] arose following the S.R.A.A. and whose main purpose was the dissemination of Institution's principles among the natives. David Fernandez was commissioned to inaugurate the lodge and the new Master, Habib Naggar, had words of recognition for the work carried out by G.O.I. In January 1901, Ettore Ferrari visited the Egyptian lodges, after being in Thessaloniki and Istanbul during the previous year, with the aim of verifying the state of the art.

Nel gennaio del 1901 Ettore Ferrari visitò le logge egiziane, dopo essersi recato nel corso dell'anno precedente presso le logge di Salonicco e di Istanbul, con lo scopo di verificare lo stato in cui versavano le logge.

7.6.2 Il Nilo

After the first Masonic practice by "Caio Gracco," "Fratelli Repetti," and "Alleanza dei Popoli," actually not long-eve, Italian Masons founded other lodges, more favorable in the course. "Il Nilo" [The Nile] was one of these; although its foundation date is unknown, it was still pretty alive during the reign of Fuad. Numerous his philanthropic engagements, including: the beginning of a social assistance service, polyclinics, a first aid roadside assistance, and the civil cemetery in Alessandria.

In the '80s of nineteenth century, the lodge was literally overwhelmed; did its utmost to encourage the entry of the Egyptians in it and for this, in July 1880, the lodge had requested to perform its functions in two distinct but supportive sections, one formed by the Europeans and the other by natives claiming it.[688]

In 1890, the lodge went through a period of crisis due to internal disagreements and Italian Freemasonry stated its dissolution with a special decree prescribing to reconstitute it immediately endorsing mason Fortunato Ventura.

7.6.3 Nuova Pompeia

The prominent Italian atelier in the Egyptian territory was the "Nuova Pompeia" [*New Pompeia*], representing for decades a key reference for

---

688 ASGOI, *Missive, Loggia Il Nilo al Grande Oriente d'Italia*, July 22.

Italian Masonry abroad. Uncertain is its foundation date—however before 1861—depended on Italian Obedience according to the Scottish Rite Ancient and Accepted.[689]

In 1864, it fronted a crisis influencing eight masons—who pronounced for the detachment from Italian Grand Orient[690]—to ride off. After this plight, however promptly resolved, the National Obedience conferred it the rank of Capitulary Mother Lodge, with the name of "Nuova Pompeia."

In 1872, returned to its original prosperity, after a span of internal struggles undermining the steadiness. Its dynamism expressed in many initiatives such as providing primary learning to masons and illiterate initiates.

The Italian lodge was on good terms with many foreign cells, such as the Greek "Socrates," whose Worshipful was invited to attend the works for the installing of new offices.

In 1875, on offices renewal appointment, a discourse was read—raising the possibility for masonry to become a single body by the various national Obediences.

"Pompeia" was dissolved and founded several times in its existence due of serious disagreements amid members until Italian Obedience entrusted some Brethen from "Cincinnato" to provide yet another reconstitution, hoping that many of the retreated masons would return.[691]

In 1891, the atelier was still dissolved and reformed; in November 1896, mason Tito Figari came from Cairo to preside over the housing in a new temple. Demolished again in 1898 despite the efforts of its member Alberto Alby, Worshipful Master, since composing the contradictions was uncanny he resigned. Recurring again, the lodge was officially canceled from G.O.I. records by the decree n. 156 of December 9, 1903.

In July 1909, it started one more time and in 1918, it turned out still active; after that date, no more certain facts are listed.

---

689 ASGOI, *Alessandria d'Egitto*, in "Rivista della Massoneria Italiana", n. 23, year 4, 1873, p. 8.

690 ASGOI, *Missive, Grande Oriente d'Italia alla loggia Pompeia*, March 11, 1864.

691 *La loggia Nuova Pompeia*, in "Rivista della Massoneria Italiana", n. 7–8, year 21, 1890, p. 120.

7.6.4 *Cincinnato*

The Egyptian masonic community was fully swinging in 1880—its activities were almost frenetic—new foundations in a row, not ceasing even in this fairly delicate period for Egypt. Italians built "Cincinnato" lodge in Alexandria during 1882, which followed the Symbolic Rite and had inside broadly European partakers.

In 1886, Honorary Worshipful in "Cincinnato" were Grand Master Ferdinando Oddi—of the Rite of Memphis—Dionisi Iconomopoulo, GM of the Grand National Lodge of Egypt, and Eugenio Polzi, head of the Chapter of Alexandria.[692] Same year the lodge was dissolved due to internal disputes but, by decree n. 53 of September 24, 1886, was promptly reconstituted by a group already militating there. G.O.I. declared the reconstitution took place under the best auspices and the young Worshipful drove the atelier vigorously and profitably. Despite this, the lodge lived a doomed fate between 1892 and 1906, crossing in 1901 a crisis that serious the lodge was canceled from the general records of Italian communion, without providing—as usual—the chance of a prompt re-foundation.[693]

The 1906 rebirth is due to the struggle by Brethen Raffaele Camerini, Anselmo Morpurgo, Tullio Zacutti, Aristodemo Petrini, Alfredo Tivoli, Oscar Goldenberg, and Max Saphir. In 1937, the lodge was still active, thanks to the Mastery of Davide Augusto Albarin, managing to gather around him the anti-fascist share of the community. In the '40s of twentieth century, Albarin himself became a key Italian freemason, when he was elected Grand Master of G.O.I. from lodges in exile, since reputed exempt from the conditioning of fascism, besides that—Capitulations rescinded—Italian citizens were no longer subject to homeland sovereignty, but only to the Egyptian government. Albarin was Grand Master of the G.O.I. in exile from 1940 to 1944. He began in 1909 inside "Cincinnato II" lodge, founded in 1905; lived almost entirely his life in Alexandria in Egypt, just expelled in 1957 because of the crisis in the Suez Canal and took refuge in France where he died two years later.

---

692 *Notizie massoniche della comunione*, in "Rivista della Massoneria Italiana", year 17, n. 31, p. 246.

693 ASGOI, *Decreto Grande Oriente d'Italia n. 57*, May 1901.

7.6.5 Italian Masonry in Port Said and Suez

The keenness of Italian Freemasonry also showed off in a small center of Egypt, Port Said, where in 1907, "Il Progresso" [*Growth*] was installed by the restless Menotti Rimediotti.[694] Its built-up was hard according to the Worshipful, since that district didn't number masons willing to form one. Masons were but a few and the locals were not as culturally boosted as in Alexandria or Cairo.

In the end, when he was about to give the idea off, Rimediotti found few but valid contributors, mostly from the Italian community, with some other French element. Once the lodge was founded, no coincidence it was flanked by the already existing French and English lodges in Port Said. In his opening address, the Worshipful Rimediotti emphasized the active alliance amid diverse European lodges, with Italians tight to French Masons in pursuit of lay schools French were setting up in Port Said. The Masonry of G.O.I. went to Suez too, where the "Klysma" was founded in 1905.

7.7 Tunisia Masonic Ground

7.7.1 The Italian Settlement in Tunisia Before Fascism Rising

Amid the national minorities in Tunisia in the last two centuries, the Italian one was the prime for longevity and bulk. Its organized presence dates back to a hundred years before the French occupation, only in May 1881.

The structure of the Italian group is assorted, the first settlers were of Ligurian origin and practiced coral fishing on the island of Tabarca, near the northern shores close to the border with Algeria. During the eighteenth century, many Jews came to Tunisia from Leghorn, an organized and solid nucleus, distinguishing itself from the Israelis already in Tunisia. Leghorn Jews can be considered the core of the Italian collectivity.[695] Called *grana*, they were mostly bankers, traders, and freelancers and in the Regency (Province) of Tunis covered prominent rules.

Many were in the court of Tunisian Bey, like Giuseppe Maria Raffo, for about 30 years in charge of relations with foreign consuls. Even in the military, the presence was primary, mostly during the Janissary revolts, under

---

694 *La loggia di Port Said*, in "Rivista Massonica", 1908, year 39, nn. 1–2, p. 17.
695 Patrizia Manduchi, *La presenza italiana in Tunisia e il suo ruolo nello sviluppo*, p. 83.

Bey Hamuda who, to defeat the garrison, turned to the French army, actually enlisting a handful of Italians.

In 1838, a military school was established, the Military Polytechnic, by the Italian Luigi Calligaris. Upon the request of the Sardinian vice-consul Giovannetti, he accepted the duty of Tunisian troops trainer.

Italian emigration, due to financial reasons, was flanked by political emigration, largely in the first half of the nineteenth century, after the failure of Risorgimento movements, when many young Carbonari and Mazziniani took the road to exile finding in Tunisia a brand new land.

In Tunis, the environment was favorable to continue the struggle for the Italian cause, without endangering as at home.

These refugees were often sort in masonic lodges and the Italian community—leaning on cultured bourgeoisie as a backbone—was on good terms with the indigenous population, thanks to the plenty of welfare institutions. Italians established credit institute and cooperatives, while Dante Alighieri company—with proxies in Tunis, Sfax, and Bizerte—was mainly involved in the establishment of Italian colleges and classes, also frequently held in French schools. The opening of Italian schoolhouses is to be dated around the second half of the nineteenth century to the initiative of political expatriates and some Jews from Leghorn.

Dante Alighieri's engagement also outcome in other areas—libraries, clinics, and hospitals such as the Italian Colonial Hospital, flagship of Tunisian health.

After the French settlement, there arose the Chamber of Commerce and Arts, from 1900 releasing a periodical bulletin. Italian distinguished also in the press, scoring a progressive growth with the arrival of political defectors. Italian idiom, already in used for trade and politics, became the tongue of culture utmost. The first newspaper released in Tunis on March 21, 1838, "Il Giornale di Tunisi e Cartagine" [*Tunis and Carthage Journal*], was linked to Italian Freemasonry and edited by two printers of Neapolitan rise, Romeo and Malatesta. He went out for a single number, as bey Ahmed forbade its circulation right away. In 1859 "Il Corriere di Tunisi" [*Tunis Courier*] debuted, published until 1881; over the years, many other publications in Italian were seen. Each of them portrayed a social group or an activity soon becoming an instrument of protection and promotion to the Italian minority. Official organ of the whole groups became "L'Unione"

[*The Union*], shut only in 1943, after its headquarters have being invaded by fascist legates.

Political bonds amid Italy and Tunisia were guided by the Treaty of Schooner, signed in the homonymous locality on September 8, 1868, stating the issue of the "most favored nation" to benefit Italy. The purpose was the enhancement of economic exchanges between the two in support of Italian broad community already dwelled in Tunisia and the boost of Italian move, with regard to the small and middle-class bourgeoisie.

7.7.2 The Italian Outpost During Fascism

Italians are considerable even between the two world wars, their community yet overcome French one, though powerful thanks to the Protectorate.[696] Fascism also developed in Tunisian colony, but the homologation of society—due to its scattering—was not as deep as homeland.

However, the main opponent in Tunisia have been masonic lodges, at least until 1925, the year of G.O.I. induced dissolution, even though the related decree concerned only lodges operating in the peninsula.

There a progressive dispersion starts; many members over time became fascists. Some of the older founded the "Mazzini e Garibaldi" lodge, amid them anarchist Giulio Barresi who, counting on socialists and communists endorsement, was a fundamental reference character for the diverse anti-fascist in Tunisia.[697]

Another insurgent, filed by the fascist police as a potential terrorist, was Enrico Forti, a native of Leghorn though born in Tunis in 1892 and later a French naturalized.

With the racial laws of 1938, the Italian Jewish community increase its political awareness even though, conscious of Italian Jews strength in Tunisia, the fascist executive itself considerably milds the tones of anti-Semitic propaganda. Italian newspapers, even linked to fascism, dampen the aggressiveness of Italian racial politics and even Consul Giacomo Silimbani sought during his mandate to avoid an enfeebling of Italian Jewish community, whom the French one would have benefited from.

---

696 Lucia Valenzi (edited), *Italiani e antifascisti in Tunisia negli anni trenta*, Liguori editore, Napoli, 2008, p. 1.

697 Santi Fedele, *Massoneria Italiana ...* , op. cit., p. 53.

7.7.3 The Birth of Freemasonry in Tunisia

Historians disagree in fixing a date of masonry blossoming in the North African country; some authors close to Jewish circles postulate it was in 1773, when *grana* arrived in Tunis,[698] but the historian Dudley Wright sets the year 1821.

To him, Freemasonry got with the resettlement in Tunis of massive Neapolitan groups, yet active members of the Grand Orient of Naples.

Since 1860, Masonry knew a period of huge spread; Italian, French, and English lodges began to multiply.

7.7.4 The Early Lodges

The Italian Grand Orient first and following the Grand Orient of Italy built in their early spread in Tunisia "Attilio Regolo" in 1862, "Il Risorgimento" in 1870, "Concordia e Progresso" [*Concord and Growth*] in 1867, "Fede e Costanza" [*Belief and Firmness*], and "Cartagine e Utica" [*Carthage and Utica*] in 1862. Record sources relating to these are scarce, we learn only "Il Risorgimento" in 1879 expressed as Worshipful Guglielmo Funaro[699] and the following year Giuseppe Ayra, who—on his election—pronounced a speech on the aim of Masonry and masons's mandatory skills. A part of the address was focused on the activity Freemasonry would play in a land like Tunisia, where distinct cultures and religions coexisted and "con interessi sovente diametralmente opposti".[700]

G.O.I. was close with it, sending in 1882 to the Italian obedience a missive describing the Tunisian Masonic life during that harsh span due to riots fronting Europeans and indigenous peoples. Here, the Brethen were urged not to give in to provocation and to do everything in their power to reconcile to make masonry flourish in Tunisia.[701] In 1887 its temple, shared with

---

698 Laroussi Mizouri, *La Naissance de la Franc-maçonnerie dans la Tunisie précoloniale*, in "Revue de l'Istitut des Belles Lettres Arabes", n. 173, t. 57, 1994, p. 73.

699 *Tunisi*, in "Rivista della Massoneria Italiana", year 10, n. 19, 1879, p. 298.

700 "often with diametrically adverse concernes" [translator's note]. *Libro d'oro della massoneria italiana, loggia Il Risorgimento, Tunisi*, in "Rivista della Massoneria Italiana", year 11, nn. 5–6, p. 79.

701 *Lettera del Gran Segretario al G. M. della R. L. Il Risorgimento, Mallesopulo*, in "Rivista della Massoneria Italiana", 1882, p. 45.

the English lodge Ancient Chartage n. 1717, was destroyed by a fire whose causes were unknown; the English lodge suffered the greatest damage, losing a capital of 20,000 liras.

"Il Risorgimento" was on good terms also with Spanish masonic organs and in 1886, its Worshipful Giuseppe Ayra received from the Supreme Council of Spain the Kadosch Knight patent—30th degree of S.R.A.A.—to thank him for his works to the rescue of the Spanish cholera patients; besides Ayra, the Supreme Council of Spain conferred same recognition to Luciano Bignas, Worshipful of the Ancient Carthage lodge and dependent on the Grand Lodge of England, to Philippe Caillat, Worshipful of the Nouvelle Carthage lodge and employee of the Grand Orient of France, and to Italian Antonio Ferretti, Worshipful of "Fede e Costanza." Ferretti endowed the recognition to his lodge, as quintessential masonic devotedness.

"Fede e Costanza" was in restless deals with G.O.I. and in 1887, the lodge was pleased by the unity of Italian Freemasonry in the fight against clericalism, long-lasting enemy of the institution. The "Rivista della Massoneria Italiana"[702] [*Journal of Italian Freemasonry*] assumes 1885 as the year of this lodge opening, though the constitution activity began the year before on behalf of Antonio Ferretti.[703]

In 1889, both "Il Risorgimento" and "Fede e Costanza" were dissolved to allow the birth of a unitary lodge,[704] welcoming the request the officers of both[705] presented to G.O.I.

In the mid-60s of nineteenth century, Tunisia was affected by a severe economic crisis, foreigners took the road home, lodges stopped working, and just five years afterwards, Masonry gained again possession of the abandoned temples, preparing for a new era of development and flourishing.

7.7.5 *Cartagine e Utica*

According to some references, the first regular lodge implanted in Tunisia by Italian Obedience was "Cartagine e Utica"[706] [*Carthage and Utica*]. To

---

702 *Tunisi*, in "Rivista della Massoneria Italiana", year 18, n. 3, 1887, p. 23.

703 *A Tunisi*, in "Rivista della Massoneria Italiana", year 15, nn. 45–48, anno 1884, p. 375.

704 ASGOI, *Decree n. 36*, March 3, 1889.

705 "Il Risorgimento" was represented by Ercole Marinelli, First Superintendent acting as Worshipful, "Fede e Costanza" spoke on behalf of its Worshipful Riccardo Costa.

706 ASGOI, *Minute*, May 26, 1863, Roma.

collect members, it would have drawn from the Italian resettlement after Naples uprisings of 1821, with the arrival of numerous masonic political expatriates from the Orient of Naples. Thus, in Tunis, a prominent Italian Masonic center operated, without the permission of the Bey, meeting secretly on city outskirts or near the ancient Roman tanks close to the ruins of Carthage.

In 1845, the loggia was renamed "Figli scelti di Cartagine e Utica" [*Picked Sons of Carthage and Utica*], flanked by two other lodges: "Nuova Cartagine" [*New Carthage*] and "Attilio Regolo." "Figli scelti di Cartagine e Utica" was a bulwark of Freemasonry in Tunisia and acted as a link between the Italian outlander masons and G.O.I., benefiting from the choice of many Italians to leave French lodges to erect new under the Italian Obedience. The new lodge was "Attilio Regolo," who asked for the foundation patent in 1862.[707] To open it and to chair over the oath, the Great Council of Italian Grand Orient commissioned Quintilio Mugnaini, Worshipful of "Figli scelti di Cartagine e Utica." "Attilio Regolo" gained then the invitation to partake in the Masonic summons held in 1862 and there represented by mason Rebuffi.

On years following records are spare; in 1876, the lodge was active but unsteady, for years, the economic scenery is precarious[708]—especially for foreigners—yet the Grand Orient of Italy encourages the lodge to continue its activity.[709]

7.7.6 *Progress of Italian Masonry*

In early twentieth century, G.O.I. founded numerous lodges, such as "Veritas," "Fides," and "Mazzini." This new phase of Masonic development came after a span when Italian lodges—wholly the Tunisian masonic system—suffered from the strains amid Italian and French communities. This renewed vitality was esteemed a step toward the plain cooperation between the two, although the end of WWI actually re-establish full cooperation between Obediences. This thanks to the treaty signed on February 15, 1920, by the officials of G.O.I. and the Grand Lodge of France.

---

707 ASGOI, *Minute, tenuta del Gran Consiglio*, April 6, 1862, Roma.

708 *Tunisi*, in "Rivista della Massoneria Italiana", year 7, 1876, nn. 13–14, p. 10.

709 *Tunisi*, in "Rivista della Massoneria Italiana", year 5, 1874, n. 24, p. 15.

7.7.7 *Veritas*

Gathering the most influential members of the Italian community in Tunis, it was founded in 1900 ensuing a long and arduous plot by masons from "Il Progresso di Susa" [*Growth of Susa*]. The temple opened on January 21, 1901, when Brethen of "Antiqua Agape" handed over the foundation patent to the dignitaries of the new atelier. As a tradition, some members addressed about Freemasonry and its aims, and the evening after a dinner was offered including members' families. The following year "Veritas" sent a dispatch to his Mother Lodge in Rome, to announce its solemn inauguration.

Ateliers in Tunis then complained of serious problems, their activities were slow, the whole masonic system was in need of a boost, thus the foundation of "Veritas."

More than 60 Masons came from the old Italian lodges, as most esteemed elements of Italian community, with a broad presence of Italian Jewish initiates. The meetings discussed disparate topics and—in the meeting on November 2, 1901—the founding of a newspaper to give voice to the Liberal Party. Sequent session discussed the chance for the Italian government to give off schools running in Tunisia in favor of missionaries.

Like many of Italian ateliers, lodge was on good terms with French ones, so much so that in 1903, "Veritas" met its peer *Nouvelle Carthage* and *Volonté* to celebrate the anniversary of the fall of papal Rome. Relations with the French became tight after WWII, when "Veritas," impoverished of most of its members since 1925 law, joined the French "La Volonté," giving rise to a new lodge *La Volonté et Veritas Réunies*.

7.7.8 *Ateliers in Tunisi: Concordia e Mazzini-Garibaldi*

In 1916, lodges in Tunis merged into one, "Concordia" [*Concord*]; the activities were immediately well underway, with Tunisian masonic community always on the front line in matters concerning Italians. Engaged in philanthropic ventures, it worked with ease and in 1917, solemnly honored the anniversary of Garibaldi's death.[710] Throughout the duration of WWI, it held its affairs, with several initiations and growth in rank among its members; at the end of the conflict, mason Herdenberg was elected Worshipful,

---

710 64ª *Commemorazione di Garibaldi*, in "Rivista massonica", year XL, 1917, n. 6, p. 182.

confirming activities did not languish during the war. The scenery altered with the advent of fascism and the arrival, since 1922, of its legates in Tunisia, even in the most farfetched boroughs to settle the party. This diffuse action was directed at subdue European citizens, on the spread of the fascist demands strengthening of the Italian influence on Tunisia. Even "Concordia" was hit by this wave and many Brethen were overwhelmed by the new political and cultural climate ending up adhering to fascism.

In 1920 and 1921, Salvatore Calò was its Worshipful; in 1924, "Concordia" partook in the foundation of "Pensiero e Azione" [*Thought and Deed*], solemnly built on October 17.[711]

At the opening of its offices, diverse foreign masons intervened, French mostly.[712] Calò was named Worshipful even there, but replaced almost immediately by Domenico Scalera. The news on "Pensiero e Azione" stopped in 1925, when together with "Concordia" celebrated with a conference Giuseppe Garibaldi. "Concordia" meanwhile was in trouble since fascist propaganda, only very few loyal to Freemasonry did not adhere to fascism and, in 1925, stated to carry on masonic work in secret, founding in 1926, after the ill-famed law that prohibited the cult, "Mazzini-Garibaldi" atelier, also with the contribution of some members of the Italian Consulate. Founded after the establishment of G.O.I. in exile, to Khayat was born from the merger of "Giuseppe Mazzini," "Garibaldi e Patria"[713] [*Garibaldi and Homeland*]. The newborn lodge was in constant turmoil, its activity consisting also in the outlawed deliver to homeland of anti-fascist propaganda pamphlets through mason Sante Zammitto, Merchant Marine officer, often traveling on the Tunisi-Palermo trade route.

The leaflets were printed in France by "Giustizia e Libertà" [*Justice and Freedom*].

The very foundation of the lodge was itself a challenge to fascism and, amid founders, Giulio Barresi and Enrico Forti played an important role. Barresi, born in 1885 in Tunisia though native of Trapani, was commodities surveyor in the port of Tunis. He was a key exponent of Italian community, southern population mostly, recognized itself in the anarchic thought of Nicolò

---

711 ASGOI, *Minute,* February 28, 1920 and *Minute,* May 23, 1921.

712 *Cerimonia d'insediamento delle cariche della nuova loggia Pensiero e Azione all'oriente di Tunisi,* in "Rivista Massonica", year 54, n. 9, 1924, p. 208.

713 Michel Khayat, *Storia della Massoneria ...* , op. cit., p. 59.

Converti. Heading the lodge for a long time, due to his Masonic merits, in 1938, he was elevated to the 33rd degree of Scottish Rite.

7.8 The Grand Orient of Italy in Lybia

I talian masonry was in Libya far before the colonial initiative Italy followed there after the first decade of the twentieth century. This institution showed the Italian presence in those lands as a national outpost abroad. No wonder lodges were always founded in cities or pivotal places where Italian presence was deep, gathering outstanding persons in the Italian community with no records about native admissions.

The first lodge endorsed by the G.O.I. named "Stella Africana" [*African Star*] was founded in Tripoli in 1862, following the Symbolic Rite. One of the forefathers was Aronne Morpurgo. In 1863, it was abided by G.O.I. in Turin; *Gazzetta Ufficiale* notices its communications were to be posted to Livorno, proving the tight relation between Livorno's Hebrews ad their coreligionists spread in North Africa including non-native Hebrews in Libya. The life of this lodge was not that long and unluckily scarce are the items we dispose to draw its story. In 1867, it can't intervene to the Founding and Executive assembly in Naples since the representative was busy elsewhere; in those years, Worshipful was Isach Lati.

After a few years, in 1872, activities ceased as reported thus the year after the item disappears from the list of lodges in the Italian Commune. The first masonic outcome in Libya therefore ends as a short but vain experience since in Tripoli, another lodge started following its footsteps—the "Abramo Lincoln," in 1866—despite a few facts are supplied: the sole solid one is the institution was not existing anymore in 1891. Keeping on the discussion on freemasonic life in Libya, "Cirenaica" comes up, established in Tripoli on February 3 1887,[714] formerly noticed as upcoming on the outstanding Italian masonic review. It was a Symbolic Rite lodge; Giuseppe Ayra, mastering the only astronomical observatory between Tunis and Alessandria in Egypt—one of the most skilled in the Mediterranean—was one of the founders.

As often when clashes happen in an atelier, the office was suspended in 1895 from masonic working groups up to a brand new issue. During this gap, Worshipful was Eugenio Riccard. In this role, he donated 40 liras to

---

714 *Loggia Cirenaica*, in "Rivista della massoneria italiana", 1887, p. 96.

earthquake victims in Calabria, to testify the liveliness of the institution, despite the hanging due to heavy conflicts between the Worshipful and the First Knight Commander. On August, same year, the lodge overcame the crisis and reinstate in its masonic profile. According to freemasonry year-books, this was not active in 1902 (even if the 1902 RMI states the re-action). Record books trace a sole working one—"La Vigilanza" [*The Vigilance*]—founded in 1900, following the Scottish Rite Ancient and Accepted, located to the house of Professor Giannetto Paggi, Prevost of the Italian Male School.[715] Members were former adherents to Cirenaica. Worshipful was Giuseppe Ayra, while in 1902, Paggi succeeded; during his tenure, 50 liras are devolved to the needy of Martinica. The lodge was "demolished" at the end of 1902, no witnessing of it on following Freemasonry yearbooks. Despite the diffuse bright, the masonic entourage is always yeasty: on 1902, after the G.O.I. fiat n. 123 of December the 24th by the appointment of "Propaganda Massonica" [*Masonic Propaganda*] lodge based in Rome, a Triangle is established, running from 1903 to 1911.[716] The address to refer to Triangle was to one of the most relevant profile of Italian Freemasonry, Adriano Lemmi, in Florence.

7.8.1 *The Grand Orient of Italy Lodges After the Taking of Libya*

To spectate to the very bloom of Italian lodges in Libya, we should wait the gap from 1914, after conquer at the expense of the Ottoman Empire, to the outcome of fascism that ceased the initiative.

A few months after the Italian settlement in Libya, the "Cinque Ottobre" [*October V*] lodge is founded to the Orient in Tripoli (1912). The name recalls the day Italians occupied Tripoli, inflaming conflict in Tripolitania.

The lodge followed the Scottish rite and in the year, it started was able to devolve 20 liras to help the families of Tripolitania war victims. In 1913, Worshipful was Professor Giannetto Paggi, endorsed on 1894 and already effective in "La Vigilanza" [*The Watch*] lodge accomplishments. Perhaps in 1914, Worshipful was Eusebio Eusebione, in charge on artillery and during 1915, in the core of WWI taking part in the foundation of a Triangle in Zuara. The following years—with "Progresso" [*Progress*]—celebrated Brother Tito Marconcini for his masonic engagement in Libya.[717] In 1918

---

715 ASGOI, *Masonic Yearbook of G.O.I.*, 1902.

716 ASGOI, *Masonic Yearbook*, 1911, p. 111.

717 *Solenne voto di plauso*, in "Rivista Massonica", 1916, pp. 200–201.

took up residence to Vincenzo Campo Ingrao, in 1919–1920 Worshipful was Carlo Smith, while the year after Vincenzo G, De Meo succeeded. In 1921 merged with Leptis Magna freshly renaming as "Cinque Otto-bre-Leptis Magna."

Freemasonry was constantly widening, thus in 1912, two Triangles started, one in Tobruk and the other in Derna: the former didn't generate any other cell while in Derna after a few time, "Dante Alighieri" atelier was spawned.

A pivotal lodge of Italian Commune in Libya was "Cirene," founded in Bengasi in 1914. Its minute books have been carefully preserved, thus, a deep investigation is achievable due to catch its arrangement, members, geographical origins of affiliated, profession, endorsement, and advancement. Asking the issues, it's easily fair on a bunch of 126 Brethen attending the lodge since the very beginning up to November 1923—when the last advance is recorded—all members were Italians, only three born in a Libyan city (Tripoli and Bengasi): by chance second-generation Italians. All the rest were born in Italy, with a major presence from Southern lands. Just one mason was born in Lebanon showing a clear Greek lineage by the surname. On profession structure, soldierly was heading—counting 66 men among infantry, engineers, army, cavalry, riflemen, and doctors—while the others were retailers, employees, attorneys, accountants, and students.

Fair was the relation with the Obedience it was depending, despite the physical distance; some representatives took part to Achille Ballori funerals as he was killed on October 31, 1917, in Palazzo Giustiniani.

Lodge records, minutes letters and telegrams, show an overview on customary activities able to line up the accomplishment of lodges and reveal—to mention—that during WWI Giuseppe Bosco, a member born in Lampircello in 1891 and artillery official admitted in 1915[718] bravely fell in Santa Lucia di Tolmino on October 31, 1917.

In 1919–1920, Worshipful was Engineer Rocco Maurizio Lanzi and its agenda is pretty rich.[719] Then, one after the other, Carlo Ragazzi, Adolfo de Palme, Giuseppe Sboto—replaced by Vincenzo Grana—while in the last year, 1923–1924, Emanuele Sartorio Nicolosi is mentioned. In 1922, the

---

718 ASGOI, *Enrollment lists, Cirene lodge, Orient of Bengasi.*

719 Archivio Storico Centro ricerche Storiche Libera Muratoria, Torino (ASCRSLM), *Collection G.O.I., Lodges abroad, telegram.*

lodge domiciles to an Italian Club, Humanitarian and Culture Society.[720] Last facts from the lodge are set in 1925, as fascist persecutions addressed some members. A letter Carlo Regazzi sent to "Cirene" Worshipful drawn the "dark" moment, the Institution is in due to fascist repression. Being a freemason was equal as being in danger, the whole Italian community was split between supporting the national government and the freedom ideals masonry carried on. Mostly, by a letter sent by the deputies of "Cirene" to the Grand Orient of Italy appears many official documents found in the Worshipful dwelling were seized by fascists and afterward many freemasons were called back homeland. Thus, the lodge went through much harm in keeping the activity on. One of the people addressed to this application was Giuseppe Della Cà, eminent figure in "Cinque Ottobre" and deputy chancellor in Tripoli's government, tribute office employee. Della Cà complained on arguments used to his forced repatriation, straightly accusing General Ernesto Mombelli (1867–1932) as subdued to Fascism will, since the Governor himself charged Della Cà, accused to report facts he was able to cover, cause of its role, directly to the high levels of freemasonry Order against the government. Clearly, Della Cà remitted any charge. After he left we lack any records on lodges, beaten for sure by the pushy fascist presence, since no sources state ateliers activities after 1925, possibly as a result of archives requisition again by fascist initiative. Proving the situation abovementioned, a letter sent by Della Cà to Cirene on behalf of Sovereign Rosicrucian Chapter "Le due Palme" [Two Palms], where Della Cà reports about no more adhesions "anche per impedire che il Neofita, necessariamente lasciato a sé ed incapace di auto evolversi non si ingannasse sul fine e sullo scopo dell'Istituzione".[721]

The Grand Orient of Italy—conscious of the situation the masonry suffered in Libyan colony—thus asks to Giuseppe della Cà to reach Rome office to testify about the situation and inviting him to act to support the Rosicrucian Chapter to go on even without him. Due to records lack, we can't state any progress about. Della Cà corresponded with Giuseppe Leti, who blamed him about the inaccurate keeping of documents; he replies he did every effort to prevent the accident even some papers were safe at least.

---

720 ASCRSLM, *Ivi, Missive January 15, 1925.*

721 "furthermore to avoid the Initiate—necessarily discarded and unable to develop in his status—misunderstood the aim of the Institution" [translator's note]. ASCRSLM, *Ivi, Missive* September 24, 1925.

Retracing through time freemasonry events, in 1913, a distinguished fact takes place: in Derna "Dante Alighieri" is founded (formerly a Triangle), while some of its members start a Triangle in Marsa Susa. This cell played for ten years, following the S.R.A.A. and represented by Mr Alberico Esperty, chancellor to the region court. To grab some infos on this lodge, we have to wait till 1919, since sources are almost missing for the whole WWI. That year atelier was referring to Professor Fulvio Contini, Prevost to the Royal Primary Schools. In 1922, worshipful was Alessandro Sportelli, head of the Royal estate office in Derna. The following year, the lodge office was to Attn. Guido Panighetti, thus probably he was the new Worshipful.

During WWI in Tripoli, "Leptis Magna" is established, whose name recalls the ancient name of the city close to Tripoli and nowadays known as Homs. Previously endorsed by the Serenissima Gran Loggia Nazionale d'Italia [*Serenissima National Grand Lodge of Italy*], (Piazza del Gesù), then formalized in 1917 under the Grand Orient of Italy. In 1918 was addressed to Marino Nardi dwelling, born in Portici in 1887 and attorney to the war court. Its activities didn't stop during the fights. Soon after war, Worshipful was Renzo Testori and Edoardo Morvillo the year after. In 1921 merged with sister "Cinque Ottobre."

During 1914, again in Tripoli, "Progresso" lodge is given to birth—following the Scottish rite.

Unluckily, on a few lodges under the G.O.I., we are but able to gather complete infos, anyway—to give a complete overview—below are reported the brief facts collected.

In 1918, "Cesare Battisti" was founded, taking the name from the irredentist martyr—born Austrian and enrolled as volunteer in the Italian Army, prisoned and hanged for high treason in 1916 as a member of the Austrian Chamber of Deputies. In 1921 to the Tripoli, Orient Italia lodge of Scottish rite was established, made mostly by army officers. As freshly instituted, Worshipful was Antonio Coppolino—Customs Official with G.O.I. roll 43966, in 1914 entered in "Cinque Ottobre" records—while in 1923/1924 was accountant Arrigo Modena.

The very last lodge sorted by records is Lebda to the Homs Orient, taking the name by the ruins of ancient Leptis Magna occupied by Italians in

1912: in 1922/1923 Worshipful Master was Eliodoro Guastella[722] and in 1924/1925 Tommaso De Crescenzo.

The above mentioned was the depiction of Italian lodges in Libya since 1862—year of foundation of the first lodge subdued to the Obedience to the Grand Orient of Italy—up to 1925, last year of recorded facts on Italian Institutions. Unfortunately, the found documents give us just a blink on the masonic scenario in Libya. The scarcity of papers doesn't allow us to go deep to offer a comprehensive overlook on this phenomenon. Despite the lacks we can draw up a conclusion: Libya can be thought as a quintessential masonic land. The only masonry was Italian, first with GOI—soon after its starting in Turin—*in secundis* a few obeying to Piazza del Gesù, to testify the vitality of freemasonry. These were founded beginning from 1918, after WWI, tailing just a decade the Obedience in Italy. Two Obedience coexisting allow us to catch the importance of this Institution, enduring and able to gather the outstanding personalities in the Italian community. By the check of enrollment books, we can resume the kind of members and state that often, mostly after the catch by Italy in 1911, the very of them were part of the laical word depicting our nation in those territories: army, admins, teachers in Italian schools.

This bright activity, starting from the '20s, was contrasted by the pushiness of fascists as well as in homeland. Many shakedowns and many commandeering of masonic stuff happened. In this hard moment, Italian Institutions were but undammed by the political issues from fascism, set against the freemasonry. The review ends its investigation on Libya masonry history in 1925, when due to fascism repression, the deeds were stopped, as well as in Italy: in November 1925, an act suppressing secret societies—thus including masonry—was released. The eco reached Institutions abroad with the only exception of Egyptian lodges: iconic was Davide Augusto Albarin, Grand Master of G.O.I., who saved the tradition from the oblivion. In 1925, this chapter ends, despite the numbers and the coexistence of two diverse Italian Obediences. More than 60 years of masonic history, whose remembrance focuses *in primis* on the Institution life itself and the role played in the Italian community, as a bind destroyed only cause of the violence endorsed by laws and endured by fascist squads, to demolish the Libyan masonic network.

---

722 ASGOI, *Masonic Yearbook*, 1923, p. 34.

7.9 Italian Masonry in Eritrea

Italian Freemasonry established lodges also in Eritrea; despite the unique scenery of the colony, where there were few elements with proper cultural background to be initiated to the Institution, since 1887, the possibility of founding lodges obeying to G.O.I. had been argued. In January 1891, "Eritrea" lodge by the Orient of Massaua saw the light, a focal point of the Italian community for decades. At the end of its first year, the lodge partakes into the founding the Mutual and Rescue Company, numbering 150 members at the very beginning, and inaugurated its Masonic Temple. Its success is doubtless; the high number of affiliates bears witness to this, around 40 only in the first year. In 1892, together with other ateliers, it funds a hospital for foreigners. After a span of six active years, the lodge goes burst and is demolished in 1896; three years later, it's reformed.

Next to this, another one is listed in Massaua, the "Cocab el Sciargh" [*Star of the East*] in 1892. There is little records on this sister atelier. In 1892–1893, Worshipful was Ahmed El Ghul. From its incomplete records of masons acting in it's assumed were all natives. "Cocab el Sciargh" was running when in 1895 delivered 40 liras for the Calabrian earthquake; the following year, its activities held and in 1899, it was demolished by decree n. 127 of May 12, 1899. Some of its members entered the ranks of the Eritrea lodge at the time of reconstitution.

Beyond Massawa, another Eritrean city saw the flourishing of Italian masonic labor: Asmara. Here, two lodges were founded, "Avvenire Eritreo" [*Eritrean Future*], under the Scottish rite; facts on interrupt any update in 1905.

The second one—in order of foundation—is Eritrea, established in 1909 with decree n. 165 of January 15 (same year) under G.O.I. From 1909 to 1911, attorney Eteocle Cagnassi is the Worshipful. Ending 191 the lodge made a contribution of 150 liras to the kins of fallen and wounded in the tripolitan war.[723]

In 1918, this atelier set up the Eritrean committee for the air fleet, head by Giuseppe de Rossi. The body raised 1,121.25 liras to purchase a military aircraft to steady the Italian air fleet.[724]

---

723 Archivio Storico Ministero Affari Esteri, (ASMAE), *Lodge session minutes*, Collection Eritrea, envelope 616, December 2, 1911.

724 ASMAE, *Comittee session minutes*, Collection Eritrea, envelope 616, undetectable day, 1918.

In 1919–1920, it's led by one of the prominent players of the Italian community, Giuseppe Latilla. The latest records referring to it come from a missive from G.O.I. dated 1923, where the lodge dignitaries are asked about the progress of masonic activities.[725]

---

725 ASMAE, *Missive of Grand Orient of Italy,* Collection Eritrea, envelope 726, April 23, 1918.

8. MASONIC SOLIDARITY IN THE LIBERAL AGE: EDUCATION AND PHILANTHROPY

Demetrio Xoccato

The ethical–philosophical processing held within lodges after the birth of modern Masonry often came out in "profane" society. The effort lavished on the improvement and individual upgrading was inevitably widened and came to comprise the whole of humanity. The consequence was the emergence of a particular attention and social sensitivity, which resulted in a significant civil commitment.

During the nineteenth century, and in the early years of the twentieth, this inspiration entangled with hygienist and positivist movements, and gave rise to several successful outcomes. Although there were also many abortive attempts to disseminate, under the vessel of Progress (a real deity), moral and material well-being among the masses. Of this Masonic commitment, we will focus on two distinct but complimentary areas: the spheres of education and welfare.

8.1 Education

The Constituent Assembly of Italian Grand Orient, held in Turin in December 1861, was the first appointment to discuss how the reborn freemasonry should behave toward profane society. David Levi, one of the partakers, said the Brethren had a moral duty to promote kindergartens, night schools, and institutes teaching a profession.[726]

This theme was certainly felt, but the unclear conditions of fresh Freemasonry did not prompt an immediate and effective commitment. Six years had to pass before the official documents of the Italian body—now Grand

---

726 David Levi, *Programma massonico adottato dalla Mas ∴ Ital ∴ ricostituita presentato al G ∴ O ∴ I ∴ nella seduta dell'anno della V ∴ L ∴ 5861 dal G ∴ Segr ∴ D ∴ L ∴*, s.l., s.e., 1861, p. 6.

Orient of Italy—would return to address the educational issue. In a leaflet, the Grand Master Lodovico Frapolli[727] reminded all members, with a drift to progress, that the lodges would have to promote schools for youngsters and laborers.[728]

The first effect, however, was received only in 1866, with the foundation of the Associazione Nazionale Italiana per l'Istruzione ed Educazione Popolare, prompted by the "Dante Alighieri" lodge in Turin. The purpose was to promote the establishment of school for continuing education and current libraries in all municipalities, pressing local admins. Until 1871, the Turin committee served as a national executive, directed, above all, to factories and countryside, where literacy was low or even null.[729]

The plan addressed all Masons, regardless of their belonging to the Grand Orient of Italy or the Supreme Council of Palermo (a manifestly republican organization). If the first institution gave its support, the second, through the mouth of its Grand Master Federico Campanella,[730] recognized the need to overcome the sharp divergence in the support of such pedagogical ventures.[731]

Running parallel, Freemasonry decided to support the green Italian section of the Teaching League. Founded in Belgium in 1864 on masonic input, this organization was able to settle quickly, first taking root in France (1866), and then moving on to Italy. Given its origin, it's not surprising

---

727 Lodovico Frapolli (1815–1878). Raised in an environment of the high Milanese bourgeoisie, he first attended the military school of Olmütz and then graduated in Paris in mining engineering. In 1848, when the revolts broke out in his hometown, he became one of the representatives of the provisional government. After this experience, the following year he compromised with the Roman Republic and thus expelled from France. After moving to Switzerland, he remained there until the second war of independence (1859) when he joined the Piedmontese government. With the unification of Italy, he entered Parliament, sitting in opposition (1865–1874). He went to Paris to support the French Republic that arose after the battle of Sedan, and when he returned to Italy, he was unable to be re-elected.

728 *Circolare*, in "Bollettino del Grande Oriente della Massoneria in Italia", vol. II ,1867, p. 212.

729 Associazione nazionale italiana per l'istruzione, *Statuto e regolamenti*, Torino, s.e., 1868; Gildo Valeggia, *Storia della loggia massonica fiorentina Concordia (1861–1911)*, Bertieri e Vanzetti, Milano, 1911, pp. CXIV–CXV.

730 See chapter 3, note 46.

731 Camillo Bezzi, *Orientamenti della massoneria intorno al 1870*, in *Chiesa e religiosità in Italia dopo l'Unità (1861–1878)*, Edizioni Vita e Pensiero, Milano, 1973, pp. 336–337.

that, amid its tasks—the dissemination of culture, through night and professional schools—, there was also the fight against clerical influence, regarded as an impediment to progress and education.[732]

In 1869, the "Bollettino ufficiale del Grande Oriente d'Italia" issued a paper showing this reality, asking them to subscribe to the official magazine printed in France. A short time later, the masonic periodical published a plea from the League claiming education to be free and universal.[733]

Again, Turin was the city that first mobilized and, thanks to the doctor Secondo Laura (member of "Dante Alighieri"), set the basis for the foundation of a local committee. In 1868, an extremely ambitious project was also sketched: a "Masonic high school," open to all—including the "profanes"—and which would have availed itself of the most avant-garde pedagogical techniques. This plan, by "Nuova Campidoglio" Lodge of Florence, did not get the necessary support and therefore had to be rejected within a short time.[734]

The failure of this initiative, which aimed to be nationwide, shows the leadership of G.O.I. did not believe a "vertical" approach was appropriate. In fact, the following Federal Councils, beyond the usual concern for the scope of education and Masonic action, left room for manoeuvre within local initiatives.

Again in 1874, GM Giuseppe Mazzoni[735] just urged lodge presence—financially sustaining teachers and providing supplies—without issuing clear guidelines.[736]

---

732 Roger Desmed, *La Franc-Maçonnerie belge et la laïcisation de l'enseignement (1830–1914). Un exemple: la loge des "Amis philanthropes" de Bruxelles*, in Jean Préaux (edited), *Église et enseignement. Actes du Colloque du Xe anniversaire de l'Institut d'histoire du christianisme de l'Université libre de Bruxelles (avril 22–23, 1976)*, Editions de l'Université de Bruxelles, Bruxelles, 1977, pp. 197–222.

733 *Lega per l'istruzione*, in "Bollettino del Grande Oriente della Massoneria in Italia", fold. III-IV, 1868–1869, pp. 601–602; *La Lega italiana d'insegnamento in Italia*, in "Rivista della massoneria italiana", n. 20, 1870, pp. 1–4.

734 Marco Novarino, *Massoneria ed educazione a Torino in età liberale*, in "Annali di storia dell'educazione e delle istituzioni scolastiche", vol. XI, 2004, p. 82.

735 Giuseppe Mazzoni (1808–1880). Tuscan lawyer and journalist of republican leaning. In 1848, he entered as a volunteer in the first war of independence. Back in Florence, he was Minister of Grace and Justice. After the run of Grand Duke Leopoldo II in 1849, he became a triumvir of the provisional government. He fled to France, briefly stayed in Spain until, in 1859, he returned to Tuscany, where he opposed Piedmont's takeover. MP since 1870, in 1879 he was appointed senator of the Kingdom.

736 Archivio Centrale dello Stato di Roma, Fund Pianciani, envelope 58, f. 59, *Circular ,*

1868 was a year of caesura since, after the unfeasible attempts, a first concrete outcome was finally achieved to spread the education offering: the birth of the Istituto Nazionale per le Figlie dei Militari in Turin. In a convergence of the different elites, this college welcomed girls aged 8–18 within three structures, with diverse courses depending on social status.

At Villa della Regina young aristocracy and upper bourgeoisie were hosted, while daughters of small and middle bourgeoisie were located in Casa Magistrale. Finally, there was the Casa Professionale. In this place, the girls from the poorer classes followed training based on practical skills that could be used both in family management (hence the bookkeeping lessons) and in business (tailoring and sewing, for instance).[737]

Since the subalpine Masonry—deputy Tommaso Villa[738] and professor Ariodante Fabretti—was just one of the involved entities (there were also the Savoy court and the moderate world), the institute could not be wholly different from colleges of the time: the only secular drive was the narrowing of both religious personnel and time dedicated to Mass and religious teaching. The female model itself was a mix of tradition and modernity, focused on the domestic and patriotic dimensions.[739]

In 1870, Rome, occupied by the Savoy troops, became part of the Kingdom of Italy. The fall suddenly created the circumstances for secular initiatives. Already in the years following, there were the first tryouts. In 1871, a group of people, led by engineer Mario Moretti (enrolled in "Giordano Bruno" lodge), promoted a circulating library. The year after, the Società Didascalica Italiana was founded, aimed at spreading education among the commoners, thanks to the opening of kindergartens and lending libraries throughout the territory.[740]

March 12, 1874.

737 Vittorio Guyot, *Istituto nazionale per le figlie dei militari italiani. Cenni storici, amministrativi e statistici*, Tip. Speirani, Torino, 1881, pp. 48–49.

738 See chapter 3, note 110.

739 Demetrio Xoccato, *Monumento alle vicende risorgimentali e laboratorio di un'identità femminile: l'Istituto nazionale per le figlie dei militari di Torino (1868–1914)*, in "Storia delle Donne", fasc. 12, 2016, pp. 207–231.

740 Daniela Fantozzi, *Il movimento per le biblioteche popolari nell'Italia postunitaria*, in "Ricerche Storiche", fasc. 3, 1995, pp. 543–611; *Statuto della società didascalica italiana di Roma approvato nell'adunanza generale del giorno 17 ottobre 1872*, Società cooperativa fra tipografi ed arti affini, Milano-Roma, 1872.

Thanks to the involvement of the Roman workers' societies and some lodges—"Universo", "Tito Vezio," and "Uguaglianza"—in 1875, Lega Romana per l'Istruzione del Popolo was born. This association had providing support to destitute families as its target, and, thanks to cash provisions, allowed students to continue their courses. The improvement of adults' training was also significant, and was covered by several university professors of the capital, including Antonio Labriola[741] among others.

The disposability of academics outside the institutional premises was not restrained to this, with the birth and diffusion in Italy of the Popular Universities. Since its birth, this venture was closely linked to local Masonry: among its members were Biagio Placidi (city councilor and first president), the aforementioned Moretti and Luciano Molpurgo (forthcoming head of the company).[742]

With the first accomplishments, the board decided to set up commissions in every district of the capital. As this was too ambitious for the institution, in the end a single person was in charge for each zone. In addition to this re-asset, during 1876, a professional school was opened in Rione Ponte. The institute welcomed boys seven aged and up, offering them a working outlet in textiles and woodworking. Though flowing from a clearly secular body, the school's dean kept the image of Christ on the cross in classrooms.[743]

With this mission, the League essentially exhausted its role within the Roman educational scene, since, beyond the courses, the pursuit focused on awarding cash and rallies in favor of compulsory schooling.

As seen, beginning the 70s, a spirit of intense engagement had spread, leading to several attempts, some unfruitful indeed.

It is concerning to note the "Rivista della massoneria italiana" appeared to catch this broad overthrow and, in the spring of 1874, decided to open a column to host news on pedagogical initiatives supported by the Breth-

---

741 *La Lega d'insegnamento*, in "Rivista della massoneria italiana", n. 22–23, 1875, pp. 3–4.

742 Biagio Placidi, *Resoconto morale ed economico, fatto dal presidente della lega romana per l'istruzione del popolo Biagio Placidi, all'assemblea generale dei soci nel giorno 26 marzo 1876 nel teatro Argentina*, Tip. della pace, Roma, 1876, p. 9.

743 Giancarlo Rocca, *Istruzione, educazione e istituzioni educative della massoneria a Roma dal 1870 all'avvento del fascismo*, in "Annali di storia dell'educazione e delle istituzioni scolastiche", vol. XI, 2004, p. 42.

ren.[744] It was most likely to promote emulation among members, thus stimulating new ideas and projects.

The city of Milan replied with the foundation of a headline, "La Famiglia e la Scuola. Foglio settimanale di istruzione e di educazione" under the direction of Ludovico Coiro, member of "La Ragione". It was an unfavorable initiative, closing as early as 1878, though providing essential insights for the ventures to come.[745]

In the same circumstance, Milanese Freemasonry—above all the "La Ragione" lodge—began to support meeting-places trying to be a laic version of Catholic oratories. To this end, Brethen Decio Nulli—member of the radical party—and Gaetano Pini—physician and founder of Istituto dei Rachitici—were charged with studying this topic and drafting two studies on their practice.[746]

After a biennium of planning, in 1879, the first Ricreatorio Festivo was solemnly inaugurated. Housed within the premises of the civic school of Monastero Maggiore, it had the same opening hours as the parish youth clubs and offered the students a place to spend their time reading and partaking in secular and civilian events.

Despite the first outcome, these youth clubs did not successfully disseminate within the city (the maximum was five). This explains, over time, a progressive disengagement which favored groups linked to the radical and socialist world.[747] To confirm this failure, in 1892, on the occasion of the Congress of Lay Youth Clubs held in Pavia, a text circulated where the lack of results achieved was bitterly noted.[748]

The Roman situation, however, turned out to be much more promising.

---

744 *struzione*, in "Rivista della massoneria italiana", n. 10, 1874, p. 8.

745 Angelo Robbiati, *I ricreatori festivi a Milano (1876–1906)*, in "Annali di storia dell'educazione e delle istituzioni scolastiche", vol. XI, 2004, p. 105.

746 Decio Nulli, *Gli oratori cattolici a Milano. Relazione ad una società filantropica*, Civelli, Milano, 1877; Gaetano Pini, *Gli oratori e gli educandati femminili a Milano. Relazione ad una società filantropica*, Civelli, Milano, 1877.

747 To draw the complex raltionship between socialism and Freemasonry, refer to Marco Novarino, *Tra squadra e compasso e Sol dell'avvenire. Influenze massoniche sulla nascita del socialismo italiano*, Università Popolare di Torino, Torino, 2013; Marco Novarino, *Compagni e liberi muratori. Socialismo e massoneria dalla nascita del Psi alla grande guerra*, Rubbettino, Soveria Mannelli, 2015.

748 Angelo Robbiati, *I ricreatori festivi a Milano*, op. cit., p. 111.

Already in 1883, on the Milanese experience, the Brethren in the capital had discussed the chance to open such centers. The "Universo" lodge was favorable to this project and its echo had reached the headquarters of the G.O.I. In fact, during a meeting held on November 4—the same year—the council gave its approval on the matter.[749] Despite all this emphasis, it took ten years before it became a reality.

The first institute was "Enrico Pestalozzi" (1893), followed by several others over the course of time. Although not all were ascribable to Freemasonry, 17 were strictly linked to the association (approximately 60% of all those born between 1880 and 1920).[750]

The facilities, welcoming children aged 10–18, were open every day from 18:00 to 21:00, including Sundays. This fact confirmed the willingness to act as a valid alternative to the oratory, a place of sociality and training par excellence. On closer inspection, however, their laic character wasn't shown too strongly, fearing perhaps a loss of appeal and support. The only exception was the female club "Anita Garibaldi," whose statute clearly shared its nonreligious profile.[751]

A starting reflection also comes from their management. As in the army, every body had a distinctive uniform, its own flag, and a musical band. If the "Duca degli Abruzzi" adopted the riflemen body garments, "Adelaide Cairoli" had chosen the red shirt of the Garibaldi troops. Consistent with this martial spirit, centrality was given to physical activities (gym, cycling, shooting, etc.). The theory was nevertheless left out as courses of singing, history, morality, physics, and chemistry were foreseen.[752]

A special case concerned, instead, the "Umberto I" Kindergarten. Inaugurated in 1878, it first gravitated into the Catholic orbit and then underwent a shift. In a lapse, Freemasonry acquired full control, giving a decidedly secular turn, by the presidency of an Israelite (Achille Levi) and through the financial support provided directly by G.O.I., which started from 1907.[753]

---

749 ASGOI, *Minute*, November 4, 1883.

750 Demetrio Xoccato, *Il Grande Oriente d'Italia e l'educazione: l'azione delle logge nelle grandi città (1868–1925)*, in "Revista de Estudios Históricos de la Masonería Latino-americana y Caribeña", fasc. 1, 2017, pp. 69–71.

751 Ricreatorio femminile Anita Garibaldi, *Relazione morale e finanziaria (1908–1909)*, Tip. Centenari, Roma, 1910, p. 1.

752 Giancarlo Rocca, *Istruzione, educazione*, op. cit., p. 56.

753 Achille Levi, *L'opera pia educativa di carattere laico*, Bodoni, Roma, 1910.

In the spirit of educational offers, in the 1890s, in addition to the youth clubs, so-called boarding schools arose. The first of these was born in 1887, thanks to a city commitment, obtaining wide response and providing the grounds for the practice that followed. Of 24 structures, built in Rome between 1890 and WWI, and covering almost the entire metropolitan area, half are addressed to the commitment lavished by Masonry: Roman lodges were very active—all over the "Rienzi," "Roma," and "Universo"—and many Brethren assumed top positions within.

The Obedience took on the lead of this project, as shown by the direct involvement of several prominent members. The "Roma" boarding school is the perfect example of this commitment. Among its main animators included sculptor Ettore Ferrari (Grand Master from 1904 to 1917), deputy Salvatore Barzilai (chairman of the Republican party), doctor Achille Ballori (Sovereign Grand Commander of the Ancient and Accepted Scottish Rite), and Senator Antonio Cefaly (vice-president of the Italian Symbolic Rite). [754]

Essentially, the criterion was the same everywhere. Six to ten year olds were welcomed from indigent households, strictly separated by gender (the only exception was "Alberico Gentili"). The activities, scheduled between 14:30–18:00, were the most varied: from civics classes to manual activities and physical exercises.[755]

Returning to the Piedmont capital, 1887 was defined by an educational initiative bound to the local manufacture world, the foundation of Scuole Officine Serali. This institution was designed to meet the emerging industrial needs of Turin by training professionals able to work in the most diverse sectors: construction, woodworking, metalworking, printing, and the textile industry. Attended every year by about 600 students, they boasted multiple labs where each student could improve his manual skills. The active involvement of Freemasonry had a surge in the early century, when the leadership was made up of Obedience members (vice president, secretary, and treasurer).[756]

---

754 Educatorio Roma, *Statuto approvato nell'assemblea ordinaria del 2 marzo 1906*, Tip. latina, Roma, 1907.

755 Giancarlo Rocca, *Istruzione, educazione*, op. cit., pp. 54–55.

756 Demetrio Xoccato, *Ars et Labor. Le Scuole Officine Serali di Torino (1887–1925)*, in "Cahiers di Scienze Sociali", n. 3, 2015, pp. 234–249.

A specific feature of this society was the support of the subalpine lodges—"Pietro Micca-Ausonia," "Cavour," and "Dante Alighieri" in Turin, along with others located in neighboring areas, such as "Giordano Bruno" in Pinerolo, "Giuseppe Garibaldi" in Novara, and "Andrea Vochieri" from Alessandria.[757]

The birth of Società Italiana per l'Educazione Laica della Gioventù in Milan in 1892 was a new opportunity, after the experiences of the 60s, to support a nationally oriented organization that—guessing from the name—promoted textbooks that were absolutely nondenominational, without any religious influence. Another crucial initiative was the enhancement of new and modern school facilities throughout the territory.

Despite the support of the Grand Orient of Italy, as evidenced by the wide emphasis given on the "Rivista della masoneria italiana", this entity was not that lucky and was soon forgotten.[758]

Definitely more relevant, for the history of Milanese philanthropy, was the Società Umanitaria. Founded in 1893 with the aim of offering the deprived access to education and work, it initially received little attention from the Brethren. Who was there acted on his own initiative (the aforementioned Nulli, enrolled in "La Ragione," Angelo Tondini, of "Carlo Cattaneo", and Osvaldo Gnocchi Viani).

The limited masonic influence meant the school entered the orbit of the socialists and the labor movement—a major social force—and became an iffy place to the public security forces. The Milanese riots of 1898, born to protest against the harsh conditions of life and which were roughly repressed, provided the pretext for the public authority to take control of the institute, removing the previous board.[759]

Again autonomous in 1901, it enjoyed a revived momentum from the following year, opening employment offices, providing legal, and medical assistance—for the weakest—, as well as supporting those making their way abroad. In the latter case, this service was backing up the General Commissariat of Emigration, a fresh national structure with the task of survey-

---

757 Demetrio Xoccato, *Il Grande Oriente d'Italia e l'educazione*, op. cit., p. 62.

758 *Società italiana per l'educazione laica della gioventù in Milano*, in "Rivista della massoneria italiana", n. 4–6, 1892, pp. 60–62.

759 Fabio Pruneri, *L'Umanitaria e la massoneria*, in "Annali di storia dell'educazione e delle istituzioni scolastiche", vol. XI, 2004, p. 142.

ing migration flows. This complementarity would have reached its peak in 1920, when two Brethen, Augusto Osimo and Giuseppe De Michelis, were at the top of the two organizations.[760]

With the establishment of the Casa del Lavoro in 1907, a bed for those in need of shelter was even possible for a few days.

Equally significant was the engagement in construction of public housing, built according to the criteria of the hygienist movement, to accommodate laborers at low cost.[761]

The strength was, however, another: training courses. Workshops at Umanitaria were largely directed at unskilled adults with three years' work experience and who wished to qualify, and increased their knowledge base.[762] There were classes dedicated to handiworks, such as woodworking, ironwork, decoration of fabrics, and jewelry. Furthermore, in 1904, the Scuola del Libro started its courses, where the most advanced typographic techniques were taught.

In 1910, the Umanitaria merged with the People's House, headquarters to all the social initiatives for the salaried (Lega Nazionale delle Cooperative, Federazione delle Società di Mutuo Soccorso e Camera del Lavoro).[763]

The decision to link to a obvious socialist network shows how the relationship with this world had remained strong. As a matter of fact, until 1924, the masonic attendance within the board was limited, with the notable exception of Luigi Della Torre (chairman in the first post-war period). This spread out a certain commonality of interests between the two blocks and the role of Brethren in an indirect intervention (on a financial basis) was preferable to direct management. In this regard, it is exemplary that, at the beginning of the century, all Freemasons belonging to "Carlo Cattaneo" lodge entered in the society as members.[764]

Another distinctly educational phenomenon was that of Popular Universities. The spread of this model benefitted from a certain durability and sig-

760 Gerardo Padulo, *Contributo alla storia della massoneria da Giolitti a Mussolini*, in "Annali dell'Istituto italiano per gli studi storici", n. 84, 1983, p. 328.

761 Fabio Pruneri, *L'Umanitaria e la massoneria*, op. cit., p. 144.

762 Augusto Osimo, *Il fenomeno della disoccupazione e la Società Umanitaria*, in "Nuova Antologia", vol. CCIX, 1906, pp. 244–246.

763 Fabio Pruneri, *L'Umanitaria e la massoneria*, op. cit., p. 147.

764 Gerardo Padulo, Contributo alla storia della massoneria, op. cit., p. 328.

nificant diffusion, of which Britain and Denmark had been the forerunners. In 1844, lifted by Kristian Flor, a professor at the University of Kiel, the very first institution of this kind was established in Redding, with the involvement of academics in the agenda of conferences, courses, and lectures open to the public. Six years later, the second university had risen in Rjislinge, whose calendars were designed according to the intended audience (winter session for farmers and summer for women). The intake in the early century was decidedly impressive: about 60,000 students, aged between 18 and 25, into 68 institutions.[765]

As far as the United Kingdom is concerned, 20 years had to pass before city's elite and intellectuals were interested in spreading this model.

In 1870, the universities of Cambridge, Oxford, London, and Victoria had arranged what would be known as "university extension": a panel of conferences and evening or festive courses—for a fee[766]—managed by a board of teachers consisting of young graduates. Specific to the course was the option to collect a diploma to access a final exam for possible enrolment in state universities.[767]

From this overview, the Austrian and the Spanish cases are also stimulating, and are closer to the Italian one. In 1893, a group of professors from the University of Vienna met and decided to hold evening classes on a range of subjects (natural sciences, medicine, chemistry, physics, mathematics, Latin, law, history, and literature). With the appointment of the central government—providing them an annual subsidy of 6,000 florins—the consortium was able to print and share programs and posters, and buy advertising space in newspapers.[768]

In Oviedo, Spain, the first center of the movement was followed by other alma maters in neighboring towns (Avilles, Gijon, Felguara). Between 1903 and 1904, new units were launched in Valencia—thanks to the ef-

---

765 Enrico Miletto, "... la coltura per il popolo." L'Università Popolare di Torino (1900–1930), Università Popolare di Torino, Torino, 2013, p. 8.

766 The deal was different for each participant according to their economic status. Carlo Sforza, Le Università Popolari. Un nuovo movimento, in "Nuova Antologia", vol. IV, 1901, p. 345.

767 Enrico Miletto, "... la coltura per il popolo," op. cit., p. 4.

768 Riccardo Marini, L'Università Popolare in Italia, Tip. Degli Artigianelli, Torino, 1900, p. 13.

forts of the novelist, and Mason, Vicente Blasco Ibáñez[769]—and in Madrid. Something similar also happened in Barcelona with popular athenaeums.

The Italian case, therefore, fits fully within this frame. This formula was perceived as a great innovation, to be replicated within the national context. A debate came up, involving specialized headlines from different parties that helped to raise public awareness.[770]

These premises led to the birth of the Università Popolare di Torino. The first of its kind in Italy, it set, in line with European teachings, the goal of spreading scientific and literary culture among all social strata, especially the lowers, who were unable to enroll in ranked universities. The key players were four, all Freemasons: the socialist Donato Bachi, the doctors Pio Foà[771] and Amedeo Herlitzka, and the astronomy academic Francesco Porro.[772]

Open to the public in 1900, the school offered, under tuition, several courses to all those having the primary school license. The positivist philosophy managers and teachers—mostly university professors—belonged to, meant education focused on practical and scientific subjects, while ignoring the humanistic aspect. The lessons, therefore, dealt with issues such as hygiene, disease prevention, and basic notions of electricity, chemistry, and commercial law. Laborers appeared to appreciate the training offered: they represented 38% of the participants in the courses; higher than the European average that was around 30%.[773]

Based on the results seen in Turin, even the Roman lodges decided to support the opening of a local popular university. A major input in favor of

---

769 Eugènia Ventura Gayete, *Aurelio Blasco Grajales, Vicente Dualde Furió y Vicente Blasco Ibáñez: masones y periodistas*, in José Antonio Ferrer Benimeli (a cura di), *La masonería española en el 2000 una revisión histórica, IX Symposium Internacional de Historia de la Masonería Española*, vol. I, Zaragoza, Gobierno de Aragón, Departamento de Educación, Cultura y Deporte, 2001, pp. 395–406.

770 Enrico Miletto, "... *la coltura per il popolo*," op. cit., p. 10.

771 Pio Foà (1848–1923). Graduated in Pavia alma mater in Medicine and Surgery, he began his career as a pathological anatomist. After a chair at Modena, in 1884, he was called to teach in Turin, where he remained until his death. National member of the Lincei (1892), in 1908 he was appointed senator of the Kingdom and, in this role he entered in the debate on the prophylaxis and treatment of tuberculosis. He was the curator of the fundamental *Trattato di anatomia patologica generale e speciale*.

772 Enrico Miletto, "... *la coltura per il popolo*," op. cit., pp. 17–19.

773 Enrico Miletto, *Laici e solidali. Massoneria e associazionismo in Piemonte (1861–1925)*, FrancoAngeli, Milano, 2018, p. 43.

the establishment of such a body came from the Associazione fra i Liberi Docenti Romani, whose president was Brother Nunzio Nasi,[774] at that time also Minister of Education. In 1903, the Council of G.O.I. also contributed, through financial support, to the institute.[775]

The courses here were indeed not necessarily aimed at salaried men, but to employees and traders. The goal, therefore, was to broaden the cultural skill of the middle-class, whose Masonry was largely an expression.

Several teachers, who lent their work for free, covered—or would later—prominent roles within Freemasonry, demonstrating the social commitment that was affecting everyone, including the high spheres: among all Teresio Trincheri—president of the Italian Symbolic Rite in 1909–1912—and Gustavo Canti—Deputy Grand Master from 1912 to 1916.

8.2 Aid to the Needy

O nce the pedagogical field had been accomplished, the Masonic commitment turned to analyze improvement measures for weaker people. In the next pages, we will focus—in particular—on the most significant solutions.

Abreast these, however, it should not be forgotten that Italian lodges retained, during the entire liberal span, the practice of donating cash or assets during certain appointments. On December 25, 1912, for example, "Fratelli Bandiera" lodge in Milan, together with the "Cavalieri di Scozia" and Brother Francesco Gondrand,[776] offered a meal to about 500 Milanese

---

774 Nunzio Nasi (1850–1935). Born in Trapani from a middle-class family, after graduating in law, he began to teach in a technical institute of which he became dean. In 1878, he was the head of the "Gazzetta di Trapani," headline of the liberal and radical world. He entered the city council of his own town (1883–1926); in 1886, he became MP, Minister of Posts (1898–1899) and then of Education (1900–1903). In 1908, he was convicted of embezzlement.

775 ASGOI, *Minute*, July 23, 1903.

776 Francesco Gondrand (1840–1926). Born in Savoy by a local family, once accomplished upper education courses he was hired by a friend of his father, in charge of customs procedures. After Savoy's transfer to France, he moved to Milan where he founded a transport company in 1866. Within 15 years, the firm was prosperous enough to widen in Europe and Americas too. In addition to land transport, Gondrand also took an interest in maritime transfers by acquiring agencies from foreign companies. The entrepreneur was able to develop over time many other many backing activities, such as the sale of foodstuffs and iced confections.

needy people, to give them the chance to celebrate Christmas.[777]

That said, the first institution to practice the philanthropic intervention program, which succeeded in matching assistance to the needy and literacy, arose—once again—in Turin. With the death, in 1869, of French merchant Carlo Alfonso Bonafous, "Dante Alighieri"—in the person of Fabretti—undertook his last wishes, so that even the Piedmontese capital would provide an agricultural school that would host, and then reintroduce, derelict and delinquent children into civil society. The explicit reference was to the two French colonies of Mettray, near Tours, and Oullins, near Lyon.[778]

The first community took mainly minors involved in minor crimes who were on bail. A consortium of citizens in Paris founded the institution in 1839 under the name of Société Paternelle, led by Frédéric-Auguste De Metz and Viscount Bréttignères De Courteilles. The headquarters was a large enclosure in the Turenne countryside, made by a quadrangular yard on whose two parallel sides stood the housing lodges.

The activity had its core in cultivation, plus workshops for tool crafting and fixing. Students were taught how to do laundry, to cook, to breed domestic animals, even to erect sewerage works. The Société Paternelle exercised its protection even when young people left the colony, endeavoring to find a place and, as an alternative, to offer a refuge in the case of need.

The luck and the recognition—even abroad—of Mettray, explains why, within a short time, similar institutions sprouted in other European countries, including the two Redhill shelters-colonies and the Reformatory School in England, the Ruysselède and Berneem schools in Belgium, and the Mettray Neerlandais in the Netherlands.[779]

The Oullins workshop, otherwise, was responsible for youngsters who had seen their convictions commuted in a rehab outside the prison. This colony was peculiar in its cultivation of orchards and gardens.

Returning to Turin, the testament of Bonafous meant the city would receive the significant amount of 1,248,805 liras for such rehabilitative pur-

---

777 *Notizie sull'attività delle Officine di Rito Simbolico Italiano*, in "Bollettino del rito simbolico italiano", n. 43, 1913, p. 4.

778 Demetrio Xoccato, *Un'educazione all'insegna della modernità: il caso torinese (1868–1925)*, in "L'Impegno. Rivista di storia contemporanea", n. 1, 2015, pp. 23.

779 Pietro Baricco, *Torino*, vol. II, Paravia, Torino, 1869, p. 837.

poses. Thanks to the efforts made by Villa—and after a troubled process—this sum was used to purchase Lucento manor, on the outskirts of the city, which became the headquarters of the Bonafous Agricultural Institute. Therefore, in 1871, the male school arose, admitting young people aged between 10 and 18, from orphanages or disastrous families. Here, parted in small groups, they received an education designed to train highly qualified agronomists, able to handle the latest techniques.

Together with this professional path, boys followed a brief curriculum of primary education that coexisted with the work needs in the fields.[780]

The institute distinguished itself throug important reform work in the field of rural management. Between 1913 and 1924, for example, a course was organized—in parallel with the others—in which pupils learned to type, to perfect themselves in calligraphy, and to manage bookkeeping. Moreover, the most promising were sent to the Royal Academy of Agriculture to attend classes on grafting and fruit growing.[781]

Unlike the case of the Istituto per le Figlie dei Militari, the Turin Brethren kept out of the factual management, considering it more profitable to cover only the philanthropic role. The only element that emerged from their presence was the open recognition for non-Catholic youths to have their own ministers of worship.[782]

The birth of the Casa Benefica per i Giovani Derelitti was, instead, due to the civil commitment of the lawyer and magistrate Luigi Martini. This Brother, working closely with destitute youth—often faulty—took up the belief that these children should be helped to have a future and a chance for social reintegration. Thanks to his commitment, in 1889, the association was officially opened, receiving wretched pupils aged between 7 and 16. The primary purpose was to guarantee them an education—professional mostly—and a job outlet. Working-age boys worked in workshops, and their salaries were deposited in personal passbooks, which were delivered once they left the institute.[783]

---

780 Istituto Bonafous di Torino, *Origine ed ordinamento attuale (1872–1912)*, Stab. Arti grafiche Torelli, Casale Monferrato, 1912, p. 17.

781 Ivi, pp. 17–18.

782 Istituto Bonafous, *Regolamento interno dell'Istituto Bonafous approvato dal consiglio comunale nella seduta del 19 luglio 1871*, Tip. Botta, Torino, 1871, p. 22.

783 Marcella Filippa, Giorgina Levi, *"Eravamo come uccelli sperduti". Cento anni di storia*

The masonic influence was quite small, though always present. In addition to the founder, who chaired until his death (1894), there were executives—including the inevitable Villa—and lawyer Felice Tedeschi (vice president in 1920).

Pioneering, and absolutely unique, was Filantropia Senza Sacrifici, founded in Milan in 1877. Inspired by the Austrian and Swiss experiences—where some charitable companies recycled and sold tobacco left in cigar butts—the promoters thought about collecting and reselling old newspapers, books, and paper scraps, and delivering the income to philanthropic organizations.[784]

Citizens reacted well to this venture and donations of sheets, cuttings, and books took on significant proportions. In 1881, the company recovered 100 illustrated volumes and 250 quintals of paper, for a total value of more than 2,200 liras.[785]

Observing its organigram, the Milanese Freemasonry played a pivotal role. Amid 18 members of the board, in 1886, five of them were initiates. Although apparently a small number, they still covered all the key positions and were thus able to direct the plot: members of Masonry were, in fact, the president (Malachia De Cristoforis, outstanding person in the city and in Italy), the vice president, and the treasurer.[786]

The birth of a small kindergarten for stunted children in Turin provided Pini the inspiration to sensitize the Milanese audience to this serious social scourge. The lodges of the Lombard capital—as first "La Ragione"—gave important support to the foundation of the Istituto dei Rachitici. Officially opened in January 1875, its fundraising saw the support also of distant lodges, who could not actually enjoy the positive effects of proximity to the health facility. "L'Unità" e "Garibaldi" di Palermo, for example, paid 40 liras.[787]

---

della Casa Benefica di Torino (1889–1989), Cooperativa di Consumo e Mutua Assistenza Borgo Po e Decoratori, Torino, 1989.

784 La filantropia senza sagrifici [sic] a Milano, in "Rivista della beneficenza pubblica e degli Istituzioni di previdenza", fasc. 2, 1877, p. 166.

785 L'Istituzione "Filantropia senza sacrifici" in Milano, in "Rivista della beneficenza pubblica e delle Istituzioni di previdenza", fasc. 2, 1881, p. 189.

786 Guida di Milano per l'anno 1886, Tip. Bernardoni, Milano, s.d., pp. 589–590, 620–621.

787 Notizie Massoniche, in "La Luce. Eco della costituente massonica", n.37, 1874, p. 24.

The first years were quite harsh, and the association was initially conceived as a kind of school-clinic, which welcomed kids from five to ten years, and subjected them to some orthopedic therapies. The makeover into a hospital complex took place progressively as a result of greater financial contributions from the city's philanthropic forces. Beginning in the 1890s, the establishment grew in remark and its activity was allotted into three pavilions: outpatient (reception, count, and first aid), school (didactic, orthopedics, and gym exercises), and infirmary (surgery).[788]

Another medical endeavor centered on the Piedmontese capital. Here, thanks to 100 liras collected by "Dante Alighieri," Dr. Laura was able to found, in 1883, the first infant hospital in Italy, "Regina Margherita." Divided into two units, medicine and surgery, the clinic provided care for needy children aged 2–10, and was entirely free. The positive reaction led to the expansion of facilities and services. In the first decade, more than 3,000 children were hospitalized, plus other 68,000 adolescents supported by counseling and treatments.[789]

A corollary of this fervent activity was the birth, again in Turin, of Green Cross. These volunteers, since 1907, provided a pioneering first aid service on accidents at work through the use of vehicles. Between the nineteenth and twentieth centuries, these incidents had been the main cause of illness among civilians, and had assumed the traits of a real emergency.[790]

The main animators of this initiative was a group of prompt people, including the local tycoon—and Brother—Gino Olivetti, and the criminologist Cesare Lombroso who, although not a mason, shared the same ideals and battles. The latter was named president of the association but, shortly thereafter, left the post for health reasons.[791]

In 1910, the election of Olivetti represented a caesura and gave a strong impulse to the initiative, thanks to his charisma and the contemporary ap-

---

788 Giorgio Cosmacini, *Due istituzioni, un uomo: la "Ca' Granda," i "Rachitici" e Gaetano Pini*, in "La ca' granda", fasc. 2, 2004, pp. 15–17.

789 Annibale Nota, *Resoconto clinico statistico della sezione chirurgica dell'ospedale infantile Regina Margherita in Torino dal 1 gennaio 1894 al 31 dicembre 1899*, Tip. Salesiana, Torino, 1900; Ospedale infantile Regina, Margherita, *Resoconto clinico statistico, Sessennio 1 gennaio 1884 al 31 dicembre 1889*, Tip. Salesiana, Torino, 1900.

790 Marino Properzi, Patrizio Abrate, Vassili Bonucci, *90 anni di storia verde (1907–1997)*, Croce Verde, Torino, 1997, p. 9.

791 Augusto Comba, *La massoneria tra filantropia e pedagogia*, in Augusto Comba, Emma

pointment as secretary of the Italian Confederation of Industry (gathering all the entrepreneurs of the Kingdom).

Support for the poor could not help tackling another essential theme – food: malnutrition and food scarcity were widespread among the urban population. The first Popular Kitchen, which provided the packaging and sale of foodstuffs at raw costs, was born in Leipzig (Germany) in 1849, inspired by the English-based cooperative societies. Here, a group of city's leading class opened, in the Royal Square of the village, a room—equipped with a kitchen and a refectory—where people could buy and consume a packed meal. In the first year of activity, the kitchen delivered 122,000 rations while the average, over the following 22 years of service, stood at 177,000.[792] These rates are substantial and prove why, within a short time, another branch was founded. The model spread to other countries, including France and Switzerland. In Geneva, a group of workers set down in societies, opened a place for food preparation in the town that also provided a free supply of wood and salt. After only three months, the alliance could fund itself without communal support and purchase wholesale food supplies for retail at cost price.

The Popular Kitchen of Grenoble was instead the result of a commitment from Frédéric Taullier, academic and mayor. Beginning in 1851, the young institution also enjoyed considerable success, and, within three years, was able to pay off all debts for commissioning and no longer depend on public economic aid.[793]

After Geneva and Grenoble, it was up to the Scottish city of Glasgow. As for the French case, thanks to the initiative of a philanthropist—the industrialist Thomas Corbett—the essential capital for the enterprise was gathered. At the opening of the first kitchen in September 1860, others followed quickly, bringing the whole deal to thirteen. This growth allowed Corbett not only to recover the sum disbursed, but also to gain a net (in 1862, the profit amounted to 4,000 francs). Soon, similar establishments were installed in other cities in UK: Birmingham, Liverpool, and Manchester.

Mana, Serenella Nonnis Vigilante (edited), *La morte laica. Storia della cremazione a Torino (1880–1920)*, vol. II, Scriptorium, Torino, 1998, p. 213.

792 In just 1849, the institution delivered over 3,000 meals per day. *Le cucine economiche*, in "Rivista della beneficenza pubblica e delle Istituzioni di previdenza", fasc. 2, 1881, p. 187.

793 Enrico Miletto, *Laici e solidali*, op. cit., pp. 86–87.

A last interesting case, analog with the Italian events, is the Belgian one. Here, local Masonry then acted firmly in support of the Brussels canteen. The two eminent city lodges—*Les Amis philanthropes* and *Vrais Amis de l'Union et du Progres Réunis*—gave life, in 1867, to the Atelier Réunis, with the express purpose of managing a popular kitchen, and gave it a large sum (3,000 francs). The municipality, for its part, gave the land for the premises of food supply as early as the following year.

Its results were remarkable: in its wake, similar organisms were born throughout the state (Liège, Antwerp, Namur, and Ghent). [794]

Re-addressing the Italian scene, the first Italian city to host such a food supplier was Modena in 1880. After this first experience, within a few years, many others, almost all concentrated in the center-north, sprouted. Amid them stood out those of Milan (1881), Genoa (1884), Florence (1885), Udine (1886), and Venice (1887).[795]

In 1884, the Popular Kitchens of Turin and Novara were founded, both backed by local Freemasonry. The first one had notable growth, opening branches in different districts of the city and reaching a total of nine in 1891. This impetuous rose, also due to the first president—the hygienist physician and professor Luigi Pagliani[796]—then experienced a sharp decline. Despite the tireless work of the entrepreneur Cesare Goldmann, the condition only worsened since the city hall—its main supporter—dramatically reduced the payments (from the early 12,000 liras to 3,000 in 1899), and resulted in closure in 1900.[797]

Notably, the Turin kitchen also became a recruitment area for Masonry, displaying the osmosis between social commitment and the decision to be-

---

794 Victor Serwy, *La Coopération en Belgique. Le développement de la coopération (1914–1940)*, vol. III, Les propagateurs de la coopération, Bruxelles, 1948, p. 7; *Le cucine economiche*, in "Rivista della beneficenza pubblica e delle Istituzioni di previdenza", fasc. 2, 1881, p. 187; Enrico Miletto, *Laici e solidali*, op. cit., p. 87.

795 Alessandro De Brun e Carlo De Mattia, *Le istituzioni filantropiche: cucine economiche, albegrhi popolari, case operaie*, UTET, Torino, 1914.

796 Luigi Pagliani (1847–1932). Graduated as a doctor in Turin (1868), he was appointed professor of the first Hygiene chair in Italy (a position he held from 1881 to 1924). Called to Rome by Prime Minister Crispi, set at the head of the General Directorate of Health. Here, he obtained outstanding goals in the fight against cholera, which mainly affected southern Italy, and in the diagnosis of Ancylostomiasis. With Crispi, in 1888, he rafted the first act on the protection of public health hygiene.

797 Enrico Miletto, *Laici e solidali*, op. cit., pp. 83–103.

come a Brother. Key executives, in fact, registered over time in G.O.I.: the mentioned Pagliani (initiated in 1889 to "Rienzi" of Rome) and Goldmann (in 1890 member of "Pietro Micca-Ausonia").

The Cucine di Novara deserves specific focus. Here, Freemasonry had already been engaged for some years in the food sector, supporting the introduction of Cooperative Ovens for baking bread, thus gaining a solid experience.

Unlike the Turin case, the management—with Attilio Carotti and Francesco Gastaldi from "Ugo Foscolo" and Secondo Perone from "Indipendenza"—opted for financial independence through the sale of stock to the community.

The Brethren of this medium-sized urban center showed considerable dynamism while supporting other drives in parallel. Inspired by the near Milan, in 1878, Angelo Pogliano, leader of the "Ugo Foscolo," gave birth to Filantropia senza Sacrifici, whom the Comitato di Soccorso alle Madri Lattanti Povere came from, which distributed free milk to deprived mothers who had to wean their children.[798]

The support offered to homeless and needy, however, could not be limited solely to the provision of a hot meal. Thus, the need to provide a suitable place to sleep swiftly ensued.

Once again Europe—and specifically France—provided important suggestions. The *Societé Philanthropique* had existed in Paris for a long time; in 1878, it opened the first night shelter on the continent. This place welcomed anyone who came, offering hospitality, clothes, food, and, where possible, a decent work placement. The following year a special women's section was built and, in 1886, the situation in Paris had become pretty assorted: the facilities had become six (three by gender), with a total of 394 beds for men, 190 for women, and 50 cots. According to data from the "Rivista della beneficenza pubblica e delle Istituzioni di previdenza", almost 58,000 people were helped in 1884.[799]

The importance of this experience was recognized both internationally—

---

798 Marco Novarino, *Fratellanza e solidarietà. Massoneria e associazionismo laico in Piemonte dal Risorgimento all'avvento del fascismo*, Sottosopra, Torino, 2008, p. 299.

799 *Gli Asili notturni a Parigi e a Londra*, in "Rivista della beneficenza pubblica e delle Istituzioni di previdenza", fasc. 2, 1886, p. 167.

the English magazine "Public Health" in 1896 included a report on it[800]— and inland.

The broad emphasis given to the Parisian structure and its operation in the Italian scientific and hygiene magazines—"L'ingegneria sanitaria" published an article about it in 1891[801]—shows the idea of providing temporary shelters was welcomed as an urging concern also in the "Bel Paese."

The first night shelter of certain significance was Raffaele Sonzogno Asylum of Rome. Strongly desired by the publisher Edoardo Sonzogno, as a tribute to his deceased brother, it was officially installed on February 6, 1887.[802]

Inside the mansion—located in Via Flaminia—the unemployed, beggars, and work-impaired people found decent housing, hot water, and "good readings." The success was almost immediate, since in the first trimester, around 3,504 people (mostly young, 15 to 25 aged, mothers with infants too) found hospitality.

The masonic hold within it is easily identifiable, since the GM Adriano Lemmi[803] himself was personally involved here, as chairman of the executive committee.[804]

Close to the opening of the Raffaele Sonzogno, Turin also procured a similar structure. Starting in January 1888, the Asilo Notturno Umberto I proposed to welcome both the local homeless and the poor foreigners, who were not able to afford a better stay than a bench inside the public gardens.[805]

The guests were first recorded, then taken to a changing room while their clothes were sterilized and after they underwent a medical examination.

---

800 *A municipal night shelter in Paris*, in "Public Health", vol. 8, 1896, p. 23.

801 *L'asilo notturno Umberto I in Torino*, in "L'ingegneria sanitaria", n. 7, 1891, pp. 101–102.

802 *L'Asilo notturno R. Sonzogno a Roma*, in "Rivista della beneficenza pubblica e delle Istituzioni di previdenza", fasc. 2, 1887, pp. 153–154.

803 Adriano Lemmi (1822–1906). Infused with patriotic feelings since childhood, he left Tuscany purposely going into exile where he was devoted to trade. In 1847, he met Mazzini and, two years later, joined him in Rome backing the Republic. Compromising with the insurrectional attempt of 1853, he repaired to Switzerland and, later, to Constantinople. In 1860, during the Expedition of the Thousand, he received from Garibaldi the franchise on a railway and later on a tobacco monopoly.

804 *L'asilo notturno Raffaele Sonzogno—Rapporto trimestrale*, in "Rivista della massoneria italiana", n. 23–24, 1887, p. 191.

805 *L'Asilo notturno Umberto I in Torino*, op. cit., p. 101.

The span of stays was set at four consecutive nights, though—in special cases—extensions were considered.[806]

The number of patients grew, going from 1,080 in the first year to a peak of 7,425 in 1911. Notwithstanding, in 1915—also due to the negative influence of the Great War—the amount collapsed and in 1918 reached its minimum (3,256 guests), but was to slowly rise again.[807]

Apart from the industrial Giulio Peyrot (one of the founders), in the first years, Masonry remained fairly separate. It was only from the 1910s that it rose up to assume responsibility of the institute in the 1920s, with the presidency of Giuseppe Chiesa (member of "Propaganda" lodge).

This behavior can be explained by its role as mediator between the two groups that contributed the most: Jewish and Protestant.

The outcome of this temporary care facility was successful enough to be exported to minor cities too. A notable example is Leghorn. The Tuscan city, small but with a long-living and deeply rooted masonic presence, was also experiencing a significant industrial development and the resultant emergence of workers' suburbs. Fronting the asset troubles of the "working poor" in 1893, at the incitement of the local Comitato Filantropia Senza Sacrifici, this center was equipped with a night shelter.

These promoters were a direct emanation of local Masonry: almost all its members were Brethen, mostly from the "Garibaldi-Avvenire" lodge (the entrepreneur Rosolino Orlando,[808] future mayor, stood out).

Open to both men and women—strictly separated into two dormitories—it could hold a capacity of 300 people. As for Turin guests, they could be accommodated for a maximum number of consecutive nights (here five), after which they were directed elsewhere to find a less temporary arrangement.[809]

806 Società Asili Notturni in Torino, *Statuto e regolamenti*, Officina Grafica Elzeviriana, Torino, 1923.

807 Enrico Miletto, *Laici e solidali*, op. cit., p. 149.

808 Rosolino Orlando (1860–1924). Exponent of the local notability, after a law degree at the University of Genoa, he entered the management of family affairs, the Orlando Shipyard of Leghorn. After the discord within the family nucleus, in 1904, he left the company, undertaking a managerial career in many notable enterprises (Cementiera Italiana, Ilva, Società Siderurgica of Savona, Società Anonima Torbiere d'Italia). As mayor of the city (1895–1897, 1915–1920), he committed many important infrastructural plants.

809 *Gli asili notturni in Livorno*, in "Rivista della massoneria italiana", n. 18–20, 1893, pp.

Six years after its inception, Grand Master Ernesto Nathan[810] himself, with the director of the "Rivista della masoneria italiana" Ulisse Bacci, on an appointment for the memorial to Luigi Orlando, decided to visit the institute, admiring the progress and providing a contribution: a clear sign of the approval by G.O.I.[811]

Parallel to the opening of night shelters, in Milan, the lodges were about to form the Soccorso Fraterno. The idea—from Pini—came after a petition to help a small group of homeless families who were hit by the harsh winter of 1879. The promoter committee set itself the ambitious goal of providing a series of services to fight the hardship and the scourges of poverty: subsidies and treatments for those unable to work, defense from domestic violence and exploitation in the workplace, recruitment support, and decontamination of the popular neighborhoods.[812]

Six local committees sprang to sort help requests and provide the necessary support. A few years after its birth, the balance was barely positive: in just 1881, 231 applications were admitted and more than 1,700,000 liras paid.[813]

There was initially a very close connection with Masonry—many were members of lodges—but there was a hapless drift in 1886. A severing hit the Milanese lodges leading to the creation of a new Masonic organism (in the mid-90s it would be called Italian Grand Orient). This inner break up led to the indictment of President Pini who, mistrusted about the management, presented his resignation in July.[814]

278–280.

810 Ernesto Nathan (1845–1921). Born in London to an Italian mother and a naturalized English German, he spent his first years abroad and then reverted to Italy in 1859. In 1871, summoned by Mazzini, he moved to Rome as officer in "La Roma del popolo" headline. Granted the Italian citizenship in 1888, he fully entered into political and cultural life of the Capital. Elected mayor in 1907, he kept the charge until 1913, distinguishing himself for the urban planning program and for the municipalization of public facilities.

811 *A Livorno. Feste massoniche per l'inaugurazione del monumento al F∴ Luigi Orlando 33..*, in "Rivista della massoneria italiana", n. 1–2, 1899, p. 23.

812 Ambrogio Viviani, *Storia della Massoneria lombarda dalle origini al 1962*, Bastogi, Foggia, 1992, p. 127.

813 *L'Istituzione "Il Soccorso Fraterno" in Milano*, in "Rivista della beneficenza pubblica e delle Istituzioni di previdenza", fasc. 3, 1882, p. 285.

814 *Soccorso fraterno*, in "Humanitas", n. 3, 1886, pp. 8–9.

Only in 1888 was the crisis definitively resolved and the association re-founded. In a short time, the Soccorso Fraterno was strengthened and could broaden its activities, both new and those already active. The first step was a service of book and stationery provision to deprived students, followed by a legal aid service to those workers affected by injuries owing to third parties.

As a further development, social bakeries (the first in Cuggiono, in the outskirts) and then a Magazzino Benefico were opened, where workers could buy garments and tools at cost price.[815]

Because of the knotty economic scenery seen at the end of the nineteenth century, beggary reached its peak. It was thus predictable that this juncture stimulated the birth of new bodies in an attempt to alleviate the conditions on the margins of society. Already in 1875, an institute had arisen in Florence where needy people received clothing and groceries, further equipped with workshops where men could find paid craft work.[816]

In 1896, the lawyer Ettore Obert, son-in-law of the founder of Casa Benefica and Master Mason in "Cavour", gave life to a committee whose action would beget—three years later—the Istituto contro l'Accattonaggio Pane Quotidiano in Turin.[817]

The main purpose was to provide immediate assistance to beggars, offering them—with other civic charitable institutions—food, and support for possible return to their homeland, or to find decent employment.[818]

The response was encouraging and the number of recipients grew steadily with, in 1902, its peak: 38,254 people rescued, 99,377 meal rations, 107,449 bread portions, 10,935 of wine, and 5,256 of milk.[819]

815 Il "Soccorso fraterno a Milano," in "Rivista della massoneria italiana", n. 14–17, 1894, p. 268.

816 La Società per la prevenzione e per la repressione dell'accattonaggio in Firenze, in "Rivista della beneficenza pubblica e delle Istituzioni di previdenza", fasc. 7, 1884, pp. 643–646.

817 Archivio Storico della Città di Torino, Affari gabinetto del sindaco, Istituto contro l'Accattonaggio Pane Quotidiano, inventory 2034, folder 161 bis, file 84, Statuto, concorso municipale, 1899.

818 Istituto contro l'accattonaggio Pane quotidiano, Cronologia documentata dall'anno della sua fondazione al gennaio 1904, Torino, Tip. Wolf, 1904.

819 Enrico Miletto, Marco Novarino, "Senza distinzione politica e religiosa". Repertorio bibliografico e archivistico sull'associazionismo laico a Torino e provincia (1848–1925),

The ever-increasing requests led, in 1903, to the opening of an additional structure in a different district. More than food distribution, a tailor workshop was created for unemployed laborers to fix used clothes.[820]

Another Brother of the highest level within this organization was the rubber and electrical facilities industrial Francesco Martiny, who was vice-president first, then officer, and, finally, advisor.

Similarly, in the capital, the same institution became a widespread inspiration, and was assisted by some Masonic input: the charter compiler was Guido Cavaglieri, director of the "Rivista italiana di sociologia" and a member of the "Universe."[821] After a couple of years of growth, the Società contro l'Accattonaggio of Rome was born and the first outcomes were significant. From January 26 to June 12, 1898, 103,796 people were rescued, corresponding to an average of 756 needy per day. Some labor engagement was required in exchange, with the exception of disabled. A farming colony was established for the purpose on the Capo di Bove estate, where the recipients were to be conveyed.[822]

Closely linked to the begging problem and the hygienic campaign, another institution was established in Turin in 1887: the Public Baths.

In the need to combat the spread of infections, the board of Popular Kitchen decided to devote an adjacent building to provide showers and bathrooms at reasonable prices. After the first few years, the positive reaction encouraged the opening of other plants in the districts of Borgo Dora (1899) and San Donato (1900), as well as in the center. The municipal interest toward the initiative led to a civic ownership, giving rise to new branches and the change of name to Bagni Municipali (1913).[823]

In closing, it is worth mentioning the commitment of Freemasonry, which also embraced a financially difficult sector, social housing. This discourse mentioned already the work carried out in this field by Umanitaria and

---

Centro Studi Piero Calamandrei, Torino, 2011, p. 95.

820 Enrico Miletto, *Laici e solidali*, op. cit., p. 111.

821 *La Società contro l'accattonaggio in Roma*, in "Rivista della beneficenza pubblica e delle Istituzioni di previdenza e di igiene sociale", fasc. 4–5, 1896, pp. 372–379.

822 *Società contro l'accattonaggio in Roma*, in "Rivista della beneficenza pubblica e delle Istituzioni di previdenza e di igiene sociale", fasc. 3, 1899, p. 293.

823 *I Bagni popolari di Torino*, Tip. Cooperativa, Torino, 1888; Enrico Miletto, Marco Novarino, "... *Senza distinzione politica e religiosa*", op. cit., p. 87.

something similar happened in other cities. In 1902, the Società Torinese per le Abitazioni Popolari saw the light, thanks to the commitment of the usual Pagliani. This venture built up and purchased housing estates with the most advanced social-health requirements that were rented or sold directly to low-income households.[824]

8.3 An Assessment

All the initiatives promoted by the Brethren in the relief and care of the poorest and most literacy deficient were part of the broad design of a laic assistance system ideally—and polemically—adverse to the world of Catholic facilities. Masonic action was indeed not conceived as a "forma di carità, ma di filantropia".[825] While the clericals acted in the frame of "decorum" and charity (intended as almsgiving), freemasons fulfilled their mission in the name of "rationality" and solidarity (as human and material elevation). In 1874, a magazine stated that actually helping people in distress meant "toglierli all'abbandono, all'inerzia, alle sofferenze, ridonandoli utili cittadini a sé stessi ed alla patria".[826]

The deal of this theoretical elaboration, however, turned out to be hard and—as seen in this essay—the resulting picture is an anthology of composite and contradictory initiatives. After the first ephemeral and impromptu initiatives by individual Brethen and lodges, starting from the 1880s a more systematic approach provided lasting results, thanks to the successful experiences from beyond the Alps lending ideas and models (i.e. popular universities, popular kitchens, and night shelters). This greater emphasis on philanthropic offerings, however, had to clash with the diverse socio-economic scene and produced discordant results: the disappointing achievements in Milan were reverse to the success of the Roman lay youth clubs.

Due to the distinctions made, the issue from the analysis is that at the end of the Belle Époque, a dense laic association network—alternative to the Catholic world—had been forged to respond to most of the edu-

---

824 Maria D'Amuri, *Le case per il popolo a Torino. Dibattiti e realizzazione (1849–1915)*, Carocci, Roma, 2006.

825 "form of charity, but of philanthropy" [translator's note].

826 "to relieve them from dereliction, inertia, pain, and rehabilitate them as citizens and patriots" [translator's note]. *Notizie Massoniche*, in "La Luce. Eco della costituente massonica", n. 35, 1874, p. 16.

cational needs and assistance of the population. On the rise of fascism, therefore, Italian Masonry could boast a leading role in welfare and social life.

ADDENDA

I. GRAN MASTERS | GRAND ORIENT OF ITALY

Eugenio di Beauharnais, 1805–1814;

Filippo Delpino, (*interim*) 20-12-1859/20-05-1860;

Livio Zambeccari, (*interim*) 1860;

Felice Govean, (acting regent) 12-1861/07-1863;

Costantino Nigra, 08-10-1861/12-1861;

Livio Zambeccari, (*interim*) 08-10-1861/01-03-1862;

Filippo Cordova, 01-03-1862/06-08-1863;

Celestino Peroglio, 06-08-1863/24-05-1864;

Giuseppe Garibaldi, 24-05-1864/08-08-1864;

Francesco De Luca, (regent) 09-1864/05-1865 • 28-05-1865/20-06-1867;

Filippo Cordova, 21-06-1867/02-07-1867;

Lodovico Frapolli, (acting) 02-08-1867/31-05-1869 • 31-05-1869/07-09-1870 (resigned);

Giuseppe Mazzoni, 07-09-1870/27-01-1871 (acting) • 27-01-1871/11-05-1880 (deceased);

Giuseppe Petroni, 12-05-1880/16-01-1885;

Adriano Lemmi, 17-01-1885/31-05-1896;

Ernesto Nathan, 01-06-1896/14-02-1904;

Ettore Ferrari, 14-02-1904/25-11-1917 (resigned);

Ernesto Nathan, 25-11-1917/22-06-1919;

Domizio Torrigiani, 23-06-1919/30-08-1932;

Giuseppe Meoni, (chairman Warrant Commitee) 09-1926/1929;

Eugenio Chiesa, 12-01-1930/22-06-1930;

Arturo Labriola, 23-06-1930/29-11-1931;

Alessandro Tedeschi, 29-11-1931/19-08-1940;

Mastery Committee: Umberto Cipollone, Guido Laj, Gaetano Varcasia, 1943/1945;

Davide Augusto Albarin, 19-08-1940/10-06-1944;

Guido Laj, 18-09-1945/05-11-1948;

Umberto Cipollone, (*pro tempore*) 05-01-1949/18-03-1949;

Ugo Lenzi 19-03-1949/21-03-1953;

Carlo Speranza, (acting regent) 21-03-1953/05-04-10-1953;

Publio Cortini, 04-10-1953/26-05-1956 • 26-05-1956/27-09-1956 (resigned);

Umberto Cipollone, 30-11-1957/28-05-1960;

Giorgio Tron, 29-05-1960/29-04-1961;

Corrado Mastrocinque, (*pro tempore*) 29-04-1961/16-07-1961;

Giordano Gamberini, 17-07-1961/21-03-1970;

Lino Salvini, 21-03-1970/27-03-1973 • 27-03-1973/01-03-1976 • 01-03-1976/18-11-1978 (resigned);

Ennio Battelli, 18-11-1978/28-03-1982;

Armando Corona, 28-03-1982/30-03-1985 • 30-03-1985/10-03-1990;

Giuliano Di Bernardo, 10-03-1990/16-04-1993 (expelled);

Regency Committee, 05-05-1993/18-12-1993, **Deputy Grand Masters: Eraldo Ghinoi** (regent), **Ettore Loizzo**;

Virgilio Gaito, 18-12-1993/21-03-1999;

Gustavo Raffi, 21-03-1999/02-04-2004 • 02-04-2004/03-04-2009 • 03-04-2009/06-04-2014;

Stefano Bisi, 06-04-2014 /03-03-2019 • 03-03-2019

II.Reference Bibliography

Bacci Ulisse, *Il libro del massone italiano*, Vita Nova, Roma, 1922.

Casano Nicoletta, *Libres et persécutés. Francs-maçons et laïques italiens en exil pendant le fascisme*, Garnier, Paris, 2016.

Cazzaniga Gian Mario (edited), *La Massoneria. Storia d'Italia*, Annali, XXI, Einaudi, Torino, 2006.

Cazzaniga Gian Mario, *La religione dei moderni*, Ets, Pisa, 1999.

Ciuffoletti Zeffiro, *Il complotto massonico e la Rivoluzione francese*, Edizione Medicea, Firenze, 1989.

Conti Fulvio, *Italia immaginata. Sentimenti, memorie e politica fra Otto e Novecento*, Pacini, Ospedaletto, 2017.

Conti Fulvio, *La massoneria a Firenze: dall'età dei lumi al secondo Novecento*, Bologna, Il Mulino, 2007.

Conti Fulvio, *Laicismo e democrazia. La massoneria in Toscana dopo l'Unità (1860–1900)*, Centro Editoriale Toscano, Firenze, 1990.

Conti Fulvio, Novarino Marco (edited), *Massoneria e Unità d'Italia. La Libera Muratoria e la costruzione della nazione*, Il Mulino, Bologna, 2011.

Conti Fulvio, *Storia della massoneria italiana. Dal Risorgimento al fascismo*, Il Mulino, Bologna, 2003.

Cuzzi Marco, *Dal Risorgimento al Mondo nuovo. La massoneria nella Prima guerra mondiale*, Mondadori education, Firenze, 2017.

Delogu Giulia, *La poetica della virtù. Comunicazione e rappresentazione del potere in Italia tra Sette e Ottocento*, Milano, Mimesis, 2017.

Esposito Rosario Francesco, *La massoneria e l'Italia dal 1800 ai nostri giorni*, Paoline, Roma, 1969.

Fedele Santi, Giovanni Greco (edited), Massoneria ed Europa. 300 anni di storia, Bonanno, Acireale, 2017.

Fedele Santi, *La massoneria italiana nell'esilio e nella clandestinità (1927–1939)*, FrancoAngeli, Milano, 2005.

Fedele Santi, *La massoneria italiana tra Otto e Novecento*, Bastogi, Foggia, 2011.

Francovich Carlo, *Storia della Massoneria in Italia. Dalle origini alla rivoluzione francese*, La Nuova Italia, Firenze, 1974.

Giarrizzo Giuseppe, *Massoneria e Illuminismo nell'Europa del Settecento*, Marsilio, Venezia, 1994.

Isastia Anna Maria (edited), *Il progetto liberal-democratico di Ettore Ferrari*, Angeli, Milano, 1997.

Isastia Anna Maria, Alessandro Visani, L'idea laica tra Chiesa e Massoneria. La questione della scuola, Atanòr, Roma, 2008.

Isastia Anna Maria, *Massoneria e fascismo*, Libreria Chiari, Firenze, 2003.

Isastia Anna Maria, *Scritti politici di Ernesto Nathan*, Bastogi, Foggia, 1998.

Leti Giuseppi, *Carboneria e massoneria nel risorgimento italiano*, Res Gestae, Milano, 2016.

Locci Emanuela, La massoneria nel Mediterraneo. Egitto, Tunisi e Malta, BastogiLibri, Roma, 2014.

Manenti Luca Giuseppe, *Massoneria e irredentismo. Geografia dell'associazionismo patriottico in Italia tra Otto e Novecento*, Isrml FVG, Trieste, 2015.

Miletto Enrico, Novarino Marco, «...*Senza distinzione politica e religiosa». Repertorio bibliografico e archivistico sull'associazionismo laico a Torino e provincia (1848–1925)*, Centro Studi Piero Calamandrei, Torino, 2011.

Mola Aldo Alessandro (edited), La massoneria nella storia d'Italia, Atanòr, Roma, 1981.

Mola Aldo Alessandro, *Adriano Lemmi, Gran Maestro della nuova Italia (1885–1896)*, Erasmo, Roma, 1985.

Mola Aldo Alessandro, *Storia della massoneria in Italia. Dal 1717 al 2018. Tre secoli di un ordine iniziatico*, Bompiani, Milano, 2018.

Novarino Marco, *All'Oriente di Torino. La rinascita della massoneria italiana tra moderatismo cavouriano e rivoluzionarismo garibaldino*, Chiari, Firenze, 2003.

Novarino Marco, *Compagni e liberi muratori. Socialismo e massoneria dalla nascita del Psi alla grande guerra*, Rubbettino, Soveria Mannelli, 2015.

Novarino Marco, Giuseppe M. Vatri, *Uomini e logge nella Torino capitale. Dalla fondazione della loggia «Ausonia» alla rinascita del Grande Oriente Italiano (1859-1862)*, L'Età dell'Acquario, Torino, 2009.

Novarino Marco, *Grande Oriente d'Italia. Due secoli di presenza liberomuratoria*, Erasmo, Roma, 2006.

Novarino Marco, *Nel nome del grande statista. Le Logge Cavour di Torino dall'Unità d'Italia ai giorni nostri*, Sottosopra, Torino, 2011.

Novarino Marco, *Progresso e Tradizione Libero Muratoria. Storia del Rito Simbolico Italiano (1859-1925)*, Pontecorboli, Firenze, 2009.

Polo Friz Luigi, *La massoneria italiana nel decennio post unitario. Lodovico Frapolli*, Angeli, Milano, 1998.

Rizzardini Massimo, Vento Andrea (edited), *All'Oriente d'Italia. Le fondamenta segrete del rapporto fra Stato e Massoneria*, Rubbettino, Soveria Mannelli, 2013.

Trampus Antonio, *La massoneria nell'età moderna*, Laterza, Roma, 2001.

www.ingramcontent.com/pod-product-compliance
Lightning Source LLC
Chambersburg PA
CBHW021616270326
41931CB00008B/729